Harriet Beecher Stowe

Stories and Sketches for the Young

Harriet Beecher Stowe

Stories and Sketches for the Young

ISBN/EAN: 9783337004637

Printed in Europe, USA, Canada, Australia, Japan

Cover: Foto ©Thomas Meinert / pixelio.de

More available books at **www.hansebooks.com**

Riverside Edition

THE WRITINGS OF

HARRIET BEECHER STOWE

*WITH BIOGRAPHICAL INTRODUCTIONS
PORTRAITS, AND OTHER
ILLUSTRATIONS*

IN SIXTEEN VOLUMES
VOLUME XVI

STORIES AND SKETCHES
FOR THE YOUNG

BY

HARRIET (BEECHER) STOWE

bien ou
Tout . . . rien
The Riverside Press

BOSTON AND NEW YORK
HOUGHTON, MIFFLIN AND COMPANY
The Riverside Press, Cambridge
1896

The Riverside Press, Cambridge, Mass., U. S. A.
Electrotyped and Printed by H. O. Houghton & Co.

CONTENTS

PAGE

INTRODUCTORY NOTE vii

QUEER LITTLE PEOPLE.

    THE HEN THAT HATCHED DUCKS 1

    THE NUTCRACKERS OF NUTCRACKER LODGE 11

    THE HISTORY OF TIP-TOP 19

    MISS KATY-DID AND MISS CRICKET 29

    MOTHER MAGPIE'S MISCHIEF 36

    THE SQUIRRELS THAT LIVED IN A HOUSE 42

    HUM, THE SON OF BUZ 49

    OUR COUNTRY NEIGHBORS 58

    OUR DOGS 66

    DOGS AND CATS 102

    AUNT ESTHER'S RULES 110

    AUNT ESTHER'S STORIES 114

    SIR WALTER SCOTT AND HIS DOGS 121

    COUNTRY NEIGHBORS AGAIN 127

    THE DIVERTING HISTORY OF LITTLE WHISKEY . . 134

LITTLE PUSSY WILLOW 139

THE MINISTER'S WATERMELONS 233

A DOG'S MISSION.

    CHAP. I. THE OLD HOUSE AND THE OLD WOMAN . . 258

    II. THE DOG TAKES REFUGE WITH THE OLD WOMAN . 264

    III. SHE DISCOVERS THAT HE IS A PROVIDENCE . 268

    IV. HE MAKES HIMSELF AGREEABLE 271

    V. BLUE EYES COMES TO SEE HIM 275

    VI. THE WOMAN WHO HATES DOGS 279

    VII. BLUE EYES PURSUES HER ADVANTAGE . . 282

    VIII. A BRIGHT SATURDAY AFTERNOON . . . 285

    IX. A JOYFUL SUNDAY 290

    X. WHERE IS BLUE EYES? 292

    XI. THE THANKSGIVING DINNER 296

LULU'S PUPIL 300

THE DAISY'S FIRST WINTER 306

OUR CHARLEY AND THE STORIES TOLD HIM.

    OUR CHARLEY 313
    TAKE CARE OF THE HOOK . . . 323
    A TALK ABOUT BIRDS 326
    THE NEST IN THE ORCHARD . . . 334
    THE HAPPY CHILD 339
LITTLE CAPTAIN TROTT 346
CHRISTMAS ; OR, THE GOOD FAIRY 355
LITTLE FRED, THE CANAL BOY 365

The frontispiece (Mrs. Stowe and her daughters) is from a daguerreotype taken in 1850.

The vignette (Mrs. Stowe's first Hartford home) is from a drawing by Charles Copeland.

INTRODUCTORY NOTE

HE would be an inattentive reader of Mrs. Stowe's writings who did not see how irresistibly she would be drawn not only to the portraiture of children but to stories for their pleasure. She was distinctly a domestic woman; and she was, moreover, so acutely sensible of the world of nature, loving its flowers, trees, and all animate and inanimate objects, that her active mind and intelligent sympathy could scarcely fail to seize upon this material when she came to write for the instruction or the diversion of that part of humanity which lives nearest the earth.

The Mayflower, which has yielded so many evidences of Mrs. Stowe's native proclivities in her early life, is drawn upon here for two stories, the last in the volume; but a good many of the most characteristic creature stories, those included under *Queer Little People*, were first contributed to *Our Young Folks* and afterward gathered in a volume, which was published in 1867. The other stories were for the most part contributed to periodicals before being collected in book form, *Little Captain Trott* being a study of child life first published in *The Atlantic Monthly*. It is after all a somewhat loose classification which sets these all apart as stories and sketches for the young. Some of them might readily have been grouped with the stories, sketches, and studies comprised in the fourteenth volume of this series, just as some pieces there printed might have found as suitable a place in this volume. In truth, Mrs. Stowe was naturally a companion for young and old, without too nice a calculation of adaptation to either class.

STORIES AND SKETCHES FOR THE YOUNG

QUEER LITTLE PEOPLE

THE HEN THAT HATCHED DUCKS

ONCE there was a nice young hen that we will call Mrs. Feathertop. She was a hen of most excellent family, being a direct descendant of the Bolton Grays, and as pretty a young fowl as you should wish to see of a summer's day. She was, moreover, as fortunately situated in life as it was possible for a hen to be. She was bought by young Master Fred Little John, with four or five family connections of hers, and a lively young cock, who was held to be as brisk a scratcher and as capable a head of a family as any half-dozen sensible hens could desire.

I can't say that at first Mrs. Feathertop was a very sensible hen. She was very pretty and lively, to be sure, and a great favorite with Master Bolton Gray Cock, on account of her bright eyes, her finely shaded feathers, and certain saucy dashing ways that she had, which seemed greatly to take his fancy. But old Mrs. Scratchard, living in the neighboring yard, assured all the neighborhood that Gray Cock was a fool for thinking so much of that flighty young thing, — that she had not the smallest notion how to get on in life, and thought of nothing in the world but her own pretty feathers. "Wait till she comes to have chickens," said Mrs. Scratchard. "Then you will see. I have brought

up ten broods myself, — as likely and respectable chickens
as ever were a blessing to society, — and I think I ought
to know a good hatcher and brooder when I see her; and I
know *that* fine piece of trumpery, with her white feathers
tipped with gray, never will come down to family life.
She scratch for chickens! Bless me, she never did anything in all her days but run round and eat the worms
which somebody else scratched up for her."

When Master Bolton Gray heard this he crowed very
loudly, like a cock of spirit, and declared that old Mrs.
Scratchard was envious, because she had lost all her own
tail-feathers, and looked more like a worn-out old feather-
duster than a respectable hen, and that therefore she was
filled with sheer envy of anybody that was young and
pretty. So young Mrs. Feathertop cackled gay defiance at
her busy rubbishy neighbor, as she sunned herself under
the bushes on fine June afternoons.

Now Master Fred Little John had been allowed to have
these hens by his mamma on the condition that he would
build their house himself, and take all the care of it; and,
to do Master Fred justice, he executed the job in a small
way quite creditably. He chose a sunny sloping bank covered with a thick growth of bushes, and erected there a
nice little hen-house, with two glass windows, a little door,
and a good pole for his family to roost on. He made,
moreover, a row of nice little boxes with hay in them for
nests, and he bought three or four little smooth white china
eggs to put in them, so that, when his hens *did* lay, he
might carry off their eggs without their being missed. This
hen-house stood in a little grove that sloped down to a
wide river, just where there was a little cove which reached
almost to the hen-house.

This situation inspired one of Master Fred's boy advis-
ers with a new scheme in relation to his poultry enterprise. "Hullo! I say, Fred," said Tom Seymour, "you

ought to raise ducks, — you 've got a capital place for ducks there."

"Yes, — but I 've bought *hens*, you see," said Freddy, "so it's no use trying."

"No use! Of course there is! Just as if your hens could n't hatch ducks' eggs. Now you just wait till one of your hens wants to set, and you put ducks' eggs under her, and you 'll have a family of ducks in a twinkling. You can buy ducks' eggs, a plenty, of old Sam under the hill; he always has hens hatch his ducks."

So Freddy thought it would be a good experiment, and informed his mother the next morning that he intended to furnish the ducks for the next Christmas dinner ; and when she wondered how he was to come by them, he said, mysteriously, "Oh, I will show you how!" but did not further explain himself. The next day he went with Tom Seymour, and made a trade with old Sam, and gave him a middle-aged jack-knife for eight of his ducks' eggs. Sam, by the bye, was a woolly-headed old negro man, who lived by the pond hard by, and who had long cast envying eyes on Fred's jack-knife, because it was of extra-fine steel, having been a Christmas present the year before. But Fred knew very well there were any number more of jack-knives where that came from, and that, in order to get a new one, he must dispose of the old ; so he made the trade and came home rejoicing.

Now about this time Mrs. Feathertop, having laid her eggs daily with great credit to herself, notwithstanding Mrs. Scratchard's predictions, began to find herself suddenly attacked with nervous symptoms. She lost her gay spirits, grew dumpish and morose, stuck up her feathers in a bristling way, and pecked at her neighbors if they did so much as look at her. Master Gray Cock was greatly concerned, and went to old Doctor Peppercorn, who looked solemn, and recommended an infusion of angle-worms, and said he would look in on the patient twice a day till she was better.

" Gracious me, Gray Cock ! " said old Goody Kertarkut, who had been lolling at the corner as he passed, " a'n't you a fool ? — cocks always are fools. Don't you know what 's the matter with your wife ? She wants to set, — that 's all; and you just let her set ! A fiddlestick for Doctor Peppercorn ! Why, any good old hen that has brought up a family knows more than a doctor about such things. You just go home and tell her to set, if she wants to, and behave herself."

When Gray Cock came home, he found that Master Freddy had been before him, and established Mrs. Feathertop upon eight nice eggs, where she was sitting in gloomy grandeur. He tried to make a little affable conversation with her, and to relate his interview with the doctor and Goody Kertarkut, but she was morose and sullen, and only pecked at him now and then in a very sharp, unpleasant way ; so after a few more efforts to make himself agreeable, he left her, and went out promenading with the captivating Mrs. Red Comb, a charming young Spanish widow, who had just been imported into the neighboring yard.

" Bless my soul ! " said he, " you 've no idea how cross my wife is."

" Oh, you horrid creature ! " said Mrs. Red Comb ; " how little you feel for the weaknesses of us poor hens ! "

" On my word, ma'am," said Gray Cock, " you do me injustice. But when a hen gives way to temper, ma'am, and no longer meets her husband with a smile, — when she even pecks at him whom she is bound to honor and obey — "

" Horrid monster ! talking of obedience ! I should say, sir, you came straight from Turkey ! " and Mrs. Red Comb tossed her head with a most bewitching air, and pretended to run away, and old Mrs. Scratchard looked out of her coop and called to Goody Kertarkut, —

" Look how Mr. Gray Cock is flirting with that widow. I always knew she was a baggage."

"And his poor wife left at home alone," said Goody Kertarkut. "It's the way with 'em all!"

"Yes, yes," said Dame Scratchard, "she'll know what real life is now, and she won't go about holding her head so high, and looking down on her practical neighbors that have raised families."

"Poor thing, what'll she do with a family?" said Goody Kertarkut.

"Well, what business have such young flirts to get married?" said Dame Scratchard. "I don't expect she'll raise a single chick; and there's Gray Cock flirting about, fine as ever. Folks did n't do so when I was young. I'm sure my husband knew what treatment a setting hen ought to have, — poor old Long Spur, — he never minded a peck or so now and then. I must say these modern fowls a'n't what fowls used to be."

Meanwhile the sun rose and set, and Master Fred was almost the only friend and associate of poor little Mrs. Feathertop, whom he fed daily with meal and water, and only interrupted her sad reflections by pulling her up occasionally to see how the eggs were coming on.

At last, "Peep, peep, peep!" began to be heard in the nest, and one little downy head after another poked forth from under the feathers, surveying the world with round, bright, winking eyes; and gradually the brood were hatched, and Mrs. Feathertop arose, a proud and happy mother, with all the bustling, scratching, care-taking instincts of family-life warm within her breast. She clucked and scratched, and cuddled the little downy bits of things as handily and discreetly as a seven-year-old hen could have done, exciting thereby the wonder of the community.

Master Gray Cock came home in high spirits, and complimented her; told her she was looking charmingly once more, and said, "Very well, very nice!" as he surveyed the young brood. So that Mrs. Feathertop began to feel the world going well with her, — when suddenly in came Dame Scratchard and Goody Kertarkut to make a morning call.

" Let 's see the chicks," said Dame Scratchard.

" Goodness me," said Goody Kertarkut, " what a likeness to their dear papa ! "

" Well, but bless me, what 's the matter with their bills ? " said Dame Scratchard. " Why, my dear, these chicks are deformed ! I 'm sorry for you, my dear, but it 's all the result of your inexperience ; you ought to have eaten pebble-stones with your meal when you were setting. Don't you see, Dame Kertarkut, what bills they have ? That 'll increase, and they 'll be frightful ! "

" What shall I do ? " said Mrs. Feathertop, now greatly alarmed.

" Nothing, as I know of," said Dame Scratchard, " since you did n't come to me before you set. I could have told you all about it. Maybe it won't kill 'em, but they 'll always be deformed."

And so the gossips departed, leaving a sting under the pin-feathers of the poor little hen mamma, who began to see that her darlings had curious little spoon-bills, different from her own, and to worry and fret about it.

" My dear," she said to her spouse, " do get Dr. Pepper-corn to come in and look at their bills, and see if anything can be done."

Dr. Peppercorn came in, and put on a monstrous pair of spectacles, and said, " Hum ! Ha ! Extraordinary case, — very singular ! "

" Did you ever see anything like it, Doctor ? " said both parents, in a breath.

" I 've read of such cases. It 's a calcareous enlarge-ment of the vascular bony tissue, threatening ossification," said the doctor.

" Oh, dreadful ! — can it be possible ? " shrieked both parents. " Can anything be done ? "

" Well, I should recommend a daily lotion made of mosquitoes' horns and bicarbonate of frogs' toes, together with a powder, to be taken morning and night, of muriate of fleas. One thing you must be careful about: they must never wet their feet, nor drink any water."

" Dear me, Doctor, I don't know what I *shall* do, for they seem to have a particular fancy for getting into water."

" Yes, a morbid tendency often found in these cases of bony tumification of the vascular tissue of the mouth ; but you must resist it, ma'am, as their life depends upon it ; " — and with that Dr. Peppercorn glared gloomily on the young ducks, who were stealthily poking the objectionable little spoon-bills out from under their mother's feathers.

After this poor Mrs. Feathertop led a weary life of it; for the young fry were as healthy and enterprising a brood of young ducks as ever carried saucepans on the end of their noses, and they most utterly set themselves against the doctor's prescriptions, murmured at the muriate of fleas and the bicarbonate of frogs' toes, and took every opportunity to waddle their little ways down to the mud and water which was in their near vicinity. So their bills grew larger and larger, as did the rest of their bodies, and family government grew weaker and weaker.

" You 'll wear me out, children, you certainly will," said poor Mrs. Feathertop.

" You 'll go to destruction, — do ye hear ? " said Master Gray Cock.

" Did you ever see such frights as poor Mrs. Feathertop has got ? " said Dame Scratchard. " I knew what would come of *her* family, — all deformed, and with a dreadful sort of madness, which makes them love to shovel mud with those shocking spoon-bills of theirs."

" It 's a kind of idiocy," said Goody Kertarkut. " Poor things ! they can't be kept from the water, nor made to take powders, and so they get worse and worse."

" I understand it 's affecting their feet so that they can't walk, and a dreadful sort of net is growing between their toes; what a shocking visitation! "

" She brought it on herself," said Dame Scratchard. " Why did n't she come to me before she set? She was always an upstart, self-conceited thing, but I 'm sure I pity her."

Meanwhile the young ducks throve apace. Their necks grew glossy, like changeable green and gold satin, and though they would not take the doctor's medicine, and would waddle in the mud and water, — for which they always felt themselves to be very naughty ducks, — yet they grew quite vigorous and hearty. At last one day the whole little tribe waddled off down to the bank of the river. It was a beautiful day, and the river was dancing and dimpling and winking as the little breezes shook the trees that hung over it.

" Well," said the biggest of the little ducks, " in spite of Dr. Peppercorn, I can't help longing for the water. I don't believe it is going to hurt me, — at any rate, here goes; " — and in he plumped, and in went every duck after him, and they threw out their great brown feet as cleverly as if they had taken rowing lessons all their lives, and sailed off on the river, away, away among the ferns, under the pink azalias, through reeds and rushes, and arrow-heads and pickerel-weed, the happiest ducks that ever were born; and soon they were quite out of sight.

" Well, Mrs. Feathertop, this is a dispensation!" said Mrs. Scratchard. " Your children are all drowned at last, just as I knew they 'd be. The old music-teacher, Master Bullfrog, that lives down in Water-dock Lane, saw 'em all plump madly into the water together this morning; that 's what comes of not knowing how to bring up a family."

Mrs. Feathertop gave only one shriek and fainted dead away, and was carried home on a cabbage-leaf, and Mr.

Gray Cock was sent for, where he was waiting on Mrs. Red Comb through the squash-vines.

"It's a serious time in your family, sir," said Goody Kertarkut, "and you ought to be at home supporting your wife. Send for Doctor Peppercorn without delay."

Now as the case was a very dreadful one, Doctor Peppercorn called a council from the barn-yard of the Squire, two miles off, and a brisk young Doctor Partlett appeared, in a fine suit of brown and gold, with tail-feathers like meteors. A fine young fellow he was, lately from Paris, with all the modern scientific improvements fresh in his head.

When he had listened to the whole story, he clapped his spur into the ground, and leaning back, laughed so loud that all the cocks in the neighborhood crowed.

Mrs. Feathertop rose up out of her swoon, and Mr. Gray Cock was greatly enraged.

"What do you mean, sir, by such behavior in the house of mourning?"

"My dear sir, pardon me, — but there is no occasion for mourning. My dear madam, let me congratulate you. There is no harm done. The simple matter is, dear madam, you have been under a hallucination all along. The neighborhood and my learned friend the doctor have all made a mistake in thinking that these children of yours were hens at all. They are ducks, ma'am, evidently ducks, and very finely formed ducks I dare say."

At this moment a quack was heard, and at a distance the whole tribe were seen coming waddling home, their feathers gleaming in green and gold, and they themselves in high good spirits.

"Such a splendid day as we have had!" they all cried in a breath. "And we know now how to get our own living; we can take care of ourselves in future, so you need have no further trouble with us."

"Madam," said the doctor, making a bow with an air

which displayed his tail-feathers to advantage, "let me congratulate you on the charming family you have raised. A finer brood of young, healthy ducks I never saw. Give claw, my dear friend," he said, addressing the elder son. "In our barn-yard no family is more respected than that of the ducks."

And so Madam Feathertop came off glorious at last ; and when after this the ducks used to go swimming up and down the river like so many nabobs among the admiring hens, Doctor Peppercorn used to look after them and say, "Ah ! I had the care of their infancy !" and Mr. Gray Cock and his wife used to say, "It was our system of education did that ! "

THE NUTCRACKERS OF NUTCRACKER LODGE

MR. and Mrs. Nutcracker were as respectable a pair of squirrels as ever wore gray brushes over their backs. They were animals of a settled and serious turn of mind, not disposed to run after vanities and novelties, but filling their station in life with prudence and sobriety. Nutcracker Lodge was a hole in a sturdy old chestnut overhanging a shady dell, and was held to be as respectably kept an establishment as there was in the whole forest. Even Miss Jenny Wren, the greatest gossip of the neighborhood, never found anything to criticise in its arrangements, and old Parson Too-whit, a venerable owl who inhabited a branch somewhat more exalted, as became his profession, was in the habit of saving himself much trouble in his parochial exhortations by telling his parishioners in short to "look at the Nutcrackers" if they wanted to see what it was to live a virtuous life. Everything had gone on prosperously with them, and they had reared many successive families of young Nutcrackers, who went forth to assume their places in the forest of life, and to reflect credit on their bringing-up, — so that naturally enough they began to have a very easy way of considering themselves models of wisdom.

But at last it came along, in the course of events, that they had a son named Featherhead, who was destined to bring them a great deal of anxiety. Nobody knows what the reason is, but the fact was that Master Featherhead was as different from all the former children of this worthy couple as if he had been dropped out of the moon into

their nest, instead of coming into it in the general way.
Young Featherhead was a squirrel of good parts and a lively
disposition, but he was sulky and contrary and unreasonable, and always finding matter of complaint in everything
his respectable papa and mamma did. Instead of assist-
ing in the cares of a family, — picking up nuts and learning
other lessons proper to a young squirrel, — he seemed to
settle himself from his earliest years into a sort of lofty
contempt for the Nutcrackers, for Nutcracker Lodge, and
for all the good old ways and institutions of the domestic
hole, which he declared to be stupid and unreasonable, and
entirely behind the times. To be sure, he was always on
hand at meal-times, and played a very lively tooth on the
nuts which his mother had collected, always selecting the
very best for himself ; but he seasoned his nibbling with so
much grumbling and discontent, and so many severe remarks, as to give the impression that he considered himself
a peculiarly ill-used squirrel in having to " eat their old
grub," as he very unceremoniously called it.

Papa Nutcracker, on these occasions, was often fiercely
indignant, and poor little Mamma Nutcracker would shed
tears, and beg her darling to be a little more reasonable ;
but the young gentleman seemed always to consider himself
as the injured party.

Now nobody could tell why or wherefore Master Featherhead looked upon himself as injured and aggrieved, since
he was living in a good hole, with plenty to eat, and without the least care or labor of his own ; but he seemed rather
to value himself upon being gloomy and dissatisfied. While
his parents and brothers and sisters were cheerfully racing
up and down the branches, busy in their domestic toils, and
laying up stores for the winter, Featherhead sat gloomily
apart, declaring himself weary of existence, and feeling himself at liberty to quarrel with everybody and everything
about him. Nobody understood him, he said ; — he was a

squirrel of a peculiar nature, and needed peculiar treatment, and nobody treated him in a way that did not grate on the finer nerves of his feelings. He had higher notions of existence than could be bounded by that old rotten hole in a hollow tree; he had thoughts that soared far above the miserable, petty details of every-day life, and he *could* not and *would* not bring down these soaring aspirations to the contemptible toil of laying up a few chestnuts or hickory-nuts for winter.

"Depend upon it, my dear," said Mrs. Nutcracker solemnly, "that fellow must be a genius."

"Fiddlestick on his genius!" said old Mr. Nutcracker; "what does he *do?*"

"Oh, nothing, of course; that's one of the first marks of genius. Geniuses, you know, never can come down to common life."

"He eats enough for any two," remarked old Nutcracker, "and he never helps gather nuts."

"My dear, ask Parson Too-whit; he has conversed with him, and quite agrees with me that he says very uncommon things for a squirrel of his age; he has such fine feelings, — so much above those of the common crowd."

"Fine feelings be hanged!" said old Nutcracker. "When a fellow eats all the nuts that his mother gives him, and then grumbles at her, I don't believe much in his fine feelings. Why don't he set himself about something? I'm going to tell my fine young gentleman that, if he does n't behave himself, I'll tumble him out of the nest, neck and crop, and see if hunger won't do something towards bringing down his fine airs."

But then Mrs. Nutcracker fell on her husband's neck with both paws, and wept, and besought him so piteously to have patience with her darling, that old Nutcracker, who was himself a soft-hearted old squirrel, was prevailed upon to put up with the airs and graces of his young scrapegrace

a little longer; and secretly in his silly old heart he re-
volved the question whether possibly it might not be that
a great genius was actually to come of his household.

The Nutcrackers belonged to the old established race of
the Grays, but they were sociable, friendly people, and kept
on the best of terms with all branches of the Nutcracker
family.   The Chipmunks of Chipmunk Hollow were a very
lively, cheerful, sociable race, and on the very best of terms
with the Nutcracker Grays.   Young Tip Chipmunk, the
oldest son, was in all respects a perfect contrast to Master
Featherhead.   He was always lively and cheerful, and so
very alert in providing for the family, that old Mr. and
Mrs. Chipmunk had very little care, but could sit sociably
at the door of their hole and chat with neighbors, quite
sure that Tip would bring everything out right for them,
and have plenty laid up for winter.   Now Featherhead
took it upon him, for some reason or other, to look down
upon Tip Chipmunk, and on every occasion to disparage
him in the social circles as a very common kind of squirrel,
with whom it would be best not to associate too freely.

"My dear, " said Mrs. Nutcracker one day, when he was
expressing these ideas, " it seems to me that you are too
hard on poor Tip ; he is a most excellent son and brother,
and I wish you would be civil to him."

" Oh, I don't doubt that Tip is *good* enough," said
Featherhead, carelessly ; " but then he is so very common !
he has n't an idea in his skull above his nuts and his hole.
He is good-natured enough, to be sure, — these very ordinary people often are good-natured, — but he wants manner ; he has really no manner at all; and as to the deeper
feelings, Tip has n't the remotest idea of them.   I mean
always to be civil to Tip when he comes in my way, but
I think the less we see of that sort of people the better;
and I hope, mother, you won't invite the Chipmunks at
Christmas, — these family dinners are such a bore ! "

" But my dear, your father thinks a great deal of the Chipmunks; and it is an old family custom to have all the relatives here at Christmas."

" And an awful bore it is! Why must people of refinement and elevation be forever tied down because of some distant relationship? Now there are our cousins the High-Flyers, — if we could get them, there would be some sense in it. Young Whisk rather promised me for Christmas; but it 's seldom now you can get a flying squirrel to show himself in our parts, and if we are intimate with the Chipmunks it is n't to be expected."

" Confound him for a puppy! " said old Nutcracker, when his wife repeated these sayings to him. " Featherhead is a fool. Common, forsooth! I wish good industrious, painstaking sons like Tip Chipmunk *were* common. For my part, I find these uncommon people the most tiresome; they are not content with letting us carry the whole load, but they sit on it, and scold at us while we carry them."

But old Mr. Nutcracker, like many other good old gentlemen squirrels, found that Christmas dinners and other things were apt to go as his wife said, and his wife was apt to go as young Featherhead said; and so, when Christmas came, the Chipmunks were not invited, for the first time in many years. The Chipmunks, however, took all pleasantly, and accepted poor old Mrs. Nutcracker's awkward apologies with the best possible grace, and young Tip looked in on Christmas morning with the compliments of the season and a few beech-nuts, which he had secured as a great dainty. The fact was, that Tip's little striped fur coat was so filled up and overflowing with cheerful good-will to all, that he never could be made to understand that any of his relations could want to cut him; and therefore Featherhead looked down on him with contempt, and said he had no tact, and could n't see when he was not wanted.

It was wonderful to see how, by means of persisting in remarks like these, young Featherhead at last got all his family to look up to him as something uncommon. Though he added nothing to the family, and required more to be done for him than all the others put together, — though he showed not the smallest real perseverance or ability in anything useful, — yet somehow all his brothers and sisters, and his poor foolish old mother, got into a way of regarding him as something wonderful, and delighting in his sharp sayings as if they had been the wisest things in the world.

But at last old papa declared that it was time for Featherhead to settle himself to some business in life, roundly declaring that he could not always have him as a hanger-on in the paternal hole.

"What are you going to do, my boy?" said Tip Chipmunk to him one day. "We are driving now a thriving trade in hickory-nuts, and if you would like to join us — "

"Thank you," said Featherhead; "but I confess I have no fancy for anything so slow as the hickory trade; I never was made to grub and delve in that way."

The fact was, that Featherhead had lately been forming alliances such as no reputable squirrel should even think of. He had more than once been seen going out evenings with the Rats of Rat Hollow, — a race whose reputation for honesty was more than doubtful. The fact was, further, that old Longtooth Rat, an old sharper and money-lender, had long had his eye on Featherhead as just about silly enough for their purposes, — engaging him in what he called a speculation, but which was neither more nor less than downright stealing.

Near by the chestnut-tree where Nutcracker Lodge was situated was a large barn filled with corn and grain, besides many bushels of hazel-nuts, chestnuts, and walnuts. Now old Longtooth proposed to young Featherhead that he should nibble a passage into this loft, and there establish himself in the commission business, passing the nuts and corn to him as he wanted them. Old Longtooth knew what he was about in the proposal, for he had heard talk of a brisk Scotch terrier that was about to be bought to keep the rats from the grain; but you may be sure he kept his knowledge to himself, so that Featherhead was none the wiser for it.

"The nonsense of fellows like Tip Chipmunk!" said Featherhead to his admiring brothers and sisters. "The perfectly stupid nonsense! There he goes, delving and poking, picking up a nut here and a grain there, when *I* step into property at once."

"But I hope, my son, you are careful to be honest in your dealings," said old Nutcracker, who was a very moral squirrel.

With that, young Featherhead threw his tail saucily over one shoulder, winked knowingly at his brothers, and said, "Certainly, sir! If honesty consists in getting what you can while it is going, I mean to be honest."

Very soon Featherhead appeared to his admiring companions in the height of prosperity. He had a splendid hole in the midst of a heap of chestnuts, and he literally seemed to be rolling in wealth; he never came home without showering lavish gifts on his mother and sisters; he wore his tail over his back with a buckish air, and patronized Tip Chipmunk with a gracious nod whenever he met him, and thought that the world was going well with him.

But one luckless day, as Featherhead was lolling in his hole, up came two boys with the friskiest, wiriest Scotch terrier you ever saw. His eyes blazed like torches, and poor Featherhead's heart died within him as he heard the boys say, "Now we'll see if we can't catch the rascal that eats our grain."

Featherhead tried to slink out at the hole he had gnawed to come in by, but found it stopped.

"Oh, you are there, are you, Mister?" said the boy. "Well, you don't get out; and now for a chase!"

And, sure enough, poor Featherhead ran distracted with terror up and down, through the bundles of hay, between barrels, and over casks; but with the barking terrier ever at his heels, and the boys running, shouting, and cheering his pursuer on. He was glad at last to escape through a crack, though he left half of his fine brush behind him, — for Master Wasp, the terrier, made a snap at it just as he was going, and cleaned all the hair off of it, so that it was bare as a rat's tail.

Poor Featherhead limped off, bruised and beaten and bedraggled, with the boys and dog still after him; and they would have caught him, after all, if Tip Chipmunk's hole had not stood hospitably open to receive him. Tip took him in, like a good-natured fellow as he was, and took the best of care of him; but the glory of Featherhead's tail had departed forever. He had sprained his left paw, and got a chronic rheumatism, and the fright and fatigue which he had gone through had broken up his constitution, so that he never again could be what he had been; but Tip gave him a situation as under-clerk in his establishment, and from that time he was a sadder and a wiser squirrel than he ever had been before.

THE HISTORY OF TIP-TOP

UNDER the window of a certain pretty little cottage there grew a great old apple-tree, which in the spring had thousands and thousands of lovely pink blossoms on it, and in the autumn had about half as many bright red apples as it had blossoms in the spring.

The nursery of this cottage was a little bower of a room papered with mossy-green paper, and curtained with white muslin ; and here five little children used to come, in their white nightgowns, to be dressed and have their hair brushed and curled every morning.

First, there were Alice and Mary, bright-eyed, laughing little girls, of seven and eight years, and then came stout little Jamie, and Charlie, and finally little Puss, whose real name was Ellen, but who was called Puss, and Pussy, and Birdie, and Toddlie, and any other pet name that came to mind.

Now it used to happen, every morning, that the five little heads would be peeping out of the window, together, into the flowery boughs of the apple-tree ; and the reason was this. A pair of robins had built a very pretty, smooth-lined nest in a fork of the limb that came directly under the window, and the building of this nest had been super-intended, day by day, by the five pairs of bright eyes of these five children. The robins at first had been rather shy of this inspection ; but, as they got better acquainted, they seemed to think no more of the little curly heads in the window, than of the pink blossoms about them, or the daisies and buttercups at the foot of the tree.

All the little hands were forward to help; some threw out flossy bits of cotton, — for which, we grieve to say, Charlie had cut a hole in the crib quilt, — and some threw out bits of thread and yarn, and Allie raveled out a considerable piece from one of her garters, which she threw out as a contribution; and they exulted in seeing the skill with which the little builders wove everything in. "Little birds, little birds," they would say, "you shall be kept warm, for we have given you cotton out of our crib quilt, and yarn out of our stockings." Nay, so far did this generosity proceed, that Charlie cut a flossy, golden curl from Toddlie's head and threw it out; and when the birds caught it up the whole flock laughed to see Toddlie's golden hair figuring in a bird's-nest.

When the little thing was finished, it was so neat, and trim, and workman-like, that the children all exulted over it, and called it "our nest," and the two robins they called "our birds." But wonderful was the joy when the little eyes, opening one morning, saw in the nest a beautiful pale-green egg; and the joy grew from day to day, for every day there came another egg, and so on till there were five little eggs; and then the oldest girl, Alice, said, "There are five eggs; that makes one for each of us, and each of us will have a little bird by and by;"—at which all the children laughed and jumped for glee.

When the five little eggs were all laid, the mother-bird began to sit on them; and at any time of day or night, when a little head peeped out of the nursery window, might be seen a round, bright, patient pair of bird's eyes contentedly waiting for the young birds to come. It seemed a long time for the children to wait; but every day they put some bread and cake from their luncheon on the window-sill, so that the birds might have something to eat; but still there she was, patiently watching!

"How long, long, long she waits!" said Jamie, impatiently. "I don't believe she's ever going to hatch."

"Oh, yes, she is!" said grave little Alice. "Jamie, you don't understand about these things; it takes a long, long time to hatch eggs. Old Sam says his hens set three weeks; — only think, almost a month!"

Three weeks looked a long time to the five bright pairs of little watching eyes; but Jamie said the eggs were so much smaller than hens' eggs, that it would n't take so long to hatch them, he knew. Jamie always thought he knew all about everything, and was so sure of it that he rather took the lead among the children. But one morning, when they pushed their five heads out of the window, the round, patient little bird-eyes were gone, and there seemed to be nothing in the nest but a bunch of something hairy.

Upon this they all cried out, "O mamma, *do* come here! the bird is gone and left her nest!" And when they cried out, they saw five wide little red mouths open in the nest, and saw that the hairy bunch of stuff was indeed the first of five little birds.

"They are dreadful-looking things," said Mary; "I did n't know that little birds began by looking so badly."

"They seem to be all mouth," said Jamie.

"We must feed them," said Charlie.

"Here, little birds, here's some gingerbread for you," he said; and he threw a bit of his gingerbread, which fortunately only hit the nest on the outside, and fell down among the buttercups, where two crickets made a meal of it, and agreed that it was as excellent gingerbread as if old Mother Cricket herself had made it.

"Take care, Charlie," said his mamma; "we do not know enough to feed young birds. We must leave it to their papa and mamma, who probably started out bright and early in the morning to get breakfast for them."

Sure enough, while they were speaking, back came Mr. and Mrs. Robin, whirring through the green shadows of the apple-tree; and thereupon all the five little red mouths flew open, and the birds put something into each.

It was great amusement, after this, to watch the daily
feeding of the little birds, and to observe how, when not
feeding them, the mother sat brooding on the nest, warm-
ing them under her soft wings, while the father-bird sat on
the tip-top bough of the apple-tree and sang to them. In
time they grew and grew, and, instead of a nest full of
little red mouths, there was a nest full of little, fat, speckled
robins, with round, bright, cunning eyes, just like their
parents ; and the children began to talk together about
their birds.

"I'm going to give my robin a name," said Mary. "I
call him Brown-Eyes."

"And I call mine Tip-Top," said Jamie, "because I
know he'll be a tip-top bird."

"And I call mine Singer," said Alice.

"I 'all mine Toddy," said little Toddlie, who would not
be behindhand in anything that was going on.

"Hurrah for Toddlie!" said Charlie, "hers is the best
of all. For my part, I call mine Speckle."

So then the birds were all made separate characters by
having each a separate name given it. Brown-Eyes, Tip-
Top, Singer, Toddy, and Speckle made, as they grew bigger, a very crowded nestful of birds.

Now the children had early been taught to say in a little hymn : —

> "Birds in their little nests agree,
> And 't is a shameful sight
> When children of one family
> Fall out, and chide, and fight ;" —

and they thought anything really written and printed in a
hymn must be true; therefore they were very much astonished to see, from day to day, that *their* little birds in their
nests did *not* agree.

Tip-Top was the biggest and strongest bird, and he was
always shuffling and crowding the others, and clamoring
for the most food ; and when Mrs. Robin came in with a

nice bit of anything, Tip-Top's red mouth opened so wide, and he was so noisy, that one would think the nest was all his. His mother used to correct him for these gluttonous ways, and sometimes made him wait till all the rest were helped before she gave him a mouthful ; but he generally revenged himself in her absence by crowding the others and making the nest generally uncomfortable. Speckle, however, was a bird of spirit, and he used to peck at Tip-Top ; so they would sometimes have a regular sparring-match across poor Brown-Eyes, who was a meek, tender little fellow, and would sit winking and blinking in fear while his big brothers quarreled. As to Toddy and Singer, they turned out to be sister birds, and showed quite a feminine talent for chattering ; they used to scold their badly behaving brothers in a way that made the nest quite lively.

On the whole, Mr. and Mrs. Robin did not find their family circle the peaceable place the poets represent.

" I say," said Tip-Top one day to them, " this old nest is a dull, mean, crowded hole, and it's quite time some of us were out of it ; just give us lessons in flying, won't you, and let us go."

" My dear boy," said Mother Robin, " we shall teach you to fly as soon as your wings are strong enough."

" You are a very little bird," said his father, " and ought to be good and obedient, and wait patiently till your wing-feathers grow ; and then you can soar away to some purpose."

" Wait for my wing-feathers ? Humbug ! " Tip-Top would say, as he sat balancing with his little short tail on the edge of the nest, and looking down through the grass and clover-heads below, and up into the blue clouds above. " Father and mother are slow old birds ; keep a fellow back with their confounded notions. If they don't hurry up, I'll take matters into my own claws, and be off some day before they know it. Look at those swallows, skim-

ming and diving through the blue air! That's the way
I want to do."

"But, dear brother, the way to learn to do that is to be
good and obedient while we are little, and wait till our
parents think it best for us to begin."

"Shut up your preaching," said Tip-Top; "what do you
girls know of flying?"

"About as much as *you*," said Speckle. "However,
I'm sure I don't care how soon you take yourself off, for
you take up more room than all the rest put together."

"You mind yourself, Master Speckle, or you'll get something you don't like," said Tip-Top, still strutting in a very
cavalier way on the edge of the nest, and sticking up his
little short tail quite valiantly.

"O my darlings," said the mamma, now fluttering home,
"cannot I ever teach you to live in love?"

"It's all Tip-Top's fault," screamed the other birds in
a flutter.

"My fault? Of course, everything in this nest that goes
wrong is laid to me," said Tip-Top; "and I'll leave it to
anybody, now, if I crowd anybody. I've been sitting outside, on the very edge of the nest, and there's Speckle has
got my place."

"Who wants your place?" said Speckle. "I am sure
you can come in, if you please."

"My dear boy," said the mother, "do go into the nest
and be a good little bird, and then you will be happy."

"That's always the talk," said Tip-Top. "I'm too big
for the nest, and I want to see the world. It's full of
beautiful things, I know. Now there's the most lovely creature, with bright eyes, that comes under the tree every day,
and wants me to come down in the grass and play with her."

"My son, my son, beware!" said the frightened mother;
"that lovely seeming creature is our dreadful enemy, the
cat, — a horrid monster, with teeth and claws."

At this, all the little birds shuddered and cuddled deeper in the nest; only Tip-Top, in his heart, disbelieved it.

"I'm too old a bird," said he to himself, "to believe *that* story; mother is chaffing me. But I'll show her that I can take care of myself."

So the next morning, after the father and mother were gone, Tip-Top got on the edge of the nest again, and looked over and saw lovely Miss Pussy washing her face among the daisies under the tree, and her hair was sleek and white as the daisies, and her eyes were yellow and beautiful to behold, and she looked up to the tree bewitchingly, and said, "Little birds, little birds, come down; Pussy wants to play with you."

"Only look at her!" said Tip-Top; "her eyes are like gold."

"No, don't look," said Singer and Speckle. "She will bewitch you and then eat you up."

"I'd like to see her try to eat me up," said Tip-Top, again balancing his short tail over the nest. "Just as if she would. She's just the nicest, most innocent creature going, and only wants us to have fun. We never do have any fun in this old nest!"

Then the yellow eyes below shot a bewildering light into Tip-Top's eyes, and a voice sounded sweet as silver: "Little birds, little birds, come down; Pussy wants to play with you."

"Her paws are as white as velvet," said Tip-Top; "and so soft! I don't believe she has any claws."

"Don't go, brother, don't!" screamed both sisters.

All we know about it is, that a moment after a direful scream was heard from the nursery window. "O mamma, mamma, do come here! Tip-Top's fallen out of the nest, and the cat has got him!"

Away ran Pussy with foolish little Tip-Top in her mouth, and he squeaked dolefully when he felt her sharp teeth. Wicked Miss Pussy had no mind to eat him at once; she meant just as she said, to "play with him." So she ran off to a private place among the currant-bushes, while all the little curly heads were scattered up and down looking for her.

Did you ever see a cat play with a bird or a mouse? She sets it down, and seems to go off and leave it; but the moment it makes the first movement to get away, — pounce! she springs on it, and shakes it in her mouth; and so she teases and tantalizes it, till she gets ready to kill and eat it. I can't say why she does it, except that it is a cat's nature; and it is a very bad nature for foolish young robins to get acquainted with.

"Oh, where is he? where is he? Do find my poor Tip-Top," said Jamie, crying as loud as he could scream. "I'll kill that horrid cat, — I'll kill her!"

Mr. and Mrs. Robin, who had come home meantime, joined their plaintive chirping to the general confusion; and Mrs. Robin's bright eyes soon discovered her poor little son, where Pussy was patting and rolling him from one paw to the other under the currant-bushes; and settling on the bush above, she called the little folks to the spot by her cries.

Jamie plunged under the bush, and caught the cat with luckless Tip-Top in her mouth; and, with one or two good thumps, he obliged her to let him go. Tip-Top was not dead, but in a sadly draggled and torn state. Some of his feathers were torn out, and one of his wings was broken, and hung down in a melancholy way.

"Oh, what *shall* we do for him? He will die. Poor Tip-Top!" said the children.

"Let's put him back into the nest, children," said mamma. "His mother will know best what to do with him."

So a ladder was got, and papa climbed up and put poor

Tip-Top safely into the nest. The cat had shaken all the nonsense well out of him ; he was a dreadfully humbled young robin.

The time came at last when all the other birds in the nest learned to fly, and fluttered and flew about everywhere ; but poor melancholy Tip-Top was still confined to the nest with a broken wing. Finally, as it became evident that it would be long before he could fly, Jamie took him out of the nest, and made a nice little cage for him, and used to feed him every day, and he would hop about and seem tolerably contented ; but it was evident that he would be a lame-winged robin all his days.

Jamie's mother told him that Tip-Top's history was an allegory.

" I don't know what you mean, mamma," said Jamie.

" When something in a bird's life is like something in a boy's life, or when a story is similar in its meaning to reality, we call it an allegory. Little boys, when they are about half grown up, sometimes do just as Tip-Top did. They are in a great hurry to get away from home into the great world ; and then Temptation comes, with bright eyes and smooth velvet paws, and promises them fun ; and they go to bad places ; they get to smoking, and then to drinking ; and, finally, the bad habit gets them in its teeth and claws, and plays with them as a cat does with a mouse. They try to reform, just as your robin tried to get away from the cat ; but their bad habits pounce on them and drag them back. And so, when the time comes that they want to begin life, they are miserable, broken-down creatures, like your broken-winged robin.

" So, Jamie, remember, and don't try to be a man before your time, and let your parents judge for you while you are young ; and never believe in any soft white Pussy, with golden eyes, that comes and wants to tempt you to come down and play with her. If a big boy offers to teach you to smoke a cigar, that is Pussy. If a boy wants you to go into a billiard-saloon, that is Pussy. If a boy wants you to learn to drink anything with spirit in it, however sweetened and disguised, remember, Pussy is there ; and Pussy's claws are long, and Pussy's teeth are strong ; and if she gives you one shake in your youth, you will be like a broken-winged robin all your days."

Miss Katy-did sat on the branch of a flowering azalia, in her best suit of fine green and silver, with wings of point-lace from Mother Nature's web.

Miss Katy was in the very highest possible spirits, because her gallant cousin, Colonel Katy-did, had looked in to make her a morning visit. It was a fine morning, too, which goes for as much among the Katy-dids as among men and women. It was, in fact, a morning that Miss Katy thought must have been made on purpose for her to enjoy herself in. There had been a patter of rain the night before, which had kept the leaves awake talking to each other till nearly morning, but by dawn the small winds had blown brisk little puffs, and whisked the heavens clear and bright with their tiny wings, as you have seen Susan clear away the cobwebs in your mamma's parlor; and so now there were only left a thousand blinking, burning water-drops, hanging like convex mirrors at the end of each leaf, and Miss Kate admired herself in each one.

" Certainly I am a pretty creature," she said to herself ; and when the gallant Colonel said something about being dazzled by her beauty, she only tossed her head and took it as quite a matter of course.

" The fact is, my dear Colonel," she said, " I am thinking of giving a party, and you must help me make out the lists."

" My dear, you make me the happiest of Katy-dids."

" Now," said Miss Katy-did, drawing an azalia-leaf towards her, " let us see, — whom shall we have ? The

Fireflies, of course; everybody wants them, they are so brilliant; — a little unsteady, to be sure, but quite in the higher circles."

"Yes, we must have the Fireflies," echoed the Colonel.

"Well, then, — and the Butterflies and the Moths. Now, there's a trouble. There's such an everlasting tribe of these Moths; and if you invite dull people they're always sure all to come, every one of them. Still, if you have the Butterflies, you can't leave out the Moths."

"Old Mrs. Moth has been laid up lately with a gastric fever, and that may keep two or three of the Misses Moth at home," said the Colonel.

"Whatever could give the old lady such a turn?" said Miss Katy. "I thought she never was sick."

"I suspect it's high living. I understand she and her family ate up a whole ermine cape last month, and it disagreed with them."

"For my part, I can't conceive how the Moths can live as they do," said Miss Katy with a face of disgust. "Why, I could no more eat worsted and fur, as they do — "

"That is quite evident from the fairy-like delicacy of your appearance," said the Colonel. "One can see that nothing so gross or material has ever entered into your system."

"I'm sure," said Miss Katy, "mamma says she don't know what does keep me alive; half a dewdrop and a little bit of the nicest part of a rose-leaf, I assure you, often last me for a day. But we are forgetting our list. Let's see, — the Fireflies, Butterflies, Moths. The Bees must come, I suppose."

"The Bees are a worthy family," said the Colonel.

"Worthy enough, but dreadfully humdrum," said Miss Katy. "They never talk about anything but honey and housekeeping; still, they are a class of people one cannot neglect."

" Well, then, there are the Bumble-Bees."

" Oh, I dote on them! General Bumble is one of the most dashing, brilliant fellows of the day."

" I think he is shockingly corpulent," said Colonel Katy-did, not at all pleased to hear him praised; — "don't you ? "

" I don't know but he *is* a little stout," said Miss Katy; " but so distinguished and elegant in his manners, — something martial and breezy about him."

" Well, if you invite the Bumble-Bees you must have the Hornets."

" Those spiteful Hornets, — I detest them! "

" Nevertheless, dear Miss Katy, one does not like to offend the Hornets."

" No, one can't. There are those five Misses Hornet, — dreadful old maids! — as full of spite as they can live. You may be sure they will every one come, and be looking about to make spiteful remarks. Put down the Hornets, though."

" How about the Mosquitoes ! " said the Colonel.

" Those horrid Mosquitoes, — they are dreadfully plebeian ! Can't one cut them ? "

" Well, dear Miss Katy," said the Colonel, " if you ask my candid opinion as a friend, I should say *not*. There 's young Mosquito, who graduated last year, has gone into literature, and is connected with some of our leading papers, and they say he carries the sharpest pen of all the writers. It won't do to offend him."

" And so I suppose we must have his old aunts, and all six of his sisters, and all his dreadfully common relations."

" It is a pity," said the Colonel, " but one must pay one's tax to society."

Just at this moment the conference was interrupted by a visitor, Miss Keziah Cricket, who came in with her work-bag on her arm to ask a subscription for a poor family of

Ants who had just had their house hoed up in clearing the garden-walks.

"How stupid of them," said Katy, "not to know better than to put their house in the garden-walk; that's just like those Ants!"

"Well, they are in great trouble; all their stores destroyed, and their father killed, — cut quite in two by a hoe."

"How very shocking! I don't like to hear of such disagreeable things, — it affects my nerves terribly. Well, I'm sure I have n't anything to give. Mamma said yesterday she was sure she did n't know how our bills were to be paid, — and there's my green satin with point-lace yet to come home." And Miss Katy-did shrugged her shoulders and affected to be very busy with Colonel Katy-did, in just the way that young ladies sometimes do when they wish to signify to visitors that they had better leave.

Little Miss Cricket perceived how the case stood, and so hopped briskly off, without giving herself even time to be offended.

"Poor extravagant little thing!" said she to herself, "it was hardly worth while to ask her."

"Pray, shall you invite the Crickets?" said Colonel Katy-did.

"Who? I? Why, Colonel, what a question! Invite the Crickets? Of what can you be thinking?"

"And shall you not ask the Locusts, or the Grasshoppers?"

"Certainly. The Locusts, of course, — a very old and distinguished family; and the Grasshoppers are pretty well, and ought to be asked. But we must draw a line somewhere, — and the Crickets! why, it's shocking even to think of!"

"I thought they were nice, respectable people."

"Oh, perfectly nice and respectable, — very good people,

in fact, so far as that goes.   But then you must see the difficulty."

"My dear cousin, I am afraid you must explain."

"Why, their *color*, to be sure.   Don't you see?"

"Oh!" said the Colonel.   "That's it, is it?   Excuse me, but I have been living in France, where these distinctions are wholly unknown, and I have not yet got myself in the train of fashionable ideas here."

"Well, then, let me teach you," said Miss Katy.   "You know we republicans go for no distinctions except those created by Nature herself, and we found our rank upon *color*, because that is clearly a thing that none has any hand in but our Maker.   You see?"

"Yes; but who decides what color shall be the reigning color?"

"I'm surprised to hear the question!   The only true color — the only proper one — is *our* color, to be sure.   A lovely pea-green is the precise shade on which to found aristocratic distinction.   But then we are liberal; — we associate with the Moths, who are gray; with the Butterflies, who are blue-and-gold-colored; with the Grasshoppers, yellow and brown; — and society would become dreadfully mixed if it were not fortunately ordered that the Crickets are black as jet.   The fact is, that a class to be looked down upon is necessary to all elegant society, and if the Crickets were not black, we could not keep them down, because, as everybody knows, they are often a great deal cleverer than we are.   They have a vast talent for music and dancing; they are very quick at learning, and would be getting to the very top of the ladder if we once allowed them to climb.   But their being black is a convenience, — because, as long as we are green and they black, we have a superiority that can never be taken from us.   Don't you see, now?"

"Oh, yes, I see exactly," said the Colonel.

"Now that Keziah Cricket, who just came in here, is quite a musician, and her old father plays the violin beautifully; — by the way, we might engage him for our orchestra."

And so Miss Katy's ball came off, and the performers kept it up from sundown till daybreak, so that it seemed as if every leaf in the forest were alive. The Katy-dids, and the Mosquitoes, and the Locusts, and a full orchestra of Crickets made the air perfectly vibrate, insomuch that old Parson Too-whit, who was preaching a Thursday evening lecture to a very small audience, announced to his hearers that he should certainly write a discourse against dancing for the next weekly occasion.

The good Doctor was even with his word in the matter, and gave out some very sonorous discourses, without in the least stopping the round of gayeties kept up by these dissipated Katy-dids, which ran on, night after night, till the celebrated Jack Frost epidemic, which occurred somewhere about the first of September.

Poor Miss Katy, with her flimsy green satin and point-lace, was one of the first victims, and fell from the bough in company with a sad shower of last year's leaves. The worthy Cricket family, however, avoided Jack Frost by emigrating in time to the chimney-corner of a nice little cottage that had been built in the wood that summer.

There good old Mr. and Mrs. Cricket, with sprightly Miss Keziah and her brothers and sisters, found a warm and welcome home; and when the storm howled without, and lashed the poor naked trees, the Crickets on the warm hearth would chirp out cheery welcome to papa as he came in from the snowy path, or mamma as she sat at her work-basket.

"Cheep, cheep, cheep!" little Freddy would say. "Mamma, who is it says 'cheep'?"

" Dear Freddy, it 's our own dear little cricket, who loves us and comes to sing to us when the snow is on the ground."

So when poor Miss Katy-did's satin and lace were all swept away, the warm home-talents of the Crickets made for them a welcome refuge.

OLD MOTHER MAGPIE was about the busiest character in the forest. But you must know that there is a great difference between being busy and being industrious. One may be very busy all the time, and yet not in the least industrious ; and this was the case with Mother Magpie.

She was always full of everybody's business but her own, —up and down, here and there, everywhere but in her own nest, knowing every one's affairs, telling what everybody had been doing or ought to do, and ready to cast her advice *gratis* at every bird and beast of the woods.

Now she bustled up to the parsonage at the top of the oak-tree, to tell old Parson Too-whit what she thought he ought to preach for his next sermon, and how dreadful the morals of the parish were becoming. Then, having perfectly bewildered the poor old gentleman, who was always sleepy of a Monday morning, Mother Magpie would take a peep into Mrs. Oriole's nest, sit chattering on a bough above, and pour forth floods of advice, which, poor little Mrs. Oriole used to say to her husband, bewildered her more than a hard northeast storm.

"Depend upon it, my dear," Mother Magpie would say, "that this way of building your nest, swinging like an old empty stocking from a bough, is n't at all the thing. I never built one so in my life, and I never have headaches. Now you complain always that your head aches whenever I call upon you. It 's all on account of this way of swinging and swaying about in such an absurd manner."

"But, my dear," piped Mrs. Oriole, timidly, "the Orioles

always have built in this manner, and it suits our constitution."

"A fiddle on our constitution! How can you tell what agrees with your constitution unless you try? You own you are not well; you are subject to headaches, and every physician will tell you that a tilting motion disorders the stomach and acts upon the brain. Ask old Dr. Kite. I was talking with him about your case only yesterday, and says he, 'Mrs. Magpie, I perfectly agree with you.'"

"But my husband prefers this style of building."

"That's only because he is n't properly instructed. Pray, did you ever attend Dr. Kite's lectures on the nervous system?"

"No, I have no time to attend lectures. Who would set on the eggs?"

"Why, your husband, to be sure; don't he take his turn in setting? If he don't he ought to. I shall speak to him about it. My husband always sets regularly half the time, that I might have time to go about and exercise."

"O Mrs. Magpie, pray don't speak to my husband; he will think I 've been complaining."

"No, no, he won't! Let me alone. I understand just how to say the thing. I 've advised hundreds of young husbands in my day, and I never give offence."

"But I tell you, Mrs. Magpie, I don't want any interference between my husband and me, and I will not have it," says Mrs. Oriole, with her little round eyes flashing.

"Don't put yourself in a passion, my dear; the more you talk, the more sure I am that your nervous system is running down, or you would n't forget good manners in this way. You 'd better take my advice, for I understand just what to do," — and away sails Mother Magpie; and presently young Oriole comes home, all in a flutter.

"I say, my dear, if you will persist in gossiping over our private family matters with that old Mother Magpie — "

"My dear, I don't gossip; she comes and bores me to death with talking, and then goes off and mistakes what she has been saying for what I said."

"But you must *cut* her."

"I try to, all I can; but she won't *be* cut."

"It 's enough to make a bird swear," said Tommy Oriole.

Tommy Oriole, to say the truth, had as good a heart as ever beat under bird's feathers; but then he had a weakness for concerts and general society, because he was held to be, by all odds, the handsomest bird in the woods, and sung like an angel; and so the truth was he did n't confine himself so much to the domestic nest as Tom Titmouse or Billy Wren. But he determined that he would n't have old Mother Magpie interfering with his affairs.

"The fact is," quoth Tommy, "I am a society bird, and Nature has marked out for me a course beyond the range of the commonplace, and my wife must learn to accommodate. If she has a brilliant husband, whose success gratifies her ambition and places her in a distinguished public position, she must pay something for it. I 'm sure Billy Wren's wife would give her very bill to see her husband in the circles where I am quite at home. To say the truth, my wife was all well enough content till old Mother Magpie interfered. It is quite my duty to take strong ground, and show that I cannot be dictated to."

So, after this, Tommy Oriole went to rather more concerts, and spent less time at home than ever he did before, which was all that Mother Magpie effected in that quarter. I confess this was very bad in Tommy; but then birds are no better than men in domestic matters, and sometimes will take the most unreasonable courses, if a meddlesome Magpie gets her claw into their nest.

But old Mother Magpie had now got a new business in hand in another quarter. She bustled off down to Waterdock Lane, where, as we said in a former narrative, lived the old music-teacher, Dr. Bullfrog. The poor old Doctor was a simple-minded, good, amiable creature, who had played the double-bass and led the forest choir on all public occasions since nobody knows when. Latterly some youngsters had arisen who sneered at his performances as behind the age. In fact, since a great city had grown up in the vicinity of the forest, tribes of wandering boys broke up the simple tastes and quiet habits which old Mother Nature had always kept up in those parts. They pulled the young checkerberry before it even had time to blossom, rooted up the sassafras shrubs and gnawed their roots, fired off guns at the birds, and, on several occasions when old Dr. Bullfrog was leading a concert, had dashed in and broken up the choir by throwing stones.

This was not the worst of it. The little varlets had a way of jeering at the simple old Doctor and his concerts, and mimicking the tones of his bass-viol. "There you go, Paddy-go-donk, Paddy-go-donk — umph — chunk," some rascal of a boy would shout, while poor old Bullfrog's yellow spectacles would be bedewed with tears of honest indignation. In time, the jeers of these little savages began to tell on the society in the forest, and to corrupt their simple manners; and it was whispered among the younger and more heavy birds and squirrels, that old Bullfrog was a bore, and that it was time to get up a new style of music in the parish, and to give the charge of it to some more modern performer. Poor old Dr. Bullfrog knew nothing of this, however, and was doing his simple best, in peace, when Mother Magpie called in upon him, one morning.

"Well, neighbor, how unreasonable people are! Who would have thought that the youth of our generation should have no more consideration for established merit? Now, for my part, *I* think your music-teaching never was better; and as for our choir, I maintain constantly that it never was in better order, but — Well, one may wear her tongue out, but one can never make these young folks listen to reason."

" I really don't understand you, ma'am," said poor Dr. Bullfrog.

" What ! you have n't heard of a committee that is going to call on you, to ask you to resign the care of the parish music ? "

" Madam," said Dr. Bullfrog, with all that energy of tone for which he was remarkable, " I don't believe it,— I *can't* believe it. You must have made a mistake."

" I mistake ! No, no, my good friend ; I never make mistakes. What I know, I know certainly. Was n't it I that said I knew there was an engagement between Tim Chipmunk and Nancy Nibble, who are married this blessed day ? I knew that thing six weeks before any bird or beast in our parts ; and I can tell you, you are going to be scandalously and ungratefully treated, Dr. Bullfrog."

" Bless me, we shall all be ruined ! " said Mrs. Bullfrog ; " my poor husband — "

" Oh, as to that, if you take things in time, and listen to my advice," said Mother Magpie, " we may yet pull you through. You must alter your style a little, — adapt it to modern times. Everybody now is a little touched with the operatic fever, and there 's Tommy Oriole has been to New Orleans and brought back a touch of the artistic. If you would try his style a little, — something Tyrolean, you see."

" Dear madam, consider my voice. I never could hit the high notes."

" How do you know ? It 's all practice ; Tommy Oriole says so. Just try the scales. As to your voice, your manner of living has a great deal to do with it. I always did tell you that your passion for water injured your singing. Suppose Tommy Oriole should sit half his days up to his hips in water, as you do, — his voice would be as hoarse and rough as yours. Come up on the bank, and learn to perch as we birds do. We are the true musical race."

And so poor Mr. Bullfrog was persuaded to forego his pleasant little cottage under the cat-tails, where his yellow spectacles and honest round back had excited, even in the minds of the boys, sentiments of respect and compassion. He came up into the garden, and established himself under a burdock, and began to practise Italian scales.

The result was, that poor old Dr. Bullfrog, instead of being considered as a respectable old bore, got himself universally laughed at for aping fashionable manners. Every bird and beast in the forest had a gibe at him; and even old Parson Too-whit thought it worth his while to make him a pastoral call, and admonish him about courses unbefitting his age and standing. As to Mother Magpie, you may be sure that she assured every one how sorry she was that dear old Dr. Bullfrog had made such a fool of himself; if he had taken her advice, he would have kept on respectably as a nice old Bullfrog should.

But the tragedy for the poor old music-teacher grew even more melancholy in its termination; for one day as he was sitting disconsolately under a currant-bush in the garden, practising his poor old notes in a quiet way, *thump* came a great blow of a hoe, which nearly broke his back.

"Hullo! what ugly beast have we got here?" said Tom Noakes, the gardener's boy. "Here, here, Wasp, my boy."

What a fright for a poor, quiet, old Bullfrog, as little wiry, wicked Wasp came at him, barking and yelping. He jumped with all his force sheer over a patch of bushes into the river, and swam back to his old home among the cat-tails. And always after that it was observable that he was very low-spirited, and took very dark views of life; but nothing made him so angry as any allusion to Mother Magpie, of whom, from that time, he never spoke except as *Old Mother Mischief.*

THE SQUIRRELS THAT LIVED IN A HOUSE

ONCE upon a time a gentleman went out into a great forest, and cut away the trees, and built there a very nice little cottage. It was set very low on the ground, and had very large bow-windows, and so much of it was glass that one could look through it on every side and see what was going on in the forest. You could see the shadows of the fern-leaves, as they flickered and wavered over the ground, and the scarlet partridge-berry and wintergreen plums that matted round the roots of the trees, and the bright spots of sunshine that fell through their branches and went dancing about among the bushes and leaves at their roots. You could see the little chipping sparrows and thrushes and robins and bluebirds building their nests here and there among the branches, and watch them from day to day as they laid their eggs and hatched their young. You could also see red squirrels, and gray squirrels, and little striped chip-squirrels, darting and springing about, here and there and everywhere, running races with each other from bough to bough, and chattering at each other in the gayest possible manner.

You may be sure that such a strange thing as a great mortal house for human beings to live in did not come into this wild wood without making quite a stir and excitement among the inhabitants that lived there before. All the time it was building, there was the greatest possible commotion in the breasts of all the older population ; and there was n't even a black ant, or a cricket, that did not have his own opinion about it, and did not tell the other ants and crickets just what he thought the world was coming to in consequence.

Old Mrs. Rabbit declared that the hammering and pounding made her nervous, and gave her most melancholy forebodings of evil times. "Depend upon it, children," she said to her long-eared family, "no good will come to us from this establishment. Where man is, there comes always trouble for us poor rabbits."

The old chestnut-tree, that grew on the edge of the woodland ravine, drew a great sigh which shook all his leaves, and expressed it as his conviction that no good would ever come of it, — a conviction that at once struck to the heart of every chestnut-burr. The squirrels talked together of the dreadful state of things that would ensue. "Why!" said old Father Gray, "it's evident that Nature made the nuts for us; but one of these great human creatures will carry off and gormandize upon what would keep a hundred poor families of squirrels in comfort." Old Ground-mole said it did not require very sharp eyes to see into the future, and it would just end in bringing down the price of real estate in the whole vicinity, so that every decent-minded and respectable quadruped would be obliged to move away; — for his part, he was ready to sell out for anything he could get. The bluebirds and bobolinks, it is true, took more cheerful views of matters; but then, as old Mrs. Ground-mole observed, they were a flighty set, — half their time careering and dissipating in the Southern States, — and could not be expected to have that patriotic attachment to their native soil that those had who had grubbed in it from their earliest days.

"This race of man," said the old chestnut-tree, "is never ceasing in its restless warfare on Nature. In our forest solitudes, hitherto, how peacefully, how quietly, how regularly has everything gone on! Not a flower has missed its appointed time of blossoming, or failed to perfect its fruit. No matter how hard has been the winter, how loud the winds have roared, and how high the snow-banks have been piled, all has come right again in spring. Not the least root has lost itself under the snows, so as not to be ready with its fresh leaves and blossoms when the sun returns to melt the frosty chains of winter. We have storms sometimes that threaten to shake everything to pieces, — the thunder roars, the lightning flashes, and the winds howl and beat ; but, when all is past, everything comes out better and brighter than before, — not a bird is killed, not the frailest flower destroyed. But man comes, and in one day he will make a desolation that centuries cannot repair. Ignorant boor that he is, and all incapable of appreciating the glorious works of Nature, it seems to be his glory to be able to destroy in a few hours what it was the work of ages to produce. The noble oak, that has been cut away to build this contemptible human dwelling, had a life older and wiser than that of any man in this country. That tree has seen generations of men come and go. It was a fresh young tree when Shakespeare was born ; it was hardly a middle-aged tree when he died ; it was growing here when the first ship brought the white men to our shores ; and hundreds and hundreds of those whom they call bravest, wisest, strongest, — warriors, statesmen, orators, and poets, — have been born, have grown up, lived, and died, while yet it has outlived them all. It has seen more wisdom than the best of them ; but two or three hours of brutal strength sufficed to lay it low. Which of these dolts could make a tree ? I 'd like to see them do anything like it. How noisy and clumsy are all their movements, — chopping, pounding, rasping, hammering ! And, after all, what do they build ? In the forest we do everything so quietly. A tree would be ashamed of itself that could not get its growth without making such a noise and dust and fuss. Our life is the perfection of good manners. For my part,

I feel degraded at the mere presence of these human beings ; but, alas! I am old ; — a hollow place at my heart warns me of the progress of decay, and probably it will be seized upon by these rapacious creatures as an excuse for laying me as low as my noble green brother."

In spite of all this disquiet about it, the little cottage grew and was finished. The walls were covered with pretty paper, the floors carpeted with pretty carpets ; and, in fact, when it was all arranged, and the garden walks laid out, and beds of flowers planted around, it began to be confessed, even among the most critical, that it was not after all so bad a thing as was to have been feared.

A black ant went in one day and made a tour of exploration up and down, over chairs and tables, up the ceilings and down again, and, coming out, wrote an article for the "Crickets' Gazette," in which he described the new abode as a veritable palace. Several butterflies fluttered in and sailed about and were wonderfully delighted, and then a bumble-bee and two or three honey-bees, who expressed themselves well pleased with the house, but more especially enchanted with the garden. In fact, when it was found that the proprietors were very fond of the rural solitudes of Nature, and had come out there for the purpose of enjoying them undisturbed, — that they watched and spared the anemones, and the violets, and bloodroots, and dog's-tooth violets, and little woolly rolls of fern that began to grow up under the trees in spring, — that they never allowed a gun to be fired to scare the birds, and watched the building of their nests with the greatest interest, — then an opinion in favor of human beings began to gain ground, and every cricket and bird and beast was loud in their praise.

"Mamma," said young Tit-bit, a frisky young squirrel, to his mother one day, "why won't you let Frisky and me go into that pretty new cottage to play ? "

"My dear," said his mother, who was a very wary and careful old squirrel, "how can you think of it ? The race of man are full of devices for traps and pitfalls, and who could say what might happen if you put yourself in their power ? If you had wings like the butterflies and bees, you might fly in and out again, and so gratify your curiosity ; but, as matters stand, it's best for you to keep well out of their way."

"But, mother, there is such a nice, good lady lives there ! I believe she is a good fairy, and she seems to love us all so ; she sits in the bow-window and watches us for hours, and she scatters corn all round at the roots of the tree for us to eat."

"She is nice enough," said the old mother-squirrel, "if you keep far enough off ; but I tell you, you can't be too careful."

Now this good fairy that the squirrels discoursed about was a nice little old lady that the children used to call Aunt Esther, and she was a dear lover of birds and squirrels, and all sorts of animals, and had studied their little ways till she knew just what would please them ; and so she would every day throw out crumbs for the sparrows, and little bits of bread and wool and cotton to help the birds that were building their nests, and would scatter corn and nuts for the squirrels ; and while she sat at her work in the bow-window she would smile to see the birds flying away with the wool, and the squirrels nibbling their nuts. After a while the birds grew so tame that they would hop into the bow-window, and eat their crumbs off the carpet.

"There, mamma," said Tit-bit and Frisky, "only see ! Jenny Wren and Cock Robin have been in at the bow-window, and it did n't hurt them, and why can't we go ? "

"Well, my dears," said old Mother Squirrel, "you must do it very carefully : never forget that you have n't wings like Jenny Wren and Cock Robin."

So the next day Aunt Esther laid a train of corn from the roots of the trees to the bow-window, and then from the bow-window to her work-basket, which stood on the floor beside her; and then she put quite a handful of corn in the work-basket, and sat down by it, and seemed intent on her sewing. Very soon, creep, creep, creep, came Tit-bit and Frisky to the window, and then into the room, just as sly and as still as could be, and Aunt Esther sat just like a statue for fear of disturbing them. They looked all around in high glee, and when they came to the basket it seemed to them a wonderful little summer-house, made on purpose for them to play in. They nosed about in it, and turned over the scissors and the needle-book, and took a nibble at her white wax, and jostled the spools, meanwhile stowing away the corn in each side of their little chops, till they both of them looked as if they had the mumps.

At last Aunt Esther put out her hand to touch them, when, whisk-frisk, out they went, and up the trees, chattering and laughing before she had time even to wink.

But after this they used to come in every day, and when she put corn in her hand and held it very still they would eat out of it; and, finally, they would get into her hand, until one day she gently closed it over them, and Frisky and Tit-bit were fairly caught.

Oh, how their hearts beat! but the good fairy only spoke gently to them, and soon unclosed her hand and let them go again. So, day after day, they grew to have more and more faith in her, till they would climb into her work-basket, sit on her shoulder, or nestle away in her lap as she sat sewing. They made also long exploring voyages all over the house, up and through all the chambers, till finally, I grieve to say, poor Frisky came to an untimely end by being drowned in the water-tank at the top of the house.

The dear good fairy passed away from the house in time, and went to a land where the flowers never fade, and the birds never die; but the squirrels still continue to make the place a favorite resort.

"In fact, my dear," said old Mother Red one winter to her mate, "what is the use of one's living in this cold hollow tree, when these amiable people have erected this pretty cottage where there is plenty of room for us and them too? Now I have examined between the eaves, and there is a charming place where we can store our nuts, and where we can whip in and out of the garret, and have the free range of the house; and, say what you will, these humans have delightful ways of being warm and comfortable in winter."

So Mr. and Mrs. Red set up housekeeping in the cottage, and had no end of nuts and other good things stored up there. The trouble of all this was that, as Mrs. Red was a notable body, and got up to begin her housekeeping operations, and woke up all her children, at four o'clock in the morning, the good people often were disturbed by a great rattling and fuss in the walls, while yet it seemed dark night. Then sometimes, too, I grieve to say, Mrs. Squirrel would give her husband vigorous curtain lectures in the night, which made him so indignant that he would rattle off to another quarter of the garret to sleep by himself; and all this broke the rest of the worthy people who built the house.

What is to be done about this we don't know. What would you do about it? Would you let the squirrels live in your house, or not? When our good people come down of a cold winter morning, and see the squirrels dancing and frisking down the trees, and chasing each other so merrily over the garden-chair between them, or sitting with their tails saucily over their backs, they look so jolly and jaunty and pretty that they almost forgive them for disturbing their night's rest, and think that they will not do anything to drive them out of the garret to-day. And so it goes on; but how long the squirrels will rent the cottage in this fashion, I 'm sure I dare not undertake to say.

HUM, THE SON OF BUZ

At Rye Beach, during our summer's vacation, there came, as there always will to seaside visitors, two or three cold, chilly, rainy days, — days when the skies that long had not rained a drop seemed suddenly to bethink themselves of their remissness, and to pour down water, not by drops, but by pailfuls. The chilly wind blew and whistled, the water dashed along the ground, and careered in foamy rills along the roadside, and the bushes bent beneath the constant flood. It was plain that there was to be no sea-bathing on such a day, no walks, no rides; and so, shivering and drawing our blanket-shawls close about us, we sat down to the window to watch the storm outside. The rose-bushes under the window hung dripping under their load of moisture, each spray shedding a constant shower on the spray below it. On one of these lower sprays, under the perpetual drip, what should we see but a poor little humming-bird, drawn up into the tiniest shivering ball, and clinging with a desperate grasp to his uncomfortable perch. A humming-bird we knew him to be at once, though his feathers were so matted and glued down by the rain that he looked not much bigger than a honey-bee, and as different as possible from the smart, pert, airy little character that we had so often seen flirting with the flowers. He was evidently a humming-bird in adversity, and whether he ever would hum again looked to us exceedingly doubtful. Immediately, however, we sent out to have him taken in. When the friendly hand seized him, he gave a little faint, watery squeak, evidently thinking that his last hour was come, and that grim Death was about to carry him off to the land of dead birds. What a time we had reviving him, — holding the little wet thing in the warm hollow of our hands, and feeling him shiver and palpitate! His eyes were fast closed; his tiny claws, which looked slender as cobwebs, were knotted close to his body, and it was long before one could feel the least motion in them. Finally, to our great joy, we felt a brisk little kick, and then a flutter of wings, and then a determined peck of the beak, which showed that there was some bird left in him yet, and that he meant at any rate to find out where he was.

Unclosing our hands a small space, out popped the little head with a pair of round brilliant eyes. Then we bethought ourselves of feeding him, and forthwith prepared him a stiff glass of sugar and water, a drop of which we held to his bill. After turning his head attentively, like a bird who knew what he was about and did n't mean to be chaffed, he briskly put out a long, flexible tongue slightly forked at the end, and licked off the comfortable beverage with great relish. Immediately he was pronounced out of danger by the small humane society which had undertaken the charge of his restoration, and we began to cast about for getting him a settled establishment in our apartment. I gave up my work-box to him for a sleeping-room, and it was medically ordered that he should take a nap. So we filled the box with cotton, and he was formally put to bed with a folded cambric handkerchief round his neck, to keep him from beating his wings. Out of his white wrappings he looked forth green and grave as any judge with his bright round eyes. Like a bird of discretion, he seemed to understand what was being done to him, and resigned himself sensibly to go to sleep.

The box was covered with a sheet of paper perforated with holes for purposes of ventilation; for even humming-birds have a little pair of lungs, and need their own little portion of air to fill them, so that they may make bright, scarlet, little drops of blood to keep life's fire burning in their tiny bodies. Our bird's lungs manufactured brilliant blood, as we found out by experience; for in his first nap he contrived to nestle himself into the cotton of which his bed was made, and to get more of it than he needed into his long bill. We pulled it out as carefully as we could, but there came out of his bill two round, bright, scarlet, little drops of blood. Our chief medical authority looked grave, pronounced a probable hemorrhage from the lungs, and gave him over at once. We, less scientific, declared that we had only cut his little tongue by drawing out the filaments of cotton, and that he would do well enough in time, — as it afterward appeared he did, — for from that day there was no more bleeding. In the course of the second day he began to take short flights about the room, though he seemed to prefer to return to us, — perching on our fingers or heads or shoulders, and sometimes choosing to sit in this way for half an hour at a time. "These great giants," he seemed to say to himself, "are not bad people after all; they have a comfortable way with them; how nicely they dried and warmed me! Truly a bird might do worse than to live with them."

So he made up his mind to form a fourth in the little company of three that usually sat and read, worked, and sketched in that apartment, and we christened him "Hum, the son of Buz." He became an individuality, a character, whose little doings formed a part of every letter, and some extracts from these will show what some of his little ways were.

"Hum has learned to sit upon my finger, and eat his sugar and water out of a teaspoon with most Christian-like decorum. He has but one weakness, — he will occasionally jump into the spoon and sit in his sugar and water, and then appear to wonder where it goes to. His plumage is in rather a drabbled state, owing to these performances. I have sketched him as he sat to-day on a bit of Spiræa which I brought in for him. When absorbed in reflection, he sits with his bill straight up in the air, as I have drawn him. Mr. A—— reads Macaulay to us, and you should see the wise air with which, perched on Jenny's thumb, he cocked his head now one side and then the other, apparently listening with most critical attention. His confidence in us seems unbounded; he lets us stroke his head, smooth his feathers, without a flutter; and is never better pleased than sitting, as he has been doing all this while, on my hand, turning up his bill, and watching my face with great edification.

"I have just been having a sort of maternal struggle to make him go to bed in his box; but he evidently considers himself sufficiently convalescent to make a stand for his rights as a bird, and so scratched indignantly out of his wrappings, and set himself up to roost on the edge of the box, with an air worthy of a turkey, at the very least. Having brought in a lamp, he has opened his eyes round and wide, and sits cocking his little head at me reflectively."

When the weather cleared away, and the sun came out bright, Hum became entirely well, and seemed resolved to take the measure of his new life with us. Our windows were closed in the lower part of the sash by frames with mosquito gauze, so that the sun and air found free admission, and yet our little rover could not pass out. On the first sunny day he took an exact survey of our apartment from ceiling to floor, humming about, examining every point with his bill, — all the crevices, mouldings, each little indentation in the bed-post, each window-pane, each chair and stand; and, as it is a very simply furnished seaside apartment, his scrutiny was soon finished. We wondered,

at first, what this was all about; but, on watching him
more closely, we found that he was actively engaged in
getting his living, by darting out his long tongue hither
and thither, and drawing in all the tiny flies and insects
which in summer-time are to be found in an apartment.
In short, we found that, though the nectar of flowers was
his dessert, yet he had his roast beef and mutton-chop to
look after, and that his bright, brilliant blood was not made
out of a simple vegetarian diet. Very shrewd and keen he
was, too, in measuring the size of insects before he attempted
to swallow them. The smallest class were whisked off with
lightning speed; but about larger ones he would sometimes
wheel and hum for some minutes, darting hither and thither,
and surveying them warily; and if satisfied that they could
be carried, he would come down with a quick, central dart
which would finish the unfortunate at a snap. The larger
flies seemed to irritate him, — especially when they intimated to him that his plumage was sugary, by settling on
his wings and tail; when he would lay about him spitefully,
wielding his bill like a sword. A grasshopper that strayed
in, and was sunning himself on the window-seat, gave him
great discomposure. Hum evidently considered him an in-
truder, and seemed to long to make a dive at him; but,
with characteristic prudence, confined himself to threatening
movements, which did not exactly hit. He saw evidently
that he could not swallow him whole, and what might
ensue from trying him piecemeal he wisely forbore to essay.

Hum had his own favorite places and perches. From
the first day he chose for his nightly roost a towel-line
which had been drawn across the corner over the wash-
stand, where he every night established himself with one
claw in the edge of the towel and the other clasping the
line, and, ruffling up his feathers till he looked like a little
chestnut-burr, he would resign himself to the soundest sleep.
He did not tuck his head under his wing, but seemed to

sink it down between his shoulders, with his bill almost straight up in the air. One evening one of us, going to use the towel, jarred the line, and soon after found that Hum had been thrown from his perch, and was hanging head downward, fast asleep, still clinging to the line. Another evening, being discomposed by somebody coming to the towel-line after he had settled himself, he fluttered off; but so sleepy that he had not discretion to poise himself again, and was found clinging, like a little bunch of green floss silk, to the mosquito netting of the window.

A day after this we brought in a large green bough, and put it up over the looking-glass. Hum noticed it before it had been there five minutes, flew to it, and began a regular survey, perching now here, now there, till he seemed to find a twig that exactly suited him; and after that he roosted there every night. Who does not see in this change all the signs of reflection and reason that are shown by us in thinking over our circumstances, and trying to better them? It seemed to say in so many words: "That towel-line is an unsafe place for a bird; I get frightened, and wake from bad dreams to find myself head downwards; so I will find a better roost on this twig."

When our little Jenny one day put on a clean white muslin gown embellished with red sprigs, Hum flew towards her, and with his bill made instant examination of these new appearances; and one day, being very affectionately disposed, perched himself on her shoulder, and sat some time. On another occasion, while Mr. A —— was reading, Hum established himself on the top of his head just over the middle of his forehead, in the precise place where our young belles have lately worn stuffed humming-birds, making him look as if dressed out for a party. Hum's most favorite perch was the back of the great rocking-chair, which, being covered by a tidy, gave some hold into which he could catch his little claws. There he would sit, balancing himself cleverly if its occupant chose to swing to and fro, and seeming to be listening to the conversation or reading.

Hum had his different moods, like human beings. On cold, cloudy, gray days he appeared to be somewhat depressed in spirits, hummed less about the room, and sat humped up with his feathers ruffled, looking as much like a bird in a great-coat as possible. But on hot, sunny days every feather sleeked itself down, and his little body looked natty and trim, his head alert, his eyes bright, and it was impossible to come near him, for his agility. Then let mosquitoes and little flies look about them! Hum snapped them up without mercy, and seemed to be all over the ceiling in a moment, and resisted all our efforts at any personal familiarity with a saucy alacrity.

Hum had his established institutions in our room, the chief of which was a tumbler with a little sugar and water mixed in it, and a spoon laid across, out of which he helped himself whenever he felt in the mood, — sitting on the edge of the tumbler, and dipping his long bill, and lapping with his little forked tongue like a kitten. When he found his spoon accidentally dry, he would stoop over and dip his bill in the water in the tumbler, — which caused the prophecy on the part of some of his guardians, that he would fall in some day and be drowned. For which reason it was agreed to keep only an inch in depth of the fluid at the bottom of the tumbler. A wise precaution this proved; for the next morning I was awaked, not by the usual hum over my head, but by a sharp little flutter, and found Mr. Hum beating his wings in the tumbler — having actually tumbled in during his energetic efforts to get his morning coffee before I was awake.

Hum seemed perfectly happy and satisfied in his quarters, — but one day, when the door was left open, made a dart out, and so into the open sunshine. Then, to be sure, we thought we had lost him. We took the mosquito netting out of all the windows, and, setting his tumbler of sugar and water in a conspicuous place, went about our usual occupations. We saw him joyous and brisk among the honeysuckles outside the window, and it was gravely predicted that he would return no more. But at dinner-time in came Hum, familiar as possible, and sat down to his spoon as if nothing had happened; instantly we closed our windows and had him secure once more.

At another time I was going to ride to the Atlantic House, about a mile from my boarding-place. I left all secure, as I supposed, at home. While gathering moss on the walls there, I was surprised by a little green humming-bird flying familiarly right towards my face, and humming above my head. I called out, "Here is Hum's very brother." But, on returning home, I saw that the door of the room was open, and Hum was gone. Now certainly we gave him up for lost. I sat down to painting, and in a few minutes in flew Hum, and settled on the edge of my tumbler in a social, confidential way, which seemed to say, " O, you've got back then." After taking his usual drink of sugar and water, he began to fly about the ceiling as usual, and we gladly shut him in.

When our five weeks at the seaside were up, and it was time to go home, we had great questionings what was to be done with Hum. To get him home with us was our desire, — but who ever heard of a humming-bird traveling by railroad ? Great were the consultings; a little basket of Indian work was filled up with cambric handkerchiefs, and a bottle of sugar and water provided, and we started with him for a day's journey. When we arrived at night the first care was to see what had become of Hum, who had not been looked at since we fed him with sugar and water in Boston. We found him alive and well, but so dead asleep that we could not wake him to roost; so we put him to bed on a toilet cushion, and arranged his tumbler for morn-

ing. The next day found him alive and humming, exploring the room and pictures, perching now here and now
there ; but, as the weather was chilly, he sat for the most
part of the time in a humped-up state on the tip of a pair
of stag's horns. We moved him to a more sunny apartment ; but, alas ! the equinoctial storm came on, and there
was no sun to be had for days. Hum was blue ; the pleasant seaside days were over ; his room was lonely, the pleasant three that had enlivened the apartment at Rye no longer
came in and out ; evidently he was lonesome, and gave way
to depression. One chilly morning he managed again to
fall into his tumbler, and wet himself through ; and notwithstanding warm bathings and tender nursings, the poor
little fellow seemed to get diphtheria, or something quite as
bad for humming-birds.

We carried him to a neighboring sunny parlor, where ivy
embowers all the walls, and the sun lies all day. There he
revived a little, danced up and down, perched on a green
spray that was wreathed across the breast of a Psyche, and
looked then like a little flitting soul returning to its rest.
Towards evening he drooped ; and, having been nursed and
warmed and cared for, he was put to sleep on a green twig
laid on the piano. In that sleep the little head drooped
— nodded — fell ; and little Hum went where other bright
dreams go, — to the Land of the Hereafter.

OUR COUNTRY NEIGHBORS

WE have just built our house in rather an out-of-the-way place, — on the bank of a river, and under the shade of a patch of woods which is a veritable remain of quite an ancient forest. The checkerberry and partridge-plum, with their glossy green leaves and scarlet berries, still carpet the ground under its deep shadows; and prince's-pine and other kindred evergreens declare its native wildness, — for these are children of the wild woods, that never come after plough and harrow has once broken a soil.

When we tried to look out the spot for our house, we had to get a surveyor to go before us and cut a path through the dense underbrush that was laced together in a general network of boughs and leaves, and grew so high as to overtop our heads. Where the house stands, four or five great old oaks and chestnuts had to be cut away to let it in ; and now it stands on the bank of the river, the edges of which are still overhung with old forest-trees, chestnuts and oaks, which look at themselves in the glassy stream.

A little knoll near the house was chosen for a garden spot ; a dense, dark mass of trees above, of bushes in mid-air, and of all sorts of ferns and wild-flowers and creeping vines on the ground. All these had to be cleared out, and a dozen great trees cut down and dragged off to a neighboring saw-mill, there to be transformed into boards to finish off our house. Then, fetching a great machine, such as might be used to pull a giant's teeth, with ropes, pulleys, oxen, and men, and might and main, we pulled out the stumps, with their great prongs and their network of roots

and fibres ; and then, alas ! we had to begin with all the
pretty, wild, lovely bushes, and the checkerberries and ferns
and wild blackberries and huckleberry-bushes, and dig them
up remorselessly, that we might plant our corn and squashes.
And so we got a house and a garden right out of the heart
of our piece of wild wood, about a mile from the city of
H ——.

Well, then, people said it was a lonely place, and far
from neighbors, — by which they meant that it was a good
way for them to come to see us. But we soon found that
whoever goes into the woods to live finds neighbors of a
new kind, and some to whom it is rather hard to become
accustomed.

For instance, on a fine day early in April, as we were
crossing over to superintend the building of our house, we
were startled by a striped snake with his little bright eyes,
raising himself to look at us, and putting out his red forked
tongue. Now there is no more harm in these little garden-
snakes than there is in a robin or a squirrel ; they are poor
little, peaceable, timid creatures, which could not do any
harm if they would ; but the prejudices of society are so
strong against them, that one does not like to cultivate too
much intimacy with them. So we tried to turn out of our
path into a tangle of bushes ; and there, instead of one, we
found four snakes. We turned on the other side, and there
were two more. In short, everywhere we looked, the dry
leaves were rustling and coiling with them ; and we were
in despair. In vain we said that they were harmless as
kittens, and tried to persuade ourselves that their little
bright eyes were pretty, and that their serpentine movements were in the exact line of beauty ; for the life of us,
we could not help remembering their family name and connections ; we thought of those disagreeable gentlemen, the
anacondas, the rattlesnakes, and the copperheads, and all of
that bad line, immediate family friends of the old serpent

to whom we are indebted for all the mischief that is done in this world. So we were quite apprehensive when we saw how our new neighborhood was infested by them, until a neighbor calmed our fears by telling us that snakes always crawled out of their holes to sun themselves in the spring, and that in a day or two they would all be gone.

So it proved. It was evident they were all out merely to do their spring shopping, or something that serves with them the same purpose that spring shopping does with us; and where they went afterwards we do not know. People speak of snakes' holes, and we have seen them disappearing into such subterranean chambers; but we never opened one to see what sort of underground housekeeping went on there. After the first few days of spring, a snake was a rare visitor, though now and then one appeared.

One was discovered taking his noontide repast one day in a manner which excited much prejudice. He was, in fact, regaling himself by sucking down into his maw a small frog, which he had begun to swallow at the toes, and had drawn about half down. The frog, it must be confessed, seemed to view this arrangement with great indifference, making no struggle, and sitting solemnly, with his great unwinking eyes, to be sucked in at the leisure of his captor. There was immense sympathy, however, excited for him in the family circle; and it was voted that a snake which indulged in such very disagreeable modes of eating his dinner was not to be tolerated in our vicinity. So I have reason to believe that that was his last meal.

Another of our wild woodland neighbors made us some trouble. It was no other than a veritable woodchuck, whose hole we had often wondered at when we were scrambling through the underbrush after spring flowers. The hole was about the size of a peck-measure, and had two openings about six feet apart. The occupant was a gentleman we never had had the pleasure of seeing; but we soon learned his existence from his ravages in our garden. He had a taste, it appears, for the very kind of things we wanted to eat ourselves, and helped himself without asking. We had a row of fine, crisp heads of lettuce, which were the pride of our gardening, and out of which he would from day to day select for his table just the plants we had marked for ours. He also nibbled our young beans; and so at last we were reluctantly obliged to let John Gardiner set a trap for him. Poor old simple-minded hermit, he was too artless for this world! He was caught at the very first snap, and found dead in the trap, — the agitation and distress having broken his poor woodland heart, and killed him. We were grieved to the very soul when the poor, fat old fellow was dragged out, with his useless paws standing up stiff and imploring. As it was, he was given to Denis, our pig, which, without a single scruple of delicacy, ate him up as thoroughly as he ate up the lettuce.

This business of eating, it appears, must go on all through creation. We eat ducks, turkeys, and chickens, though we don't swallow them whole, feathers and all. Our four-footed friends, less civilized, take things with more directness and simplicity, and chew each other up without ceremony, or swallow each other alive. Of these unceremonious habits we had other instances.

Our house had a central court on the southern side, into which looked the library, dining-room, and front hall, as well as several of the upper chambers. It was designed to be closed in with glass, to serve as a conservatory in winter; and meanwhile we had filled it with splendid plumy ferns, taken up out of the neighboring wood. In the centre was a fountain surrounded by stones, shells, mosses, and various water-plants. We had bought three little goldfish to swim in our basin; and the spray of it, as it rose in the air and rippled back into the water, was the pleasantest

possible sound of a hot day. We used to lie on the sofa
in the hall, and look into the court, and fancy we saw
some scene of fairy-land, and water-sprites coming up from
the fountain. Suddenly a new-comer presented himself, —
no other than an immense bullfrog, that had hopped up
from the neighboring river, apparently with a view to
making a permanent settlement in and about our fountain.
He was to be seen, often for hours, sitting reflectively on
the edge of it, beneath the broad shadow of the calla-leaves.
When sometimes missed thence, he would be found under
the ample shield of a great bignonia, whose striped leaves
grew hard by.

The family were prejudiced against him. What did he
want there ? It was surely some sinister motive impelled
him. He was probably watching for an opportunity to
gobble up the goldfish. We took his part, however, and
strenuously defended his moral character, and patronized
him in all ways. We gave him the name of Unke, and
maintained that he was a well-conducted, philosophical old
water-sprite, who showed his good taste in wanting to take
up his abode in our conservatory. We even defended his
personal appearance, praised the invisible-green coat which
he wore on his back, and his gray vest, and solemn gold
spectacles ; and though he always felt remarkably slimy
when we touched him, yet, as he would sit still, and allow
us to stroke his head and pat his back, we concluded his
social feelings might be warm, notwithstanding a cold ex-
terior. Who knew, after all, but he might be a beautiful
young prince, enchanted there till the princess should come
to drop the golden ball into the fountain, and so give him
a chance to marry her, and turn into a man again ? Such
things, we are credibly informed, are matters of frequent
occurrence in Germany. Why not here ?

By and by there came to our fountain another visitor, —
a frisky, green young frog of the identical kind spoken of
by the poet : —

> "There was a frog lived in a well,
> Rig dum pully metakimo."

This thoughtless, dapper individual, with his bright green coat, his faultless white vest, and sea-green tights, became rather the popular favorite. He seemed just rakish and gallant enough to fulfil the conditions of the song : —

> "The frog he would a courting ride,
> With sword and pistol by his side."

This lively young fellow, whom we shall call Cri-Cri, like other frisky and gay young people, carried the day quite over the head of the solemn old philosopher under the calla-leaves. At night, when all was still, he would trill a joyous little note in his throat, while old Unke would answer only with a cracked guttural more singular than agreeable ; and to all outward appearance the two were as good friends as their different natures would allow.

One day, however, the conservatory became a scene of a tragedy of the deepest dye. We were summoned below by shrieks and howls of horror. "Do pray come down and see what this vile, nasty, horrid old frog has been doing ! " Down we came ; and there sat our virtuous old philosopher, with his poor little brother's hind legs still sticking out of the corner of his mouth, as if he were smoking them for a cigar, all helplessly palpitating as they were. In fact, our solemn old friend had done what many a solemn hypocrite before has done, — swallowed his poor brother, neck and crop, — and sat there with the most brazen indifference, looking as if he had done the most proper and virtuous thing in the world.

Immediately he was marched out of the conservatory at the point of the walking-stick, and made to hop down into the river, into whose waters he splashed ; and we saw him no more. We regret to say that the popular indignation was so precipitate in its results ; otherwise the special artist who sketched Hum, the son of Buz, would have made a sketch of the old villain, as he sat with his luckless victim's hind legs projecting from his solemn mouth. With all his moral faults, he was a good sitter, and would probably have sat immovable any length of time that could be desired.

Of other woodland neighbors there were some which we saw occasionally. The shores of the river were lined here and there with the holes of the muskrats; and, in rowing by their settlements, we were sometimes strongly reminded of them by the overpowering odor of the perfume from which they get their name. There were also owls, whose nests were high up in some of the old chestnut-trees. Often in the lonely hours of the night we could hear them gibbering with a sort of wild, hollow laugh among the distant trees. But one tenant of the woods made us some trouble in the autumn. It was a little flying-squirrel, who took to making excursions into our house in the night season, coming down chimney into the chambers, rustling about among the clothes, cracking nuts or nibbling at any morsels of anything that suited his fancy. For a long time the inmates of the rooms were awakened in the night by mysterious noises, thumps, and rappings, and so lighted candles, and searched in vain to find whence they came; for the moment any movement was made, the rogue whipped up chimney, and left us a prey to the most mysterious alarms. What could it be?

But one night our fine gentleman bounced in at the window of another room, which had no fireplace; and the fair occupant, rising in the night, shut the window, without suspecting that she had cut off the retreat of any of her woodland neighbors. The next morning she was startled by what she thought a gray rat running past her bed. She rose to pursue him, when he ran up the wall, and clung against the plastering, showing himself very plainly a gray flying-squirrel, with large, soft eyes, and wings which consisted of a membrane uniting the fore paws to the hind ones, like those of a bat. He was chased into the conservatory, and, a window being opened, out he flew upon the ground, and made away for his native woods, and thus put an end to many fears as to the nature of our nocturnal rappings.

So you see how many neighbors we found by living in the woods, and, after all, no worse ones than are found in the great world.

OUR DOGS

I

WE who live in Cunopolis are a dog-loving family. We have a warm side towards everything that goes upon four paws, and the consequence has been that, taking things first and last, we have been always kept in confusion and under the paw, so to speak, of some honest four-footed tyrant, who would go beyond his privilege and overrun the whole house. Years ago this begun, when our household consisted of a papa, a mamma, and three or four noisy boys and girls, and a kind Miss Anna who acted as a second mamma to the whole. There was also one more of our number, the youngest, dear little bright-eyed Charley, who was king over us all, and rode in a wicker wagon for a chariot, and had a nice little nurse devoted to him ; and it was through him that our first dog came.

One day Charley's nurse took him quite a way to a neighbor's house to spend the afternoon ; and, he being well amused, they stayed till after nightfall. The kind old lady of the mansion was concerned that the little prince in his little coach, with his little maid, had to travel so far in the twilight shadows, and so she called a big dog named Carlo, and gave the establishment into his charge.

Carlo was a great, tawny-yellow mastiff, as big as a calf, with great, clear, honest eyes, and stiff, wiry hair ; and the good lady called him to the side of the little wagon, and said, " Now, Carlo, you must take good care of Charley, and you must n't let anything hurt him."

Carlo wagged his tail in promise of protection, and away he trotted, home with the wicker wagon; and when he arrived, he was received with so much applause by four little folks, who dearly loved the very sight of a dog, he was so stroked and petted and caressed, that he concluded that he liked the place better than the home he came from, where were only very grave elderly people. He tarried all night, and slept at the foot of the boys' bed, who could hardly go to sleep for the things they found to say to him, and who were awake ever so early in the morning, stroking his rough, tawny back, and hugging him.

At his own home Carlo had a kennel all to himself, where he was expected to live quite alone, and do duty by watching and guarding the place. Nobody petted him, or stroked his rough hide, or said, " Poor dog ! " to him, and so it appears he had a feeling that he was not appreciated, and liked our warm-hearted little folks, who told him stories, gave him half of their own supper, and took him to bed with them sociably. Carlo was a dog that had a mind of his own, though he could n't say much about it, and in his dog fashion proclaimed his likes and dislikes quite as strongly as if he could speak. When the time came for taking him home, he growled and showed his teeth dangerously at the man who was sent for him, and it was necessary to drag him back by force, and tie him into his kennel. However, he soon settled that matter by gnawing the rope in two and paddling down again and appearing among his little friends, quite to their delight. Two or three times was he taken back and tied or chained; but he howled so dismally, and snapped at people in such a misanthropic manner, that finally the kind old lady thought it better to have no dog at all than a dog soured by blighted affection. So she loosed his rope, and said, " There, Carlo, go and stay where you like ; " and so Carlo came to us, and a joy and delight was he to all in the house.

He loved one and all; but he declared himself as more than all the slave and property of our Prince Charley. He would lie on the floor as still as a door-mat, and let him pull his hair, and roll over him, and examine his eyes with his little fat fingers; and Carlo submitted to all these personal freedoms with as good an understanding as papa himself. When Charley slept, Carlo stretched himself along under the crib; rising now and then, and standing with his broad breast on a level with the slats of the crib, he would look down upon him with an air of grave protection. He also took a great fancy to papa, and would sometimes pat with tiptoe care into his study, and sit quietly down by him when he was busy over his Greek or Latin books, waiting for a word or two of praise or encouragement. If none came, he would lay his rough horny paw on his knee, and look in his face with such an honest, imploring expression, that the professor was forced to break off to say, "Why, Carlo, you poor, good, honest fellow, — did he want to be talked to? — so he did. Well, he shall be talked to; — he's a nice, good dog;" — and during all these praises Carlo's transports and the thumps of his rough tail are not to be described.

He had great, honest, yellowish-brown eyes, — not remarkable for their beauty, but which used to look as if he longed to speak, and he seemed to have a yearning for praise and love and caresses that even all our attentions could scarcely satisfy. His master would say to him sometimes, "Carlo, you poor, good, homely dog, — how loving you are!"

Carlo was a full-blooded mastiff, and his beauty, if he had any, consisted in his having all the good points of his race. He was a dog of blood, come of real old mastiff lineage; his stiff, wiry hair, his big, rough paws, and great brawny chest, were all made for strength rather than beauty; but for all that he was a dog of tender sentiments.

Yet, if any one intruded on his rights and dignities, Carlo showed that he had hot blood in him; his lips would go back, and show a glistening row of ivories that one would not like to encounter, and if any trenched on his privileges, he would give a deep warning growl, — as much as to say, "I am your slave for love, but you must treat me well, or I shall be dangerous." A blow he would not bear from any one: the fire would flash from his great yellow eyes, and he would snap like a rifle; — yet he would let his own Prince Charley pound on his ribs with both baby fists, and pull his tail till he yelped, without even a show of resistance.

At last came a time when the merry voice of little Charley was heard no more, and his little feet no more pattered through the halls; he lay pale and silent in his little crib, with his dear life ebbing away, and no one knew how to stop its going. Poor old Carlo lay under the crib when they would let him, sometimes rising up to look in with an earnest, sorrowful face; and sometimes he would stretch himself out in the entry before the door of little Charley's room, watching with his great open eyes lest the thief should come in the night to steal away our treasure.

But one morning when the children woke, one little soul had gone in the night, — gone upward to the angels; and then the cold, pale little form that used to be the life of the house was laid away tenderly in the yard of a neighboring church.

Poor old Carlo would pit-pat silently about the house in those days of grief, looking first into one face and then another, but no one could tell him where his gay little master had gone. The other children had hid the baby-wagon away in the lumber-room lest their mamma should see it; and so passed a week or two, and Carlo saw no trace of Charley about the house. But then a lady in the neighborhood, who had a sick baby, sent to borrow the wicker wagon, and it was taken from its hiding-place to go to her. Carlo came to the door just as it was being drawn out of the gate into the street. Immediately he sprung, cleared the fence with a great bound, and ran after it. He overtook it, and poked his nose between the curtains, — there was no one there. Immediately he turned away, and padded dejectedly home. What words could have spoken plainer of love and memory than this one action ?

Carlo lived with us a year after this, when a time came for the whole family hive to be taken up and moved away from the flowery banks of the Ohio to the piny shores of Maine. All our household goods were being uprooted, disordered, packed, and sold ; and the question daily arose, "What shall we do with Carlo ? " There was hard begging on the part of the boys that he might go with them, and one even volunteered to travel all the way in baggage cars to keep Carlo company. But papa said no, and so it was decided to send Carlo up the river to the home of a very genial lady who had visited in our family, and who appreciated his parts, and offered him a home in hers.

The matter was anxiously talked over one day in the family circle while Carlo lay under the table, and it was agreed that papa and Willie should take him to the steamboat landing the next morning. But the next morning Mr. Carlo was nowhere to be found. In vain was he called, from garret to cellar ; nor was it till papa and Willie had gone to the city that he came out of his hiding-place. For two or three days it was impossible to catch him, but after a while his suspicions were laid, and we learned not to speak out our plans in his presence, and so the transfer at last was prosperously effected.

We heard from him once in his new home, as being a highly appreciated member of society, and adorning his new

situation with all sorts of dog virtues, while we wended our
ways to the coast of Maine.   But our hearts were sore for
want of him ; the family circle seemed incomplete, until a
new favorite appeared to take his place, of which I shall
tell you next month.

II

A neighbor, blessed with an extensive litter of Newfoundland pups, commenced one chapter in our family history by
giving us a puppy, brisk, funny, and lively enough, who
was received in our house with acclamations of joy, and
christened "Rover."   An auspicious name we all thought,
for his four or five human playfellows were all rovers, —
rovers in the woods, rovers by the banks of a neighboring
patch of water, where they dashed and splashed, made rafts,
inaugurated boats, and lived among the cat-tails and sweet
flags as familiarly as so many musk-rats.   Rovers also they
were, every few days, down to the shores of the great sea,
where they caught fish, rowed boats, dug clams, — both
girls and boys, — and one sex quite as handily as the other.
Rover came into such a lively circle quite as one of them,
and from the very first seemed to regard himself as part and
parcel of all that was going on, in doors or out.   But his
exuberant spirits at times brought him into sad scrapes.
His vivacity was such as to amount to decided insanity, —
and mamma and Miss Anna and papa had many grave looks
over his capers.   Once he actually tore off the leg of a new
pair of trousers that Johnny had just donned, and came
racing home with it in his mouth, with its bare-legged little
owner behind, screaming threats and maledictions on the
robber.   What a commotion !   The new trousers had just
been painfully finished, in those days when sewing was sewing and not a mere jig on a sewing-machine ; but Rover, so
far from being abashed or ashamed, displayed an impish

glee in his performance, bounding and leaping hither and thither with his trophy in his mouth, now growling and mangling it, and shaking it at us in elfish triumph as we chased him hither and thither, — over the wood-pile, into the woodhouse, through the barn, out of the stable door, — vowing all sorts of dreadful punishments when we caught him. But we might well say that, for the little wretch would never be caught; after one of his tricks he always managed to keep himself out of arm's length till the thing was a little blown over, when in he would come, airy as ever, and wagging his little pudgy puppy tail with an air of the most perfect assurance in the world.

There is no saying what youthful errors were pardoned to him. Once he ate a hole in the bed-quilt as his night's employment, when one of the boys had surreptitiously got him into bed with them; he nibbled and variously mal-treated sundry sheets; and once actually tore up and chewed off a corner of the bedroom carpet, to stay his stomach during the night season. What he did it for, no mortal knows; certainly it could not be because he was hungry, for there were five little pairs of hands incessantly feeding him from morning till night. Beside which, he had a boundless appetite for shoes, which he mumbled, and shook, and tore, and ruined, greatly to the vexation of their rightful owners, — rushing in and carrying them from the bedsides in the night-watches, racing off with them to any out-of-the-way corner that hit his fancy, and leaving them when he was tired of the fun. So there is no telling of the disgrace into which he brought his little masters and mistresses, and the tears and threats and scoldings which were all wasted on him, as he would stand quite at his ease, lolling out his red, saucy tongue, and never deigning to tell what he had done with his spoils.

Notwithstanding all these sins, Rover grew up to doghood, the pride and pet of the family, — and in truth a very handsome dog he was.

It is quite evident from his looks that his Newfoundland blood had been mingled with that of some other races ; for he never attained the full size of that race, and his points in some respects resembled those of a good setter. He was grizzled black and white, and spotted on the sides in little inky drops about the size of a three-cent piece ; his hair was long and silky, his ears beautifully fringed, and his tail long and feathery. His eyes were bright, soft, and full of expression, and a jollier, livelier, more loving creature never wore dog-skin. To be sure, his hunting blood some-times brought us and him into scrapes. A neighbor now and then would call with a bill for ducks, chickens, or young turkeys, which Rover had killed. The last time this occurred it was decided that something must be done ; so Rover was shut up a whole day in a cold lumber-room, with the murdered duck tied round his neck. Poor fellow ! how dejected and ashamed he looked, and how grateful he was when his little friends would steal in to sit with him, and " poor " him in his disgrace ! The punishment so improved his principles that he let poultry alone from that time, except now and then, when he would snap up a young chick or turkey, in pure absence of mind, before he really knew what he was about. We had great dread lest he should take to killing sheep, of which there were many flocks in the neighborhood. A dog which once kills sheep is a doomed beast, — as much as a man who has committed murder ; and if our Rover, through the hunting blood that was in him, should once mistake a sheep for a deer, and kill him, we should be obliged to give him up to justice, — all his good looks and good qualities could not save him.

What anxieties his training under this head cost us ! When we were driving out along the clean, sandy roads, among the piny groves of Maine, it was half our enjoyment to see Rover, with ears and tail wild and flying with ex-citement and enjoyment, bounding and barking, now on

this side the carriage, now on that, — now darting through
the woods straight as an arrow, in his leaps after birds or
squirrels, and anon returning to trot obediently by the carriage, and, wagging his tail, to ask applause for his performances. But anon a flock of sheep appeared in a distant
field, and away would go Rover in full bow-wow, plunging
in among them, scattering them hither and thither in dire
confusion. Then Johnny and Bill and all hands would
spring from the carriage in full chase of the rogue ; and all
of us shouted vainly in the rear; and finally the rascal
would be dragged back, panting and crestfallen, to be admonished, scolded, and cuffed with salutary discipline,
heartily administered by his best friends for the sake of
saving his life. " Rover, you naughty dog ! Don't you
know you must n't chase the sheep? You'll be killed,
some of these days." Admonitions of this kind, well
shaken and thumped in, at last seemed to reform him
thoroughly. He grew so conscientious that, when a flock
of sheep appeared on the side of the road, he would immediately go to the other side of the carriage, and turn away
his head, rolling up his eyes meanwhile to us for praise at
his extraordinary good conduct. " Good dog, Rove ! nice
dog! good fellow ! he does n't touch the sheep, — no, he
does n't." Such were the rewards of virtue which sweetened his self-denial; hearing which, he would plume up
his feathery tail, and loll out his tongue, with an air of
virtuous assurance quite edifying to behold.

Another of Rover's dangers was a habit he had of running races and cutting capers with the railroad engines as
they passed near our dwelling.

We lived in plain sight of the track, and three or four
times a day the old, puffing, smoking iron horse thundered
by, dragging his trains of cars, and making the very ground
shake under him. Rover never could resist the temptation
to run and bark, and race with so lively an antagonist;

and, to say the truth, John and Willy were somewhat of his mind, — so that, though they were directed to catch and hinder him, they entered so warmly into his own feelings that they never succeeded in breaking up the habit. Every day when the distant whistle was heard, away would go Rover, out of the door or through the window — no matter which, — race down to meet the cars, couch down on the track in front of them, barking with all his might, as if it were only a fellow-dog, and when they came so near that escape seemed utterly impossible, he would lie flat down between the rails and suffer the whole train to pass over him, and then jump up and bark, full of glee, in the rear. Sometimes he varied this performance more dangerously by jumping out full tilt between two middle cars when the train had passed half-way over him. Everybody predicted, of course, that he would be killed or maimed, and the loss of a paw, or of his fine, saucy tail, was the least of the dreadful things which were prophesied about him. But Rover lived and throve in his imprudent courses notwithstanding.

The engineers and firemen, who began by throwing sticks of wood and bits of coal at him, at last were quite subdued by his successful impudence, and came to consider him as a regular institution of the railroad, and, if any family excursion took him off for a day, they would inquire with interest, "Where's our dog? — what's become of Rover?" As to the female part of our family, we had so often anticipated piteous scenes when poor Rover would be brought home with broken paws or without his pretty tail, that we quite used up our sensibilities, and concluded that some kind angel, such as is appointed to watch over little children's pets, must take special care of our Rover.

Rover had very tender domestic affections. His attachment to his little playfellows was most intense ; and one time, when all of them were taken off together on a week's excursion. and Rover left alone at home, his low spirits were really pitiful. He refused entirely to eat for the first day. and finally could only be coaxed to take nourishment. with many strokings and caresses, by being fed out of Miss Anna's own hand. What perfectly boisterous joy he showed when the children came back ! — careering round and round, picking up chips and bits of sticks, and coming and offering them to one and another, in the fulness of his doggish heart, to show how much he wanted to give them something.

This mode of signifying his love by bringing something in his mouth was one of his most characteristic tricks. At one time he followed the carriage from Brunswick to Bath, and in the streets of the city somehow lost his way, so that he was gone all night. Many a little heart went to bed anxious and sorrowful for the loss of its shaggy playfellow that night, and Rover doubtless was remembered in many little prayers ; what, therefore, was the joy of being awakened by a joyful barking under the window the next morning, when his little friends rushed in their nightgowns to behold Rover back again, fresh and frisky, bearing in his mouth a branch of a tree about six feet long, as his offering of joy.

When the family removed to Zion Hill, Rover went with them, the trusty and established family friend. Age had somewhat matured his early friskiness. Perhaps the grave neighborhood of a theological seminary and the responsibility of being a professor's dog might have something to do with it. but Rover gained an established character as a dog of respectable habits, and used to march to the post-office at the heels of his master twice a day as regularly as any theological student.

Little Charley the second — the youngest of the brood, who took the place of our lost little Prince Charley — was yet padding about in short robes, and seemed to regard

Rover in the light of a discreet older brother, and Rover's
manners to him were of most protecting gentleness. Charley seemed to consider Rover in all things as such a model,
that he overlooked the difference between a dog and a boy,
and wearied himself with fruitless attempts to scratch his
ear with his foot as Rover did, and one day was brought
in dripping from a neighboring swamp, where he had been
lying down in the water, because Rover did.

Once in a while a wild oat or two from Rover's old sack
would seem to entangle him. Sometimes, when we were
driving out, he would, in his races after the carriage, make
a flying leap into a farmer's yard, and, if he lighted in a
flock of chickens or turkeys, gobble one off-hand, and be
off again and a mile ahead before the mother hen had recovered from her astonishment. Sometimes, too, he would
have a race with the steam-engine just for old acquaintance'
sake. But these were comparatively transient follies; in
general, no members of the grave institutions around him
behaved with more dignity and decorum than Rover. He
tried to listen to his master's theological lectures, and to
attend chapel on Sundays; but the prejudices of society
were against him, and so he meekly submitted to be shut
out, and waited outside the door on these occasions.

He formed a part of every domestic scene. At family
prayers, stretched out beside his master, he looked up reflectively with his great soft eyes, and seemed to join in
the serious feeling of the hour. When all were gay, when
singing, or frolicking, or games were going on, Rover barked
and frisked in higher glee than any. At night it was his
joy to stretch his furry length by our bedside, where he
slept with one ear on cock for any noise which it might
be his business to watch and attend to. It was a comfort
to hear the tinkle of his collar when he moved in the
night, or to be wakened by his cold nose pushed against
one's hand if one slept late in the morning. And then he

was always so glad when we woke; and when any member of the family circle was gone for a few days, Rover's warm delight and welcome were not the least of the pleasures of return.

And what became of him? Alas! the fashion came up of poisoning dogs, and this poor, good, fond, faithful creature was enticed into swallowing poisoned meat. One day he came in suddenly, ill and frightened, and ran to the friends who always had protected him, — but in vain. In a few moments he was in convulsions, and all the tears and sobs of his playfellows could not help him; he closed his bright, loving eyes, and died in their arms.

If those who throw poison to dogs could only see the real grief it brings into a family to lose the friend and playfellow who has grown up with the children, and shared their plays, and been for years in every family scene, — if they could know how sorrowful it is to see the poor dumb friend suffer agonies which they cannot relieve, — if they could see all this, we have faith to believe they never would do so more.

Our poor Rover was buried with decent care near the house, and a mound of petunias over him kept his memory ever bright; but it will be long before his friends will get another as true.

III

After the sad fate of Rover, there came a long interval in which we had no dog. Our hearts were too sore to want another. His collar, tied with black crape, hung under a pretty engraving of Landseer's, called "My Dog," which we used to fancy to be an exact resemblance of our pet.

The children were some of them grown up and gone to school, or scattered about the world. If ever the question

of another dog was agitated, papa cut it short with, " I
won't have another ; I won't be made to feel again as I
did about Rover." But somehow Mr. Charley the younger
got his eye on a promising litter of puppies, and at last he
begged papa into consenting that he might have one of
them.

It was a little black mongrel, of no particular race or
breed, — a mere common cur, without any pretensions to
family, but the best-natured, jolliest little low-bred pup
that ever boy had for a playmate. To be sure, he had the
usual puppy sins ; he would run away with papa's slippers
and boots and stockings ; he would be under everybody's
feet, at the most inconvenient moment ; he chewed up a
hearth-broom or two, and pulled one of Charley's caps to
pieces in the night, with an industry worthy of a better
cause ; — still, because he was dear to Charley, papa and
mamma winked very hard at his transgressions.

The name of this little black individual was Stromion, —
a name taken from a German fairy tale, which the Professor was very fond of reading in the domestic circle ; and
Stromion, by dint of much patience, much feeding, and very
indulgent treatment, grew up into a very fat, common-look-
ing, black cur dog, not very prepossessing in appearance
and manners, but possessed of the very best heart in the
world, and most inconceivably affectionate and good-natured.
Sometimes some of the older members of the family would
trouble Charley's enjoyment in his playfellow by suggesting
that he was no blood dog, and that he belonged to no particular dog family that could be named. Papa comforted
him by the assurance that Stromion did belong to a very
old and respectable breed, — that he was a *mongrel ;* and
Charley after that valued him excessively under this head ;
and if any one tauntingly remarked that Stromion was only
a cur, he would flame up in his defense, — " He isn't a cur,
he's a mongrel," introducing him to strangers with the

addition to all his other virtues, that he was a "pure mongrel, — papa says so."

The edict against dogs in the family having once been broken down, Master Will proceeded to gratify his own impulses, and soon led home to the family circle an enormous old black Newfoundland, of pure breed, which had been presented him by a man who was leaving the place. Prince was in the decline of his days, but a fine, majestic old fellow. He had a sagacity and capacity of personal affection which were uncommon. Many dogs will change from master to master without the least discomposure. A good bone will compensate for any loss of the heart, and make a new friend seem quite as good as an old one. But Prince had his affections quite as distinctly as a human being, and we learned this to our sorrow when he had to be weaned from his old master under our roof. His howls and lamentations were so dismal and protracted, that the house could not contain him ; we were obliged to put him into an outhouse to compose his mind, and we still have a vivid image of him sitting, the picture of despair, over an untasted mutton shank, with his nose in the air, and the most dismal howls proceeding from his mouth. Time, the comforter, however, assuaged his grief, and he came at last to transfer all his stores of affection to Will, and to consider himself once more as a dog with a master.

Prince used to inhabit his young master's apartment, from the window of which he would howl dismally when Will left him to go to the academy near by, and yelp triumphant welcomes when he saw him returning. He was really and passionately fond of music, and. though strictly forbidden the parlor, would push and elbow his way there with dogged determination when there was playing or singing. Any one who should have seen Prince's air when he had a point to carry, would understand why quiet obstinacy is called doggedness.

The female members of the family, seeing that two dogs had gained admission to the circle, had cast their eyes admiringly on a charming little Italian greyhound, that was living in doleful captivity at a dog-fancier's in Boston, and resolved to set him free and have him for their own. Accordingly they returned one day in triumph, with him in their arms, — a fair, delicate creature, white as snow, except one mouse-colored ear. He was received with enthusiasm, and christened Giglio; the honors of his first bath and toilette were performed by Mesdemoiselles the young ladies on their knees, as if he had been in reality young Prince Giglio from fairyland.

Of all beautiful shapes in dog form, never was there one more perfect than this. His hair shone like spun glass, and his skin was as fine and pink as that of a baby; his paws and ears were translucent like fine china, and he had great, soft, tremulous dark eyes; his every movement seemed more graceful than the last. Whether running or leaping, or sitting in graceful attitudes on the parlor table among the ladies' embroidery-frames, with a great rose-colored bow under his throat, he was alike a thing of beauty, and his beauty alone won all hearts to him.

When the papa first learned that a third dog had been introduced into the household, his patience gave way. The thing was getting desperate; we were being overrun with dogs; our house was no more a house, but a kennel; it ought to be called Cunopolis, — a city of dogs; he could not and would not have it so; but papa, like most other indulgent old gentlemen, was soon reconciled to the children's pets. In fact, Giglio was found cowering under the bedclothes at the Professor's feet not two mornings after his arrival, and the good gentleman descended with him in his arms to breakfast, talking to him in the most devoted manner: — "Poor little Giglio, was he cold last night? and did he want to get into papa's bed? he should be brought down stairs, that he should;"— all which, addressed to a young rascal whose sinews were all like steel, and who could have jumped from the top stair to the bottom like a feather, was sufficiently amusing.

Giglio's singular beauty and grace were his only merits; he had no love nor power of loving; he liked to be petted and kept warm, but it mattered nothing to him who did it. He was as ready to turn off with a stranger as with his very best friend, — would follow any whistle or any caller, — was, in fact, such a gay rover, that we came very near losing him many times; and more than once he was brought back from the Boston cars, on board which he had followed a stranger. He also had, we grieve to say, very careless habits; and after being washed white as snow, and adorned with choice rose-colored ribbons, would be brought back soiled and ill-smelling from a neighbor's livery stable, where he had been indulging in low society. For all that, he was very lordly and aristocratic in his airs with poor Stromion, who was a dog with a good, loving heart, if he was black and homely. Stromion admired Giglio with the most evident devotion; he would always get up to give him the warm corner, and would always sit humbly in the distance and gaze on him with most longing admiration, — for all of which my fine gentleman rewarded him only with an occasional snarl or a nip, as he went by him. Sometimes Giglio would condescend to have a romp with Stromion for the sake of passing the time, and then Stromion would be perfectly delighted, and frisk and roll his clumsy body over the carpet with his graceful antagonist, all whose motions were a study for an artist. When Giglio was tired of play, he would give Stromion a nip that would send him yelping from the field; and then he would tick, tick gracefully away to some embroidered ottoman forbidden to all but himself, where he would sit graceful and classical as some Etruscan vase, and look down superior on the humble companion who looked up to him with respectful admiration.

Giglio knew his own good points, and was possessed with the very spirit of a coquette. He would sometimes obstinately refuse the caresses and offered lap of his mistresses, and seek to ingratiate himself with some stolid theological visitor, for no other earthly purpose that we could see than that he was determined to make himself the object of attention. We have seen him persist in jumping time and again on the hard bony knees of some man who hated dogs and did not mean to notice him, until he won attention and caresses, when immediately he would spring down and tick away perfectly contented. He assumed lofty, fine-gentleman airs with Prince also, for which sometimes he got his reward, — for Prince, the old, remembered that he was a dog of blood, and would not take any nonsense from him.

Like many old dogs, Prince had a very powerful doggy smell, which was a great personal objection to him, and Giglio was always in a civil way making reflections upon this weak point. Prince was fond of indulging himself with an afternoon nap on the door-mat, and sometimes when he rose from his repose, Giglio would spring gracefully from the table where he had been overlooking him, and, picking his way daintily to the mat, would snuff at it, with his long, thin nose, with an air of extreme disgust. It was evidently a dog insult done according to the politest modes of refined society, and said as plain as words could say, — " My dear sir, excuse me, but can you tell what makes this peculiar smell where you have been lying ? " At any rate, Prince understood the sarcasm, for a deep angry growl and a sharp nip would now and then teach my fine gentleman to mind his own business.

Giglio's lot at last was to travel in foreign lands, for his young mistresses, being sent to school in Paris, took him with them to finish his education and acquire foreign graces. He was smuggled on board the Fulton, and placed

in an upper berth. well wrapped in a blanket; and the
last we saw of him was his long, thin, Italian nose, and
dark. tremulous eyes looking wistfully at us from the folds
of the flannel in which he shivered.   Sensitiveness to cold
was one of his great peculiarities.   In winter he wore little
blankets, which his fond mistresses made with anxious care,
and on which his initials were embroidered with their own
hands.   In the winter weather on Zion Hill he was often
severely put to it to gratify his love of roving in the cold
snows; he would hold up first one leg and then the other,
and contrive to get along on three, so as to save himself as
much as possible ; and more than once he caught severe
colds, requiring careful nursing and medical treatment to
bring him round again.

The Fulton sailed early in March.   It was chilly, stormy
weather, so that the passengers all suffered somewhat with
cold, and Master Giglio was glad to lie rolled in his blanket,
looking like a sea-sick gentleman.   The captain very gen-
erously allowed him a free passage, and in pleasant weather
he used to promenade the deck, where his beauty won for
him caresses and attentions innumerable.   The stewards
and cooks always had choice morsels for him, and fed him
to such a degree as would have spoiled any other dog's
figure ; but his could not be spoiled.   All the ladies vied
with each other in seeking his good graces, and after dinner he pattered from one to another, to be fed with sweet
things and confectionery, and hear his own praises, like a
gay buck of fashion as he was.

Landed in Paris, he met a warm reception at the pension
of Madame B——; but ambition filled his breast.   He
was in the great, gay city of Paris, the place where a handsome dog has but to appear to make his fortune, and so
Giglio resolved to seek for himself a more brilliant
destiny.

One day, when he was being led to take the air in the

court, he slipped his leash, sped through the gate, and away
down the street like the wind. It was idle to attempt to
follow him; he was gone like a bird in the air, and left the
hearts of his young mistresses quite desolate.

Some months after, as they were one evening eating ices
in the Champs Elysées, a splendid carriage drove up, from
which descended a liveried servant, with a dog in his arms.
It was Giglio, the faithless Giglio, with his one mouse-
colored ear, that marked him from all other dogs! He had
evidently accomplished his destiny, and become the darling
of rank and fashion, rode in an elegant carriage, and had
a servant in livery devoted to him. Of course he did not
pretend to notice his former friends. The footman, who
had come out apparently to give him an airing, led him up
and down close by where they were sitting, and bestowed
on him the most devoted attentions. Of course there was
no use in trying to reclaim him, and so they took their last
look of the fair inconstant, and left him to his brilliant
destiny. And thus ends the history of PRINCE GIGLIO.

IV

After Prince Giglio deserted us and proved so faithless,
we were for a while determined not to have another pet.
They were all good for nothing, — all alike ungrateful; we
forswore the whole race of dogs. But the next winter we
went to live in the beautiful city of Florence, in Italy, and
there, in spite of all our protestations, our hearts were
again ensnared.

You must know that in the neighborhood of Florence is
a celebrated villa, owned by a Russian nobleman, Prince
Demidoff, and that among other fine things that are to be
found there is a very nice breed of King Charles spaniels,
which are called Demidoffs, after the place. One of these,

a pretty little creature, was presented to us by a kind lady, and our resolution against having any more pets all melted away in view of the soft, beseeching eyes, the fine, silky ears, the glossy, wavy hair, and bright chestnut paws of the new favorite. She was exactly such a pretty creature as one sees painted in some of the splendid old Italian pictures, and which Mr. Ruskin describes as belonging to the race of "fringy paws." The little creature was warmly received among us ; an ottoman was set apart for her to lie on ; and a bright bow of green, red, and white ribbon, the Italian colors, was prepared for her neck ; and she was christened Florence, after her native city.

Florence was a perfect little fine lady, and a perfect Italian, — sensitive, intelligent, nervous, passionate, and constant in her attachments, but with a hundred little whims and fancies that required petting and tending hourly. She was perfectly miserable if she was not allowed to attend us in our daily drives, yet in the carriage she was so excitable and restless, so interested to take part in everything she saw and heard in the street, that it was all we could do to hold her in and make her behave herself decently. She was nothing but a little bundle of nerves, apparently all the while in a tremble of excitement about one thing or another ; she was so disconsolate if left at home, that she went everywhere with us. She visited the picture galleries, the museums, and all the approved sights of Florence, and improved her mind as much as many other young ladies who do the same.

Then we removed from Florence to Rome, and poor Flo was direfully seasick on board the steamboat, in company with all her young mistresses, but recovered herself at Civita Vecchia, and entered Rome in high feather. There she settled herself complacently in our new lodgings, which were far more spacious and elegant than those we had left in Florence, and began to claim her little rights in all the sight-seeing of the Eternal City.

She went with us to palaces and to ruins, scrambling up
and down, hither and thither, with the utmost show of interest. She went up all the stairs to the top of the Capitol,
except the very highest and last, where she put on airs,
whimpered, and professed such little frights, that her mistress was forced to carry her ; but once on top, she barked
from right to left, — now at the snowy top of old Soracte,
now at the great, wide, desolate plains of the Campagna,
and now at the old ruins of the Roman Forum down under
our feet. Upon all she had her own opinion, and was not
backward to express herself. At other times she used to
ride with us to a beautiful country villa outside of the walls
of Rome, called the Pamfili Doria. How beautiful and
lovely this place was I can scarcely tell my little friends.
There were long alleys and walks of the most beautiful
trees ; there were winding paths leading to all manner of
beautiful grottos, and charming fountains, and the wide
lawns used to be covered with the most lovely flowers.
There were anemones that looked like little tulips, growing
about an inch and a half high, and of all colors, — blue,
purple, lilac, pink, crimson, and white, — and there were
great beds of fragrant blue and white violets. As to the
charming grace and beauty of the fountains that were to be
found here and there all through the grounds, I could not
describe them to you. They were made of marble, carved
in all sorts of fanciful devices, and grown over with green
mosses and maidenhair.

What spirits little Miss Flo had, when once set down in
these enchanting fields ! While all her mistresses were
gathering lapfuls of many-colored anemones, violets, and
all sorts of beautiful things, Flo would snuff the air, and
run and race hither and thither, with her silky ears flying
and her whole little body quivering with excitement. Now
she would race round the grand basin of a fountain, and
bark with all her might at the great white swans that were

swelling and ruffling their silver-white plumage, and took
her noisy attentions with all possible composure. Then she
would run off down some long side alley after a lot of
French soldiers, whose gay red legs and blue coats seemed
to please her mightily; and many a fine chase she gave
her mistresses, who were obliged to run up and down, here,
there, and everywhere, to find her when they wanted to go
home again.

One time my lady's friskiness brought her into quite a
serious trouble, as you shall hear. We were all going to
St. Peter's Church, and just as we came to the bridge of
St. Angelo, that crosses the Tiber, we met quite a con-
course of carriages. Up jumped my lady Florence, all
alive and busy, — for she always reckoned everything that
was going on a part of her business, — and gave such a
spring that over she went, sheer out of the carriage, into
the mixed medley of carriages, horses, and people below.
We were all frightened enough, but not half so frightened
as she was, as she ran blindly down a street, followed by a
perfect train of ragged little black-eyed, black-haired boys,
all shouting and screaming after her. As soon as he could,
our courier got down and ran after her, but he might as
well have chased a streak of summer lightning. She was
down the street, round the corner, and lost to view, with
all the ragamuffin tribe, men, boys, and women, after her;
and so we thought we had lost her, and came home to our
lodgings very desolate in heart, when lo! our old porter
told us that a little dog that looked like ours had come
begging and whining at our street door, but before he could
open it the poor little wanderer had been chased away
again and gone down the street. After a while some very
polite French soldiers picked her up in the Piazza di
Spagna, — a great public square near our dwelling, to get
into which we were obliged to go down some one or two
hundred steps. We could fancy our poor Flo, frightened

and panting, flying like a meteor down these steps, till she was brought up by the arms of a soldier below.

Glad enough were we when the polite soldier brought her back to our doors ; — and one must say one good thing for French soldiers all the world over, that they are the pleasantest-tempered and politest people possible, so very tender-hearted towards all sorts of little defenseless pets, so that our poor runaway could not have fallen into better hands.

After this, we were careful to hold her more firmly when she had her little nervous starts and struggles in riding about Rome.

One day we had been riding outside of the walls of the city, and just as we were returning home we saw coming towards us quite a number of splendid carriages with prancing black horses. It was the Pope and several of his cardinals coming out for an afternoon airing. The carriages stopped, and the Pope and cardinals all got out to take a little exercise on foot, and immediately all carriages that were in the way drew to one side, and those of the people in them who were Roman Catholics got out and knelt down to wait for the Pope's blessing as he went by. As for us, we were contented to wait sitting in the carriage.

On came the Pope, looking like a fat, mild, kind-hearted old gentleman, smiling and blessing the people as he went on, and the cardinals scuffing along in the dust behind him. He walked very near to our carriage, and Miss Florence, notwithstanding all our attempts to keep her decent, would give a smart little bow-wow right in his face just as he was passing. He smiled benignly, and put out his hand in sign of blessing toward our carriage, and Florence doubtless got what she had been asking for.

From Rome we traveled to Naples, and Miss Flo went with us through our various adventures there, — up Mount Vesuvius, where she half choked herself with sulphurous smoke. There is a place near Naples called the Solfatara, which is thought to be the crater of the extinct volcano, where there is a cave that hisses, and roars, and puffs out scalding steam like a perpetual locomotive, and all the ground around shakes and quivers as if it were only a crust over some terrible abyss. The pools of water are all white with sulphur; the ground is made of sulphur and arsenic and all such sort of uncanny matters; and we were in a fine fright lest Miss Florence, being in one of her wildest and most indiscreet moods, should tumble into some burning hole, or strangle herself with sulphur; and in fact she rolled over and over in a sulphur puddle, and then, scampering off, rolled in ashes by way of cleaning herself. We could not, however, leave her at home during any of our excursions, and so had to make the best of these imprudences.

When at last the time came for us to leave Italy, we were warned that Florence would not be allowed to travel in the railroad cars in the French territories. All dogs, of all sizes and kinds, whose owners wish to have travel with them, are shut up in a sort of closet by themselves, called the dog-car; and we thought our nervous, excitable little pet would be frightened into fits, to be separated from all her friends, and made to travel with all sorts of strange dogs. So we determined to smuggle her along in a basket. At Turin we bought a little black basket, just big enough to contain her, and into it we made her go, — very sorely against her will, as we could not explain to her the reason why. Very guilty indeed we felt, with this traveling conveyance hung on one arm, sitting in the waiting-room, and dreading every minute lest somebody should see the great bright eyes peeping through the holes of the basket, or hear the subdued little whines and howls which every now and then came from its depths.

Florence had been a petted lady, used to having her own

way, and a great deal of it; and this being put up in a little black basket, where she could neither make her remarks on the scenery, nor join in the conversation of her young mistresses, seemed to her a piece of caprice without rhyme or reason. So every once in a while she would express her mind on the subject by a sudden dismal little whine; and what was specially trying, she would take the occasion to do this when the cars stopped and all was quiet, so that everybody could hear her. Where's that dog? — somebody's got a dog in here, — was the inquiry very plain to be seen in the suspicious looks which the guard cast upon us as he put his head into our compartment, and gazed about inquiringly. Finally, to our great terror, a railway director, a tall, gentlemanly man, took his seat in our very compartment, where Miss Florence's basket garnished the pocket above our heads, and she was in one of her most querulous moods. At every stopping-place she gave her little sniffs and howls, and rattled her basket so as to draw all eyes. We all tried to look innocent and unconscious, but the polite railroad director very easily perceived what was the matter. He looked from one anxious, half-laughing face to the others, with a kindly twinkle in his eye, but said nothing. All the guards and *employés* bowed down to him, and came cap in hand at every stopping-place to take his orders. What a relief it was to hear him say, in a low voice, to them: "These young ladies have a little dog which they are carrying. Take no notice of it, and do not disturb them!" Of course, after that, though Florence barked and howled and rattled her basket, and sometimes showed her great eyes, like two coal-black diamonds, through its lattice-work, nobody saw and nobody heard, and we came unmolested with her to Paris.

After a while she grew accustomed to her little traveling carriage, and resigned herself quietly to go to sleep in it;

and so we got her from Paris to Kent, where we stopped a few days to visit some friends in a lovely country place called Swaylands.

Here we had presented to us another pet, that was ever after the chosen companion and fast friend of Florence. He was a little Skye terrier, of the color of a Maltese cat, covered all over with fine, long, silky hair, which hung down so evenly, that it was difficult at the first glance to say which was his head and which his tail. But at the head end there gleamed out a pair of great, soft, speaking eyes, that formed the only beauty of the creature; and very beautiful they were, in their soft, beseeching lovingness.

Poor Rag had the tenderest heart that ever was hid in a bundle of hair; he was fidelity and devotion itself, and used to lie at our feet in the railroad carriages as still as a gray sheep-skin, only too happy to be there on any terms. It would be too long to tell our traveling adventures in England; suffice it to say that at last we went on board the Africa to come home, with our two pets, which had to be handed over to the butcher, and slept on quarters of mutton and sides of beef, till they smelt of tallow and grew fat in a most vulgar way.

At last both of them were safely installed in the brown stone cottage in Andover, and Rag was presented to a young lady to whom he had been sent as a gift from England, and to whom he attached himself with the most faithful devotion.

Both dogs insisted on having their part of the daily walks and drives of their young mistresses, and, when they observed them putting on their hats, would run, and bark, and leap, and make as much noise as a family of children clamoring for a ride.

After a few months, Florence had three or four little puppies. Very puny little things they were; and a fierce, nervous little mother she made. Her eyes looked blue as burnished steel, and if anybody only set foot in the room where her basket was, her hair would bristle, and she would bark so fiercely as to be quite alarming. For all that, her little ones proved quite a failure, for they were all stone-blind. In vain we waited and hoped and watched for nine days, and long after; the eyes were glazed and dim, and one by one they died. The last two seemed to promise to survive, and were familiarly known in the family circle by the names of Milton and Beethoven.

But the fatigues of nursing exhausted the delicate constitution of poor Florence, and she lay all one day in spasms. It became evident that a tranquil passage must be secured for Milton and Beethoven to the land of shades, or their little mother would go there herself; and accordingly they vanished from this life.

As to poor Flo, the young medical student in the family took her into a water-cure course of treatment, wrapping her in a wet napkin first, and then in his scarlet flannel dressing-gown, and keeping a wet cloth with iced water round her head. She looked out of her wrappings, patient and pitiful, like a very small old African female, in a very serious state of mind. To the glory of the water-cure, however, this course in one day so cured her, that she was frisking about the next, happy as if nothing had happened.

She had, however, a slight attack of the spasms, which caused her to run frantically and cry to have the hall-door opened; and when it was opened, she scampered up in all haste into the chamber of her medical friend, and, not finding him there, jumped upon his bed, and began with her teeth and paws to get around her the scarlet dressing-gown in which she had found relief before. So she was again packed in wet napkins, and after that never had another attack.

After this, Florence was begged from us by a lady who fell in love with her beautiful eyes, and she went to reside in a most lovely cottage in H——, where she received the devoted attentions of a whole family. The family physician, however, fell violently in love with her, and, by dint of caring for her in certain little ailments, awakened such a sentiment in return, that at last she was given to him, and used to ride about in state with him in his carriage, visiting his patients, and giving her opinion on their symptoms.

At last her health grew delicate and her appetite failed. In vain chicken, and chops, and all the delicacies that could tempt the most fastidious, were offered to her, cooked expressly for her table ; the end of all things fair must come, and poor Florence breathed her last, and was put into a little rosewood casket, lined with white, and studded with silver nails, and so buried under a fine group of chestnuts in the grounds of her former friends. A marble tablet was to be affixed to one of these, commemorating her charms ; but, like other spoiled beauties, her memory soon faded, and the tablet has been forgotten.

The mistress of Rag, who is devoted to his memory, insists that not enough space has been given in this memoir to his virtues. But the virtues of honest Rag were of that kind which can be told in a few sentences, — a warm, loving heart, a boundless desire to be loved, and a devotion that made him regard with superstitious veneration all the movements of his mistress. The only shrewd trick he possessed was a habit of drawing on her sympathy by feigning a lame leg whenever she scolded or corrected him. In his English days he had had an injury from the kick of a horse, which, however, had long since been healed ; but he remembered the petting he got for this infirmity, and so recalled it whenever he found that his mistress's stock of affection was running low. A blow or a harsh word would cause him to limp in an alarming manner ; but a few caresses would set matters all straight again.

Rag had been a frantic ratter, and often roused the

whole family by his savage yells after rats that he heard
gamboling quite out of his reach behind the partitions in the
china closet. He would crouch his head on his fore-paws,
and lie watching at rat-holes, in hopes of intercepting some
transient loafer; and one day he actually broke the back
and bones of a gray old thief whom he caught marauding
in the china closet.

Proud and happy was he of this feat; but, poor fellow!
he had to repose on the laurels thus gained, for his teeth
were old and poor, and more than one old rebel slipped
away from him, leaving him screaming with disappointed
ambition.

At last poor Rag became aged and toothless, and a shake
which he one day received from a big dog, who took him
for a bundle of wick-yarn, hastened the breaking up of his
constitution. He was attacked with acute rheumatism, and,
notwithstanding the most assiduous cares of his mistress,
died at last in her arms.

Funeral honors were decreed him; white chrysanthe-
mums and myrtle leaves decked his bier. And so Rag was
gathered to the dogs which had gone before him.

V

Well, after the departure of Madam Florence there was
a long cessation of the dog mania in our family. We concluded that we would have no more pets; for they made
too much anxiety, and care, and trouble, and broke all our
hearts by death or desertion.

At last, however, some neighbors of ours took unto themselves, to enliven their dwelling, a little saucy Scotch terrier, whose bright eyes and wicked tricks so wrought upon
the heart of one of our juvenile branches, that there was
no rest in the camp without this addition to it. Nothing

was so pretty, so bright, so knowing and cunning, as a
" Scotch terrier," and a Scotch terrier we must have, — so
said Miss Jenny, our youngest.

And so a bargain was struck by one of Jenny's friends
with some of the knowing ones in Boston, and home she
came, the happy possessor of a genuine article, — as wide-
awake, impertinent, frisky, and wicked a little elf as ever
was covered with a shock of rough tan-colored hair.

His mistress no sooner gazed on him, than she was inspired to give him a name suited to his peculiar character ;
— so he frisked into the front door announced as Wix, and
soon made himself perfectly at home in the family circle,
which he took, after his own fashion, by storm. He entered
the house like a small whirlwind, dashed, the first thing,
into the Professor's study, seized a slipper which was dang-
ling rather uncertainly on one of his studious feet, and,
wresting it off, raced triumphantly with it around the hall,
barking distractedly every minute that he was not shaking
and worrying his prize.

Great was the sensation. Grandma tottered with trembling steps to the door, and asked, with hesitating tones,
what sort of a creature that might be ; and being saluted
with the jubilant proclamation, " Why, Grandma, it 's my
dog, — a real genuine Scotch terrier ; he 'll never grow
any larger, and he 's a perfect beauty ! don't you think
so ? " — Grandma could only tremblingly reply, " Oh, there
is not any danger of his going mad, is there ? Is he generally so playful ? "

Playful was certainly a mild term for the tempest of excitement in which master Wix flew round and round in
giddy circles, springing over ottomans, diving under sofas,
barking from beneath chairs, and resisting every effort
to recapture the slipper with bristling hair and blazing
eyes, as if the whole of his dog-life consisted in keeping his
prize ; till at length he caught a glimpse of pussy's tail, —

at which, dropping the slipper, he precipitated himself after the flying meteor, tumbling, rolling, and scratching down the kitchen stairs, standing on his hind-legs barking distractedly at poor Tom, who had taken refuge in the sink, and sat with his tail magnified to the size of a small bolster.

This cat, the most reputable and steady individual of his species, the darling of the most respectable of cooks, had received the name of Thomas Henry, by which somewhat lengthy appellation he was generally designated in the family circle, as a mark of the respect which his serious and contemplative manner commonly excited. Thomas had but one trick of popularity. With much painstaking and care the cook had taught him the act of performing a somerset over our hands when held at a decent height from the floor; and for this one elegant accomplishment, added to great success in his calling of rat-catching, he was held in great consideration in the family, and had meandered his decorous way about the house, slept in the sun, and otherwise conducted himself with the innocent and tranquil freedom which became a family cat of correct habits and a good conscience.

The irruption of Wix into our establishment was like the bursting of a bomb at the feet of some respectable citizen going tranquilly to market. Thomas was a cat of courage, and rats of the largest size shrunk appalled at the very sight of his whiskers; but now he sat in the sink quite cowed, consulting with great, anxious, yellow eyes the throng of faces that followed Wix down the stairs, and watching anxiously the efforts Miss Jenny was making to subdue and quiet him.

"Wix, you naughty little rascal, you must n't bark at Thomas Henry; be still!" Whereat Wix, understanding himself to be blamed, brought forth his trump card of accomplishments, which he always offered by way of pacification whenever he was scolded. He reared himself up on his hind-legs, hung his head languishingly on one side, lolled out his tongue, and made a series of supplicatory gestures with his fore-paws, — a trick which never failed to bring down the house in a storm of applause, and carry him out of any scrape with flying colors.

Poor Thomas Henry, from his desolate sink, saw his terrible rival carried off in Miss Jenny's arms amid the applauses of the whole circle, and had abundance of time to reflect on the unsubstantial nature of popularity. After that he grew dejected and misanthropic, — a real Cardinal Wolsey in furs, — for Wix was possessed with a perfect cat-hunting mania, and, when he was not employed in other mischief, was always ready for a bout with Thomas Henry.

It is true, he sometimes came back from these encounters with a scratched and bloody nose, for Thomas Henry was a cat of no mean claw, and would turn to bay at times ; but generally he felt the exertion too much for his advanced years and quiet habits, and so for safety he passed much of his time in the sink, over the battlements of which he would leisurely survey the efforts of the enemy to get at him. The cook hinted strongly of the danger of rheumatism to her favorite from these damp quarters, but Wix at present was the reigning favorite, and it was vain to dispute his sway.

Next to Thomas Henry, Wix directed his principal efforts to teasing Grandmamma. Something or other about her black dress and quiet movements seemed to suggest to him suspicions. He viewed her as something to be narrowly watched ; he would lie down under some chair or table, and watch her motions with his head on his fore-paws as if he were watching at a rat-hole. She evidently was not a rat, he seemed to say to himself, but who knows what she may be ; and he would wink at her with his

great bright eyes, and, if she began to get up, would spring
from his ambush and bark at her feet with frantic energy,
— by which means he nearly threw her over two or three
times.

His young mistress kept a rod, and put him through a
severe course of discipline for these offenses ; after which
he grew more careful, — but still the unaccountable fascina-
tion seemed to continue ; still he would lie in ambush, and,
though forbidden to bark, would dart stealthily forward
when he saw her preparing to rise, and be under her dress
smelling in a suspicious manner at her heels. He would
spring from his place at the fire, and rush to the staircase
when he heard her leisurely step descending the stairs, and
once or twice nearly overset her by being under her heels,
bringing on himself a chastisement which he in vain sought
to avert by the most vigorous deprecatory pawing.

Grandmamma's favorite evening employment was to sit
sleeping in her chair, gradually bobbing her head lower
and lower, — all which movements Wix would watch, giving
a short snap, or a suppressed growl, at every bow. What
he would have done if, as John Bunyan says, he had been
allowed to have his "doggish way" with her, it is impossible to say. Once he succeeded in seizing the slipper
from her foot as she sat napping, and a glorious race he
had with it, — out at the front door, up the path to the
Theological Seminary, and round and round the halls consecrated to better things, with all the glee of an imp. At
another time he made a dart into her apartment, and seized
a turkey-wing which the good old lady had used for a
duster, and made such a regular forenoon's work of worrying, shaking, and teasing it, that every feather in it was
utterly demolished.

In fact, there was about Wix something so elfish and
impish, that there began to be shrewd suspicions that he
must be somehow or other a descendant of the celebrated

poodle of Faust, and that one need not be surprised some
day to have him suddenly looming up into some uncanny
shape, or entering into conversation, and uttering all sorts
of improprieties unbefitting a theological professor's family.

He had a persistence in wicked ways that resisted the
most energetic nurture and admonition of his young mistress. His combativeness was such, that a peaceable walk
down the fashionable street of Zion Hill in his company
became impossible; all was race and scurry, cackle and
flutter, wherever he appeared, — hens and poultry flying,
frightened cats mounting trees with magnified tails, dogs
yelping and snarling, and children and cows running in
every direction. No modest young lady could possibly
walk out in company with such a son of confusion. Beside this, Wix had his own private inexplicable personal
piques against different visitors in the family, and in the
most unexpected moment would give a snap or a nip to
the most unoffending person. His friends in the family
circle dropped off. His ways were pronounced too bad,
his conduct perfectly indefensible; his young mistress
alone clung to him, and declared that her vigorous system
of education would at last reform his eccentricities, and
turn him out a tip-top dog. But when he would slyly
leave home, and, after rolling and steeping himself in the
ill-smelling deposits of the stable or drain, come home and
spring with impudent ease into her lap, or put himself to
sleep on her little white bed, the magic cords of affection
gave out, and disgust began to succeed. It began to be
remarked that this was a stable-dog, educated for the coach-
boy and stable, and to be doubted whether it was worth
while to endeavor to raise him to a lady's boudoir; and so
at last, when the family removed from Zion Hill, he was
taken back and disposed of at a somewhat reduced price.

Since then, as we are informed, he has risen to fame
and honor. His name has even appeared in sporting ga-

zettes as the most celebrated " ratter " in little Boston, and his mistress was solemnly assured by his present possessor that for " cat work " he was unequaled, and that he would not take fifty dollars for him. From all which it appears that a dog which is only a torment and a nuisance in one sphere may be an eminent character in another.

The catalogue of our dogs ends with Wix. Whether we shall ever have another or not we cannot tell, but in the following pages I will tell my young readers a few **true** stories of other domestic pets which may amuse them.

DOGS AND CATS

AND now, with all and each of the young friends who have read these little histories of our dogs, we want to have a few moments of quiet chat about dogs and household pets in general.

In these stories you must have noticed that each dog had as much his own character as if he had been a human being. Carlo was not like Rover, nor Rover like Giglio, nor Giglio like Florence, nor Florence like Rag, nor Rag like Wix, — any more than Charley is like Fred, or Fred like Henry, or Henry like Eliza, or Eliza like Julia. Every animal has his own character, as marked and distinct as a human being. Many people who have not studied much into the habits of animals don't know this. To them a dog is a dog, a cat a cat, a horse a horse, and no more, — that is the end of it.

But domestic animals that associate with human beings develop a very different character from what they would possess in a wild state. Dogs, for example, in those countries where there is a prejudice against receiving them into man's association, herd together, and become wild and fierce like wolves. This is the case in many Oriental countries, where there are superstitious ideas about dogs ; as, for instance, that they are unclean and impure. But in other countries the dog, for the most part, forsakes all other dogs to become the associate of man. A dog without a master is a forlorn creature ; no society of other dogs seems to console him ; he wanders about disconsolate, till he finds some human being to whom to attach himself, and then he is a made dog, — he pads about with an air of dignity, like a dog that is settled in life.

There are among dogs certain races or large divisions, and those belonging purely to any of those races are called blood-dogs. As examples of what we mean by these races, we will mention the spaniel, the mastiff, the bulldog, the hound, and the terrier ; and each of these divisions contains many species, and each has a strongly marked character. The spaniel tribes are gentle, docile, easily attached to man ; from them many hunting dogs are trained. The bulldog is irritable, a terrible fighter, and fiercely faithful to his master. A mastiff is strong, large, not as fierce as the bulldog, but watchful and courageous, with a peculiar sense of responsibility in guarding anything which is placed under his charge. The hounds are slender, lean, wiry, with a long, pointed muzzle, and a peculiar sensibility in the sense of smell, and their instincts lead them to hunting and tracking. As a general thing, they are cowardly and indisposed to combat; there are, however, remarkable exceptions, as you will see if you read the account of the good black hound which Sir Walter Scott tells about in " The Talisman," — a story which I advise you to read at your next leisure. The terriers are, for the most part, small dogs, smart, bright, and active, very intelligent, and capable of being taught many tricks. Of these there are several varieties, — as the English black and tan, which is the neatest and prettiest pet a family of children can have, as his hair is so short and close that he can harbor no fleas, and he is always good-tempered, lively, and affectionate. The Skye terrier, with his mouse-colored mop of hair, and his great bright eyes, is very loving and very sagacious ; but alas ! unless you can afford a great deal of time for soap, water, and fine-tooth-comb exercises, he will bring more company than you will like. The Scotch terriers are rough, scraggy, affectionate, but so nervous, frisky, and mischievous that they are only to be recommended as out-door pets in barn and stable. They are capital rat-catchers, very amicable with horses, and will sit up by the driver or a coach-boy with an air of great sagacity.

There is something very curious about the habits and instincts of certain dogs which have been trained by man for his own purposes. In the mountains of Scotland, there is a tribe of dogs called shepherd-dogs, which for generations and ages have helped the shepherds to take care of their sheep, and which look for all the world like long-nosed, high-cheek-boned, careful old Scotchmen. You will see them in the morning, trotting out their flock of sheep, walking about with a grave, care-taking air, and at evening all bustle and importance, hurrying and scurrying hither and thither, getting their charge all together for the night. An old Scotchman tells us that his dog Hector, by long sharing his toils and cares, got to looking so much like him, that once, when he felt too sleepy to go to meeting, he sent Hector to take his seat in the pew, and the minister never knew the difference, but complimented him the next day for his good attention to the sermon.

There is a kind of dog employed by the monks of St. Bernard in the Alps, to go out and seek in the snow for travelers who may have lost their way ; and this habit becomes such a strong instinct in them, that I once knew a puppy of this species which was brought by a shipmaster to Maine, and grew up in a steady New England town, which used to alarm his kind friends by rushing off into the pine forest in snow-storms, and running anxiously up and down, burrowing in the snow as if in quest of something.

I have seen one of a remarkable breed of dogs that are brought from the island of Manilla. They resemble mastiffs in their form, but are immensely large and strong. They are trained to detect thieves, and kept by merchants on board of vessels where the natives are very sly and much given to stealing. They are called *holders*, and their way is, when a strange man, whose purposes they do not understand, comes on board the ship, to take a very gentle but decisive hold of him by the heel, and keep him fast until somebody comes to look after him. The dog I knew of this species stood about as high as an ordinary dining-table, and I have seen him stroke off the dinner-cloth with one wag of his tail in his pleasure when I patted his head. He was very intelligent and affectionate.

There is another dog, which may often be seen in Paris, called the Spitz dog. He is a white, smooth-haired, small creature, with a great muff of stiff hair round his neck, and generally comes into Paris riding horseback on the cart-horses which draw the carts of the washerwomen. He races nimbly up and down on the back of the great heavy horses, barking from right to left with great animation, and is said to be a most faithful little creature in guarding the property of his owner. What is peculiar about these little dogs is the entireness of their devotion to their master. They have not a look, not a wag of the tail, for any one else; it is vain for a stranger to try and make friends with them, — they have eyes and ears for one alone.

All dogs which do not belong to some of the great varieties, on the one side of their parentage or the other, are classed together as curs, and very much undervalued and decried; and yet among these mongrel curs we have seen individuals quite as sagacious, intelligent, and affectionate as the best blood-dogs.

And now I want to say some things to those young people who desire to adopt as domestic pets either a dog or a cat. Don't do it without making up your mind to be really and thoroughly kind to them, and feeding them as carefully as you feed yourself, and giving them appropriate shelter from the inclemency of the weather.

Some people seem to have a general idea that throwing

a scrap, or bone, or bit of refuse meat, at odd intervals, to a dog, is taking abundant care of him. "What's the matter with him ? he can't be hungry, — I gave him that great bone yesterday." Ah, Master Hopeful, how would you like to be fed on the same principle ? When you show your hungry face at the dinner-table, suppose papa should say, "What's that boy here for ? He was fed this morning." You would think this hard measure ; yet a dog's or cat's stomach digests as rapidly as yours. In like manner, dogs are often shut out of the house in cold winter weather without the least protection being furnished them. A lady and I looked out once, in a freezing icy day, and saw a great Newfoundland cowering in a corner of a fence to keep from the driving wind ; and I said, "Do tell me if you have no kennel for that poor creature." "No," said the lady. "I did n't know that dogs needed shelter. Now I think of it, I remember last spring he seemed quite poorly, and his hair seemed to come out ; do you suppose it was being exposed so much in the winter ? " This lady had taken into her family a living creature, without ever having reflected on what that creature needed, or that it was her duty to provide for its wants.

Dogs can bear more cold than human beings, but they do not like cold any better than we do ; and when a dog has his choice, he will very gladly stretch himself on a rug before the fire for his afternoon nap, and show that he enjoys the blaze and warmth as much as anybody.

As to cats, many people seem to think that a miserable, half-starved beast, never fed, and always hunted and beaten, and with no rights that anybody is bound to respect, is a necessary appendage to a family. They have the idea that all a cat is good for is to catch rats, and that if well fed they will not do this, — and so they starve them. This is a mistake in fact. Cats are hunting animals, and have the natural instinct to pursue and catch prey, and a cat that is a good mouser will do this whether well or ill fed. To live only upon rats is said to injure the health of the cat, and bring on convulsions.

The most beautiful and best trained cat I ever knew was named Juno, and was brought up by a lady who was so wise in all that related to the care and management of animals that she might be quoted as authority on all points of their nurture and breeding; and Juno, carefully trained by such a mistress, was a standing example of the virtues which may be formed in a cat by careful education.

Never was Juno known to be out of place, to take her nap elsewhere than on her own appointed cushion, to be absent at meal-times, or, when the most tempting dainties were in her power, to anticipate the proper time by jumping on the table to help herself.

In all her personal habits Juno was of a neatness unparalleled in cat history. The parlor of her mistress was always of a waxen and spotless cleanness, and Juno would have died sooner than violate its sanctity by any impropriety. She was a skilful mouser, and her sleek, glossy sides were a sufficient refutation of the absurd notion that a cat must be starved into a display of her accomplishments. Every rat, mouse, or ground-mole that she caught was brought in and laid at the feet of her mistress for approbation. But on one point her mind was dark. She could never be made to comprehend the great difference between fur and feathers, nor see why her mistress should gravely reprove her when she brought in a bird, and warmly commend when she captured a mouse.

After a while a little dog named Pero, with whom Juno had struck up a friendship, got into the habit of coming to her mistress's apartment at the hours when her modest meals were served, on which occasions Pero thought it would be a good idea to invite himself to make a third. He had a nice little trick of making himself amiable, by sitting up on his haunches, and making little begging gestures with his two fore-paws, — which so much pleased his hostess that sometimes he was fed before Juno. Juno observed this in silence for some time ; but at last a bright idea struck her, and, gravely rearing up on her haunches, she imitated Pero's gestures with her fore-paws. Of course this carried the day, and secured her position.

Cats are often said to have no heart, — to be attached to places, but incapable of warm personal affection. It was reserved for Juno by her sad end to refute this slander on her race. Her mistress was obliged to leave her quiet home, and go to live in a neighboring city ; so she gave Juno to the good lady who inhabited the other part of the house.

But no attentions or care on the part of her new mistress could banish from Juno's mind the friend she had lost. The neat little parlor where she had spent so many pleasant hours was dismantled and locked up, but Juno would go, day after day, and sit on the ledge of the window-seat, looking in and mewing dolefully. She refused food ; and, when too weak to mount on the sill and look in, stretched herself on the ground beneath the window, where she died for love of her mistress, as truly as any lover in an old ballad.

You see by this story the moral that I wish to convey. It is, that watchfulness, kindness, and care will develop a nature in animals such as we little dream of. Love will beget love, regular care and attention will give regular habits, and thus domestic pets may be made agreeable and interesting.

Any one who does not feel an inclination or capacity to take the amount of care and pains necessary for the well-being of an animal ought conscientiously to abstain from having one in charge. A carefully tended pet, whether dog or cat, is a pleasant addition to a family of young people ; but a neglected, ill-brought-up, ill-kept one is only an annoyance.

We should remember, too, in all our dealings with animals, that they are a sacred trust to us from our Heavenly Father. They are dumb, and cannot speak for themselves; they cannot explain their wants or justify their conduct; and therefore we should be tender towards them.

Our Lord says not even a little sparrow falls to the ground without our Heavenly Father, and we may believe that his eye takes heed of the disposition which we show towards those defenseless beings whom he thinks worthy of his protection.

In the last number I told my little friends about my good Aunt Esther, and her wonderful cat Juno, and her dog Pero. In thinking what to write for this month my mind goes far back to the days when I was a little girl, and used to spend many happy hours in Aunt Esther's parlor talking with her. Her favorite subject was always the habits and character of different animals, and their various ways and instincts, and she used to tell us so many wonderful, yet perfectly authentic, stories about all these things, that the hours passed away very quickly.

Some of her rules for the treatment and care of animals have impressed themselves so distinctly on my mind, that I shall never forget them, and I am going to repeat some of them to you.

One was, never to frighten an animal for sport. I recollect I had a little white kitten, of which I was very fond, and one day I was amusing myself with making her walk up and down the key-board of the piano, and laughing to see her fright at the strange noises which came up under her feet. Puss evidently thought the place was haunted, and tried to escape ; it never occurred to me, however, that there was any cruelty in the operation, till Aunt Esther said to me, " My dear, you must never frighten an animal. I have suffered enough from fear to know that there is no suffering more dreadful ; and a helpless animal, that cannot speak to tell its fright, and cannot understand an explanation of what alarms it, ought to move your pity."

I had never thought of this before, and then I remembered how, when I was a very, very little girl, a grown-up boy in school had amused himself with me and my little brother in much the same way as that in which I had amused myself with the kitten. He hunted us under one of the school-room tables by threatening to cut our ears off if we came out, and took out his pen-knife, and opened it, and shook it at us whenever we offered to move. Very likely he had not the least idea that we really could be made to suffer with fear at so absurd a threat, — any more than I had that my kitten could possibly be afraid of the piano ; but our suffering was in fact as real as if the boy really had intended what he said, and was really able to execute it.

Another thing which Aunt Esther strongly impressed on my mind was that, when there were domestic animals about a house which were not wanted in a family, it was far kinder to have them killed in some quick and certain way than to chase them out of the house, and leave them to wander homeless, to be starved, beaten, and abused. Aunt Esther was a great advocate for killing animals, and, tender-hearted as she was, she gave us many instructions in the kindest and quickest way of disposing of one whose life must be sacrificed.

Her instructions sometimes bore most remarkable fruits. I recollect one little girl, who had been trained under Aunt Esther's care, was once coming home from school across Boston Common, when she saw a party of noisy boys and dogs tormenting a poor kitten by the side of the frog pond. The little wretches would throw it into the water, and then laugh at its vain and frightened efforts to paddle out, while the dogs added to its fright by their ferocious barking. Belle was a bright-eyed, spirited little puss, and her whole soul was roused in indignation ; she dashed in among the throng of boys and dogs, and rescued the poor half-drowned little animal. The boys, ashamed, slunk away, and little

Belle held the poor, cold, shivering little creature, considering what to do for it. It was half dead already, and she was embarrassed by the reflection that at home there was no room for another pet, for both cat and kitten never were wanting in their family. "Poor kit," she said, "you must die, but I will see that you are not tormented ; " — and she knelt bravely down and held the little thing under water, with the tears running down her own cheeks, till all its earthly sorrows were over, and little kit was beyond the reach of dog or boy.

This was real brave humanity. Many people call themselves tender-hearted, because they are unwilling to have a litter of kittens killed, and so they go and throw them over fences, into people's back yards, and comfort themselves with the reflection that they will do well enough. What becomes of the poor little defenseless things ? In nine cases out of ten they live a hunted, miserable life, crying from hunger, shivering with cold, harassed by cruel dogs, and tortured to make sport for brutal boys. How much kinder and more really humane to take upon ourselves the momentary suffering of causing the death of an animal than to turn our back and leave it to drag out a life of torture and misery !

Aunt Esther used to protest much against another kind of torture which well-meaning persons inflict on animals, in giving them as playthings to very little children who do not know how to handle them. A mother sometimes will sit quietly sewing, while her baby boy is tormenting a helpless kitten, poking his fingers into its eyes, pulling its tail, stretching it out as on a rack, squeezing its feet, and, when the poor little tormented thing tries to run away, will send the nurse to catch dear little Johnny's kitten for him.

Aunt Esther always remonstrated, too, against all the practical jokes and teasing of animals, which many people practice under the name of sport, — like throwing a dog into the water for the sake of seeing him paddle out, dashing water upon the cat, or doing any of the many little tricks by which animals are made uncomfortable. "They have but one short little life to live, they are dumb and cannot complain, and they are wholly in our power" — these were the motives by which she appealed to our generosity.

Aunt Esther's boys were so well trained that they would fight valiantly for the rescue of any ill-treated animals. Little Master Bill was a bright-eyed fellow, who wasn't much taller than his father's knee, and wore a low-necked dress with white ruffles. But Bill had a brave heart in his little body, and so one day, as he was coming from school, he dashed in among a crowd of dogs which were pursuing a kitten, took it away from them, and held it as high above his head as his little arm could reach. The dogs jumped upon his white neck with their rough paws, and scratched his face, but still he stood steady till a man came up and took the kitten and frightened away the dogs. Master Bill grew up to be a man, and at the battle of Gettysburg stood a three days' fight, and resisted the charge of the Louisiana Tigers as of old he withstood the charge of the dogs. A really brave-hearted fellow is generally tender and compassionate to the weak; only cowards torment that which is not strong enough to fight them; only cowards starve helpless prisoners or torture helpless animals.

I can't help hoping that, in these stories about different pets, I have made some friends among the boys, and that they will remember what I have said, and resolve always to defend the weak, and not permit any cruelty where it is in their power to prevent it. Boys, you are strong and brave little fellows; but you ought n't to be strong and brave for nothing; and if every boy about the street would set himself to defending helpless animals, we should see much less cruelty than we now do.

AUNT ESTHER used to be a constant attendant upon us young ones whenever we were a little ill, or any of the numerous accidents of childhood overtook us. In such seasons of adversity she always came to sit by our bedside, and take care of us. She did not, as some people do, bring a long face and a doleful whining voice into a sick-room, but was always so bright, and cheerful, and chatty, that we began to think it was almost worth while to be sick to have her about us. I remember that once, when I had the quinsy, and my throat was so swollen that it brought the tears every time I swallowed, Aunt Esther talked to me so gayly, and told me so many stories, that I found myself laughing heartily, and disposed to regard my aching throat as on the whole rather an amusing circumstance.

Aunt Esther's stories were not generally fairy tales, but stories about real things, — and more often on her favorite subject of the habits of animals, and the different animals she had known, than about anything else.

One of these was a famous Newfoundland dog, named Prince, which belonged to an uncle of hers in the country, and was, as we thought, a far more useful and faithful member of society than many of us youngsters. Prince used to be a grave, sedate dog, that considered himself put in trust of the farm, the house, the cattle, and all that was on the place. At night he slept before the kitchen door, which, like all other doors in the house in those innocent days, was left unlocked all night; and if such a thing had ever happened as that a tramp or an improper person of any kind had even touched the latch of the door, Prince would have been up attending to him as master of ceremonies.

At early dawn, when the family began to stir, Prince was up and out to superintend the milking of the cows, after which he gathered them all together, and started out with them to pasture, paddling steadily along behind, dashing out once in a while to reclaim some wanderer that thoughtlessly began to make her breakfast by the roadside, instead of saving her appetite for the pastures, as a properly behaved cow should. Arrived at the pasture-lot, Prince would take down the bars with his teeth, drive in the cows, put up bars, and then soberly turn tail and pad off home, and carry the dinner-basket for the men to the mowing lot, or the potato-field, or wherever the labors of the day might be. There arrived, he was extremely useful to send on errands after anything forgotten or missing. "Prince! the rake is missing: go to the barn and fetch it!" and away Prince would go, and come back with his head very high, and the long rake very judiciously balanced in his mouth.

One day a friend was wondering at the sagacity of the dog, and his master thought he would show off his tricks in a still more original style; and so, calling Prince to him, he said, "Go home and bring Puss to me!"

Away bounded Prince towards the farm-house, and, looking about, found the younger of the two cats, fair Mistress Daisy, busy cleaning her white velvet in the summer sun. Prince took her gently up by the nape of her neck, and carried her, hanging head and heels together, to the fields, and laid her down at his master's feet.

"How 's this, Prince?" said the master; "you did n't understand me. I said the cat, and this is the kitten. Go right back and bring the old cat."

Prince looked very much ashamed of his mistake, and

turned away, with drooping ears and tail, and went back to the house.

The old cat was a venerable, somewhat portly old dame, and no small lift for Prince; but he reappeared with old Puss hanging from his jaws, and set her down, a little discomposed, but not a whit hurt by her unexpected ride.

Sometimes, to try Prince's skill, his master would hide his gloves or riding-whip in some out-of-the-way corner and when ready to start, would say, "Now, where have I left my gloves? Prince, good fellow, run in, and find them;" and Prince would dash into the house, and run hither and thither with his nose to every nook and corner of the room; and, no matter how artfully they were hid, he would upset and tear his way to them. He would turn up the corners of the carpet, snuff about the bed, run his nose between the feather-bed and mattress, pry into the crack of a half-opened drawer, and show as much zeal and ingenuity as a policeman, and seldom could anything be so hid as to baffle his perseverance.

Many people laugh at the idea of being careful of a dog's feelings, as if it were the height of absurdity; and yet it is a fact that some dogs are as exquisitely sensitive to pain, shame, and mortification, as any human being. See, when a dog is spoken harshly to, what a universal droop seems to come over him. His head and ears sink, his tail drops and slinks between his legs, and his whole air seems to say, "I wish I could sink into the earth to hide myself."

Prince's young master, without knowing it, was the means of inflicting a most terrible mortification on him at one time. It was very hot weather, and Prince, being a shaggy dog, lay panting, and lolling his tongue out, apparently suffering from the heat.

"I declare," said young Master George, "I do believe Prince would be more comfortable for being sheared."

And so forthwith he took him and began divesting him of his coat. Prince took it all very obediently; but when he appeared without his usual attire, every one saluted him with roars of laughter, and Prince was dreadfully mortified. He broke away from his master, and scampered off home at a desperate pace, ran down cellar, and disappeared from view. His young master was quite distressed that Prince took the matter so to heart; he followed him in vain, calling, "Prince! Prince!" No Prince appeared. He lighted a candle and searched the cellar, and found the poor creature cowering away in the darkest nook under the stairs. Prince was not to be comforted: he slunk deeper and deeper into the darkness, and crouched on the ground when he saw his master, and for a long time refused even to take food. The family all visited and condoled with him, and finally his sorrows were somewhat abated; but he would not be persuaded to leave the cellar for nearly a week. Perhaps by that time he indulged the hope that his hair was beginning to grow again, and all were careful not to destroy the illusion by any jests or comments on his appearance.

Such were some of the stories of Prince's talents and exploits which Aunt Esther used to relate to us. What finally became of the old fellow we never heard. Let us hope that, as he grew old, and gradually lost his strength, and felt the infirmities of age creeping on, he was tenderly and kindly cared for in memory of the services of his best days, — that he had a warm corner by the kitchen fire, and was daily spoken to in kindly tones by his old friends. Nothing is a sadder sight than to see a poor old favorite, that once was petted and caressed by every member of the family, now sneaking and cowering as if dreading every moment a kick or a blow, — turned from the parlor into the kitchen, driven from the kitchen by the cook's broomstick, half starved and lonesome.

O how much kinder if the poor thread of life were at once cut by some pistol-shot, than to have the neglected favorite linger only to suffer! Now, boys, I put it to you, is it generous or manly, when your old pet and playmate grows sickly and feeble, and can no longer amuse you, to forget all the good old times you have had with him, and let him become a poor, trembling, hungry, abused vagrant? If you cannot provide comforts for his old age, and see to his nursing, you can at least secure him an easy and painless passage from this troublesome world. A manly fellow I once knew, who, when his old hound became so diseased that he only lived to suffer, gave him a nice meal with his own hand, patted his head, got him to sleep, and then shot him, — so that he was dead in a moment, felt no pain, and knew nothing but kindness to the last.

And now to Aunt Esther's stories of a dog I must add one more which occurred in a town where I once lived. I have told you of the fine traits of blood-dogs, their sagacity and affection. In doing this, perhaps, I have not done half justice to the poor common dogs, of no particular blood or breed, that are called curs or mongrels; yet among these I believe you will quite as often find both affection and sagacity as among better-born dogs.

The poor mongrel I am going to tell you about belonged to a man who had not, in one respect, half the sense that his dog had. A dog will never eat or drink a thing that has once made him sick, or injured him; but this man would drink, time and time again, a deadly draught, that took away his senses and unfitted him for any of his duties. Poor little Pero, however, set her ignorant dog's heart on her drinking master, and used to patter faithfully after him, and lick his hand respectfully, when nobody else thought he was in a condition to be treated with respect.

One bitter cold winter day, Pero's master went to a grocery, at some distance from home, on pretence of getting groceries, but in reality to fill a very dreadful bottle, that was the cause of all his misery; and little Pero padded after him through the whirling snow, although she left three poor little pups of her own in the barn. Was it that she was anxious for the poor man who was going the bad road, or was there some secret thing in her dog's heart that warned her that her master was in danger? We know not, but the sad fact is, that at the grocery the poor man took enough to make his brain dizzy, and coming home he lost his way in a whirling snow-storm, and fell down stupid and drunk, not far from his own barn, in a lonesome place, with the cold winter's wind sweeping the snow-drift over him. Poor little Pero cuddled close to her master and nestled in his bosom, as if trying to keep the warm life in him.

Two or three days passed, and nothing was seen or heard of the poor man. The snow had drifted over him in a long white winding-sheet, when a neighbor one day heard a dog in the barn crying to get out. It was poor Pero, that had come back and slipped in to nurse her puppies while the barn-door was open, and was now crying to get out and go back to her poor master. It suddenly occurred to the man that Pero might find the body, and in fact, when she started off, he saw a little path which her small paws had worn in the snow, and, tracking after, found the frozen body. This poor little friend had nestled the snow away around the breast, and stayed watching and waiting by her dead master, only taking her way back occasionally to the barn to nurse her little ones. I cannot help asking whether a little animal that can show such love and faithfulness has not something worth respecting and caring for in its nature.

At this time of the year our city ordinances proclaim a general leave and license to take the lives of all dogs found in the streets, and scenes of dreadful cruelty are often enacted in consequence.   I hope, if my stories fall under the eye of any boy who may ever witness, or be tempted to take part in, the hunting down and killing a poor dog, that he will remember of how much faithfulness and affection and constancy these poor brutes are capable, and, instead of being their tyrant and persecutor, will try to make himself their protector and friend.

SIR WALTER SCOTT AND HIS DOGS

MASTER FREDERICK LITTLE-JOHN has of late struck up quite a friendship with me, and haunts my footsteps about the house to remind me of my promise to write some more dog stories. Master Fred has just received a present from his father of a great Newfoundland that stands a good deal higher in his stocking-feet than his little master in his highest-heeled boots, and he has named him Prince, in honor of the Prince that I told you about last month, that used to drive the cows to pasture, and take down the bars with his teeth. We have daily and hourly accounts in the family circle of Prince's sayings and doings ; for Master Freddy insists upon it that Prince speaks, and daily insists upon placing a piece of bread on the top of Prince's nose, which at the word of command he fires into the air, and catches in his mouth, closing the performance with a snap like a rifle. Fred also makes much of showing him a bit of meat held high in the air, for which he is requested to "speak," — the speaking consisting in very short exclamations of the deepest bow-wow. Certain it is that Prince shows on these occasions that he has the voice for a public speaker, and that, if he does not go about the country lecturing, it is because he wants time yet to make up his mind what to say on the topics of the day.

Fred is somewhat puzzled to make good the ground of his favorite with Aunt Zeroiah, who does not love dogs, and is constantly casting reflections on them as nuisances, dirt-makers, flea-catchers, and flea-scatterers, and insinuating a plea that Prince should be given away, or in some manner sold or otherwise disposed of.

"Aunt Zeroiah thinks that there is nothing so mean as a dog," said Master Fred to me as he sat with his arm around the neck of his favorite. "She really seems to grudge every morsel of meat a dog eats, and to think that every kindness you show a dog is almost a sin. Now I think dogs are noble creatures, and have noble feelings, — they are so faithful, and so kind and loving. Now I do wish you would make haste and write something to show her that dogs have been thought a good deal of."

"Well, Master Freddy," said I, "I will tell you in the first place about Sir Walter Scott, whose poems and novels have been the delight of whole generations."

He was just of your opinion about dogs, and he had a great many of them. When Washington Irving visited Sir Walter at Abbotsford, he found him surrounded by his dogs, which formed as much a part of the family as his children.

In the morning, when they started for a ramble, the dogs would all be on the alert to join them. There was first a tall old staghound named Maida, that considered himself the confidential friend of his master, walked by his side, and looked into his eyes as if asserting a partnership in his thoughts. Then there was a black greyhound named Hamlet, a more frisky and thoughtless youth, that gamboled and pranced and barked and cut capers with the wildest glee; and there was a beautiful setter named Finette, with large mild eyes, soft silken hair, and long curly ears, — the favorite of the parlor; and then a venerable old greyhound, wagging his tail, came out to join the party as he saw them going by his quarters, and was cheered by Scott with a hearty, kind word as an old friend and comrade.

In his walks Scott would often stop and talk to one or another of his four-footed friends, as if they were in fact rational companions; and, from being talked to and treated in this way, they really seemed to acquire more sagacity than other dogs.

Old Maida seemed to consider himself as a sort of president of the younger dogs, as a dog of years and reflection, whose mind was upon more serious and weighty topics than theirs. As he padded along, the younger dogs would sometimes try to ensnare him into a frolic, by jumping upon his neck and making a snap at his ears. Old Maida would bear this in silent dignity for a while, and then suddenly, as if his patience were exhausted, he would catch one of his tormentors by the neck and tumble him in the dirt, giving an apologetic look to his master at the same time, as much as to say, " You see, sir, I can't help joining a little in this nonsense."

" Ah," said Scott, " I 've no doubt that, when Maida is alone with these young dogs, he throws dignity aside and plays the boy as much as any of them, but he is ashamed to do it in our company, and seems to say, ' Have done with your nonsense, youngsters; what will the Laird and that other gentleman think of me if I give way to such foolery ? ' "

At length the younger dogs fancied that they discovered something, which set them all into a furious barking. Old Maida for some time walked silently by his master, pretending not to notice the clamors of the inferior dogs. At last, however, he seemed to feel himself called on to attend to them, and giving a plunge forward he opened his mind to them, with a deep " Bow-wow," that drowned for the time all other voices. Then, as if he had settled matters, he returned to his master, wagging his tail, and looking in his face as if for approval.

" Ay, ay, old boy," said Scott ; " you have done wonders; you have shaken the Eildon Hills with your roaring, and now you may shut up your artillery for the rest of the day. Maida," he said, " is like the big gun of Constantinople, — it takes so long to get it ready that the small ones can fire off a dozen times, but when it does go off it carries all before it."

Scott's four-footed friends made a respectful part of the company at family meals. Old Maida took his seat gravely at his master's elbow, looking up wistfully into his eyes, while Finette, the pet spaniel, took her seat by Mrs. Scott. Besides the dogs in attendance, a large gray cat also took her seat near her master, and was presented from time to time with bits from the table. Puss, it appears, was a great favorite both with master and mistress, and slept in their room at night; and Scott laughingly said that one of the least wise parts of the family arrangement was the leaving the window open at night for puss to go in and out. The cat assumed a sort of supremacy among the quadrupeds, sitting in state in Scott's arm-chair, and occasionally stationing himself on a chair beside the door, as if to review his subjects as they passed, giving each dog a cuff on the ears as he went by. This clapper-clawing was always amiably taken. It appeared to be in fact a mere act of sovereignty on the part of Grimalkin, to remind the others of their vassalage, to which they cheerfully submitted. Perfect harmony prevailed between old puss and her subjects, and they would all sleep contentedly together in the sunshine.

Scott once said, the only trouble about having a dog was that he must die; but he said it was better to have them die in eight or nine years than to go on loving them for twenty or thirty, and then have them die.

Scott lived to lose many of his favorites, that were buried with funeral honors, and had monuments erected over them, which form some of the prettiest ornaments of Abbotsford. When we visited the place, one of the first objects we saw in the front yard near the door was the tomb of old Maida, over which is sculptured the image of a beautiful hound, with this inscription, which you may translate if you like : —

> "Maidæ marmorea dormis sub imagine,
> Maida,
> Ad januam domini ; sit tibi terra levis."

Or, if you don't want the trouble of translating it, Master Freddy, I would do it thus : —

> "At thy lord's door, in slumbers light and blest,
> Maida, beneath this marble Maida rest.
> Light lie the turf upon thy gentle breast."

Washington Irving says that in one of his morning rambles he came upon a curious old Gothic monument, on which was inscribed in Gothic characters,

> "Cy git le preux Percy,"
> (Here lies the brave Percy,)

and asking Scott what it was, he replied, " Oh, only one of my fooleries," — and afterwards Irving found it was the grave of a favorite greyhound.

Now, certainly, Master Freddy, you must see in all this that you have one of the greatest geniuses of the world to bear you out in thinking a deal of dogs.

But I have still another instance. The great rival poet to Scott was Lord Byron ; not so good or so wise a man by many degrees, but very celebrated in his day. He also had a four-footed friend, a Newfoundland, called Boatswain, which he loved tenderly, and whose elegant monument now forms one of the principal ornaments of the garden of Newstead Abbey, and upon it may be read this inscription : —

> "Near this spot
> Are deposited the remains of one
> Who possessed beauty without vanity,
> Strength without insolence,
> Courage without ferocity,
> And all the virtues of man without his vices.
> This praise, which would be unmeaning flattery
> If inscribed over human ashes,
> Is but a just tribute to the memory of
> BOATSWAIN, a dog,

Who was born at Newfoundland, May, 1803,
And died at Newstead Abbey, Nov. 18, 1808."

On the other side of the monument the poet inscribed
these lines in praise of dogs in general, which I would
recommend you to show to any of the despisers of dogs : —

"When some proud son of man returns to earth
Unknown to glory, but upheld by birth,
The sculptor's art exhausts the pomp of woe,
And storied urns record who rests below.
But the poor dog, in life the firmest friend,
The first to welcome, foremost to defend,
Whose honest heart is still his master's own,
Who labors, fights, lives, breathes, for him alone,
Unhonored falls, unnoticed all his worth,
Denied in heaven the soul he held on earth.
While man, vain insect ! hopes to be forgiven,
And claims himself a sole exclusive heaven !
Ye who perchance behold this simple urn,
Pass on, it honors none you wish to mourn.
To mark a *friend's* remains these stones arise ;
I never knew but one, — and here he lies."

If you want more evidence of the high esteem in which
dogs are held, I might recommend to you a very pretty dog
story called "Rab and his Friends," the reading of which
will give you a pleasant hour. Also in a book called
"Spare Hours" the author of "Rab and his Friends" gives
amusing accounts of all his different dogs, which I am sure
you would be pleased to read, even though you find many
long words in it which you cannot understand.

But enough has been given to show you that in the high
esteem you have for your favorite, and in your determination to treat him as a dog should be treated, you are sus-
tained by the very best authority.

Do my dear little friends want to hear a word more about our country neighbors? Since we wrote about them, we have lived in the same place more than a year, and perhaps some of you may want to know whether old Unke or little Cri-cri have ever come up to sit under the lily-leaves by the fountain, or Master Furry-toes, the flying squirrel, has amused himself in pattering about the young lady's chamber o' nights? I am sorry to say that our country neighbors have entirely lost the neighborly, confiding spirit that they had when we first came and settled in the woods.

Old Unke has distinguished himself on moonlight nights in performing bass solos in a very deep, heavy voice, down in the river, but he has never hopped his way back into that conservatory from which he was disgracefully turned out at the point of Mr. Fred's cane. He has contented himself with the heavy musical performances I spoke of, and I have fancied they sounded much like "Won't come any more, — won't come any more, — won't come any more!"

Sometimes, strolling down to the river, we have seen his solemn yellow spectacles emerging from the tall water-grasses, as he sat complacently looking about him. Near by him, spread out on the sunny bottom of the pool, was a large flat-headed water-snake, with a dull yellow-brown back and such a swelled stomach that it was quite evident he had been making his breakfast that morning by swallowing some unfortunate neighbor like poor little Cri-cri. This trick of swallowing one's lesser neighbors seems to prevail greatly among the people who live in our river. Mr. Water-snake makes his meal on little Mr. Frog, and little Mr. Bullfrog follows the same example. It seems a sad state of things; but then I suppose all animals have to die in some way or other, and perhaps, if they are in the habit of seeing it done, it may appear no more to a frog to expect to be swallowed some day, than it may to some of us to die of a fever, or be shot in battle, as many a brave fellow has been of late.

We have heard not a word from the woodchucks. Ever since we violated the laws of woodland hospitality by setting a trap for their poor old patriarch, they have very justly considered us as bad neighbors, and their hole at the bottom of the garden has been " to let," and nobody as yet has ventured to take it. Our friends the muskrats have been flourishing, and on moonlight nights have been swimming about, popping up the tips of their little black noses to make observations.

But latterly a great commotion has been made among the amphibious tribes, because of the letting down of the dam which kept up the water of the river, and made it a good, full, wide river. When the dam was torn down it became a little miserable stream, flowing through a wide field of muddy bottom, and all the secrets of the underwater were disclosed. The white and yellow water-lily roots were left high and dry up in the mud, and all the musk-rat holes could be seen plainer than ever before ; and the other day Master Charley brought in a fish's nest which he had found in what used to be deep water.

"A fish's nest !" says little Tom ; " I did n't know fishes made nests." But they do, Tommy ; that is, one particular kind of fish makes a nest of sticks and straws and twigs plastered together with some kind of cement, the making of which is a family secret. It lies on the ground like a common bird's nest turned bottom upward, and has a tiny little hole in the side for a door, through which the little fishes swim in and out.

The name of the kind of fish that builds this nest I do not know; and if the water had not been drawn off, I should not have known that we had any such fish in our river. Where we found ours the water had been about five feet above it. Now, Master Tom, if you want to know more about nest-building fishes, you must get your papa and mamma to inquire and see if they cannot get you some of the little books on fishes and aquariums that have been published lately. I remember to have read all about these nests in one of them, but I do not remember either the name of the book or the name of the fish, and so there is something still for you to inquire after.

I am happy to say, for the interest of the water-lilies and the muskrats and the fishes, that the dam has only been torn down from our river for the purpose of making a new and stronger one, and that by and by the water will be again broad and deep as before, and all the water-people can then go on with their housekeeping just as they used to do, — only I am sorry to say that one fish family will miss their house, and have to build a new one; but if they are enterprising fishes they will perhaps make some improvements that will make the new house better than the old.

As to the birds, we have had a great many visits from them. Our house has so many great glass windows, and the conservatory windows in the centre of it being always wide open, the birds seem to have taken it for a piece of outdoors, and flown in. The difficulty has been, that after they had got in, there appeared to be no way of making them understand the nature of glass, and wherever they saw a glass window they fancied they could fly through; and so, taking aim hither and thither, they darted head first against the glass, beating and bruising their poor little

heads without beating in any more knowledge than they
had before. Many a poor little feather-head has thus fallen
a victim to his want of natural philosophy, and tired himself out with beating against window-panes, till he has at
last fallen dead. One day we picked up no less than three
dead birds in different parts of the house. Now if it had
only been possible to enlighten our feathered friends in
regard to the fact that everything that is transparent is not
air, we would have summoned a bird council in our conservatory, and explained matters to them at once and altogether. As it is, we could only say, " Oh ! " and " Ah ! "
and lament, as we have followed one poor victim after
another from window to window, and seen him flutter and
beat his pretty senseless head against the glass, frightened
to death at all our attempts to help him.

As to the humming-birds, their number has been infinite.
Just back of the conservatory stands an immense, high
clump of scarlet sage, whose brilliant flowers have been like
a light shining from afar, and drawn to it flocks of these
little creatures; and we have often sat watching them as
they put their long bills into one scarlet tube after another,
lifting themselves lightly off the bush, poising a moment in
mid-air, and then dropping out of sight.

They have flown into the conservatory in such numbers
that, had we wished to act over again the dear little history
of our lost pet, Hum, the son of Buz, we should have had
plenty of opportunities to do it. Humming-birds have been
for some reason supposed to be peculiarly wild and untam-
able. Our experience has proved that they are the most
disposed to put trust in us human beings of all birds in the
world.

More than once this summer has some little captive
exhausted his strength flying hither and thither against the
great roof window of the conservatory, till the whole family
was in alarm to help. The Professor himself has left his

books, and anxiously flourished a long cobweb broom in hopes to bring the little wanderer down to the level of open windows, while every other member of the family ran, called, made suggestions, and gave advice, which all ended in the poor little fool's falling flat, in a state of utter exhaustion, and being picked up in some lady's pocket handkerchief.

Then has been running to mix sugar and water, while the little crumb of a bird has lain in an apparent swoon in the small palm of some fair hand, but opening occasionally one eye, and then the other, dreamily, to see when the sugar and water was coming, and gradually showing more and more signs of returning life as it appeared. Even when he had taken his drink of sugar and water, and seemed able to sit up in his warm little hollow, he has seemed in no hurry to flee, but remained tranquilly looking about him for some moments, till all of a sudden, with one whirr, away he goes, like a flying morsel of green and gold, over our heads — into the air — into the treetops. What a lovely time he must have of it!

One rainy, windy day, Miss Jenny, going into the conservatory, heard a plaintive little squeak, and found a poor humming-bird, just as we found poor little Hum, all wet and chilled, and bemoaning himself, as he sat clinging tightly upon the slenderest twig of a grape-vine. She took him off, wrapped him in cotton, and put him in a box on a warm shelf over the kitchen range. After a while you may be sure there was a pretty fluttering in the box. Master Hum was awake and wanted to be attended to. She then mixed sugar and water, and, opening the box, offered him a drop on her finger, which he licked off with his long tongue as knowingly as did his namesake at Rye Beach. After letting him satisfy his appetite for sugar and water, as the rain was over and the sun began to shine, Miss Jenny took him to the door, and away he flew.

These little incidents show that it would not ever be a
difficult matter to tame humming-birds, — only they cannot
be kept in cages; a sunny room with windows defended
by mosquito-netting would be the only proper cage.   The
humming-bird, as we are told by naturalists, though very
fond of the honey of flowers, does not live on it entirely or
even principally.   It is in fact a little fly-catcher, and lives
on small insects; and a humming-bird never can be kept
healthy for any length of time in a room that does not ad-
mit insects enough to furnish him a living.   So you see it
is not merely toads, and water-snakes, and such homely
creatures, that live by eating other living beings, — but
even the fairy-like and brilliant humming-bird.

The autumn months are now coming on (for it is Octo-
ber while I write), — the flowers are dying night by night
as the frosts grow heavier, — the squirrels are racing about,
full of business, getting in their winter's supply of nuts;
everything now is active and busy among our country neighbors.   In a cottage about a quarter of a mile from us, a
whole family of squirrels have made the discovery that a
house is warmer in winter than the best hollow tree, and
so have gone into a chink between the wall, where Mr.
and Mrs. Squirrel can often be heard late at night chattering and making quite a family fuss about the arrangement of their household goods for the coming season.   This
is all the news about the furry people that I have to
give you.   The flying squirrel I have not yet heard from,
— perhaps he will appear yet as the weather gets colder.

Old Master Boohoo, the owl, sometimes goes on at such
a rate on moonlight nights in the great chestnut-trees that
overhang the river, that, if you did not know better, you
might think yourself miles deep in the heart of a sombre
forest, instead of being within two squares' walk of the
city lamps.   We never yet have caught a fair sight of him.
At the cottage we speak of, the chestnut-trees are very

tall, and come close to the upper windows; and one night
a fair maiden, going up to bed, was startled by a pair of
great round eyes looking into her window.   It was one of
the Boohoo family, who had been taken with a fit of grave
curiosity about what went on inside the cottage, and so set
himself to observe.   We have never been able to return the
compliment by looking into their housekeeping, as their
nests are very high up in the hollows of old trees, where
we should not be likely to get at them.

If we hear anything more from any of these neighbors
of ours, we will let you know.   We have all the afternoon
been hearing a great screaming among the jays in the woods
hard by, and I think we must go out and see what is the
matter.   So good-by.

THE DIVERTING HISTORY OF LITTLE
WHISKEY

AND now, at the last, I am going to tell you something of the ways and doings of one of the queer little people, whom I shall call Whiskey.

You cannot imagine how pretty he is. His back has the most beautiful smooth shining stripes of reddish brown and black, his eyes shine like bright glass beads, and he sits up jauntily on his hind quarters, with his little tail thrown over his back like a ruffle !

And where does he live ? Well, " that is telling," as we children say. It was somewhere up in the mountains of Berkshire, in a queer, quaint, old-fashioned garden, that I made Mr. Whiskey's acquaintance.

Here there lives a young parson, who preaches every Sunday in a little brown church, and during week-days goes through all these hills and valleys, visiting the poor, and gathering children into Sunday schools.

His wife is a very small-sized lady, — not much bigger than you, my little Mary, — but very fond of all sorts of dumb animals ; and by constantly watching their actions and ways, she has come to have quite a strange power over them, as I shall relate.

The little lady fixed her mind on Whiskey, and gave him his name without consulting him upon the subject. She admired his bright eyes, and resolved to cultivate his acquaintance.

By constant watching, she discovered that he had a small hole of his own in the grass-plot a few paces from her back door. So she used to fill her pockets with hazel-nuts, and go out and sit in the back porch, and make a little noise, such as squirrels make to each other, to attract his attention.

In a minute or two up would pop the little head with the bright eyes, in the grass-plot, and Master Whiskey would sit on his haunches and listen, with one small ear cocked towards her. Then she would throw him a hazel-nut, and he would slip instantly down into his hole again. In a minute or two, however, his curiosity would get the better of his prudence; and she, sitting quiet, would see the little brown-striped head slowly, slowly coming up again, over the tiny green spikes of the grass-plot. Quick as a flash he would dart at the nut, whisk it into a little bag on one side of his jaws, which Madame Nature has furnished him with for his provision-pouch, and down into his hole again! An ungrateful, suspicious little brute he was too; for though in this way he bagged and carried off nut after nut, until the patient little woman had used up a pound of hazel-nuts, still he seemed to have the same wild fright at sight of her, and would whisk off and hide himself in his hole the moment she appeared. In vain she called, "Whiskey, Whiskey, Whiskey," in the most flattering tones; in vain she coaxed and cajoled. No, no; he was not to be caught napping. He had no objection to accepting her nuts, as many as she chose to throw to him; but as to her taking any personal liberty with him, you see, it was not to be thought of!

But at last patience and perseverance began to have their reward. Little Master Whiskey said to himself, "Surely, this is a nice, kind lady, to take so much pains to give me nuts; she is certainly very considerate;" and with that he edged a little nearer and nearer every day, until, quite to the delight of the small lady, he would come and climb into her lap and seize the nuts, when she rattled them there, and after that he seemed to make exploring voyages all over her person. He would climb up and sit on her shoulder; he would mount and perch himself on her head; and, when she held a nut for him between her teeth, would take it out of her mouth.

After a while he began to make tours of discovery in the house. He would suddenly appear on the minister's writing-table, when he was composing his Sunday sermon, and sit cocking his little pert head at him, seeming to wonder what he was about. But in all his explorations he proved himself a true Yankee squirrel, having always a shrewd eye on the main chance. If the parson dropped a nut on the floor, down went Whiskey after it, and into his provision-bag it went, and then he would look up as if he expected another; for he had a wallet on each side of his jaws, and he always wanted both sides handsomely filled before he made for his hole. So busy and active, and always intent on this one object, was he, that before long the little lady found he had made way with six pounds of hazel-nuts. His general rule was to carry off four nuts at a time, — three being stuffed into the side-pockets of his jaws, and the fourth held in his teeth. When he had furnished himself in this way, he would dart like lightning for his hole, and disappear in a moment; but in a short time up he would come, brisk and wide-awake, and ready for the next supply.

Once a person who had the curiosity to dig open a chipping squirrel's hole found in it two quarts of buckwheat, a quantity of grass-seed, nearly a peck of acorns, some Indian corn, and a quart of walnuts; a pretty handsome supply for a squirrel's winter store-room, — don't you think so?

Whiskey learned in time to work for his living in many artful ways that his young mistress devised. Sometimes she would tie his nuts up in a paper package, which he

would attack with great energy, gnawing the strings, and
rustling the nuts out of the paper in wonderfully quick
time. Sometimes she would tie a nut to the end of a bit
of twine, and swing it backward and forward over his
head ; and, after a succession of spry jumps, he would
pounce upon it, and hang swinging on the twine, till he
had gnawed the nut away.

Another squirrel — doubtless hearing of Whiskey's
good luck — began to haunt the same yard ; but Whiskey
would by no means allow him to cultivate his young mistress's acquaintance. No indeed ! he evidently considered
that the institution would not support two. Sometimes
he would appear to be conversing with the stranger on the
most familiar and amicable terms in the back yard : but if
his mistress called his name, he would immediately start
and chase his companion quite out of sight, before he came
back to her.

So you see that self-seeking is not confined to men alone,
and that Whiskey's fine little fur coat covers a very selfish
heart.

As winter comes on, Whiskey will go down into his
hole, which has many long galleries and winding passages,
and a snug little bedroom well lined with leaves. Here
he will doze and dream away his long winter months, and
nibble out the inside of his store of nuts.

If I hear any more of his cunning tricks, I will tell you
of them.

LITTLE PUSSY WILLOW

TO

MARY, EMILY, NELLIE, and CHARLOTTE,

AND ALL MY LITTLE GIRL FRIENDS.

Here is PUSSY WILLOW in a book, just as I have promised you she should be. I send her to you as a Christmas and New Year's present, and I hope that you will all grow up to be nice good girls like her, with bright, healthy faces, and cheerful hearts, and the gift of always seeing

The Bright Side of Everything.

Your loving friend,
H. B. STOWE.

I

In a retired town of New England was a certain little green hollow among high hills; and in this little hollow stood an old brown farm-house. It was built two stories high in front, but the roof sloped a long way down behind, till it came so near the ground that any one of you might have jumped off from it without frightening the most anxious mamma.

As I have said, this house stood in a little hollow formed by ever so many high hills, which rose around it much as waves rise around a little boat in stormy weather; they looked, in fact, like green waves that had been suddenly stopped and hardened into mountains and hills. Upon their sides grew forests of pines, besides chestnut, hickory, ash, and maple-trees, which gave them a charming variety through most of the months of the year. The rocks, too, in many places were perfectly veiled and covered with the bright, glossy green leaves of the rose-laurel, while underneath the crevices were full of fern, saxifrage, rock-columbine, and all sorts of lovely things, which were most charming to explore, if one had energy enough to hunt them up.

The house had no yard round it, but stood on a smooth green turfy knoll, and was shaded by a great elm-tree, whose long branches arched over, and seemed like a broad, leafy sky. In summer this was pleasant enough, for the morning sun sent straight arrows of gold hither and thither between the boughs and branches, and carried some of the greenness as they went into the chambers of the old house, and at night the moon and stars winked and twinkled, and made a thousand pretty plays of light and shadow as they sent their rays dancing over, under, and through the elm-boughs to the little brown house.

It was somewhere about the first of March, I believe, when there was quite a stir in the ground-floor bedroom of this little brown house, because a very small young lady had just made her appearance in this world, who was the first daughter that had ever been given to John and Martha Primrose ; and, of course, her coming was a great event. Four of the most respectable old matrons in the vicinity were solemnly taking tea and quince preserves in Martha's bedroom, in honor of the great event which had just transpired, while a little bundle of flannel was carefully trotted and tended in the lap of the oldest of them, who every now and then opened the folds and peered in through her spectacles at a very red, sleepy little face that lay inside.

" Well," said Dame Toothacre, the eldest, " did I ever

know such a spell of warm weather as we had the last fortnight ? "

" Yes," said Ma'am Trowbridge, " it has fairly started
the buds. Look, that pussy willow by the window is quite
out."

" My Mary says she has seen a liverwort blossom," said
Dame Toothacre ; " and I 've heard bluebirds these two
weeks, — it 's a most uncommon season."

" If the warm weather holds on, Martha will have a good
getting-up," said Dame Johnson. " She 's got as plump
and likely a little girl as I should want to see."

And so, after a time, night settled down in the bedroom,
and one after another of the good old gossips went home,
and the little bundle of flannel was tucked warmly into
bed, and Nurse Toothacre was snoring loudly on a cot-bed
in the corner, and the moon streamed through the willow-
bush by the window, and marked the shadow of all the
little pussy buds on it clearly on the white, clean floor, —
when something happened that nobody must know of but
you and me, dear little folks ; and what it was I shall
relate.

There came in on the moonbeams a stream of fairy folk
and wood spirits, to see what they could do for the new
baby. You must know that everything that grows has its
spirit, and these spirits not only attend on their own plants,
but now and then do a good turn for mortals, — as, when
plants have good and healing properties, they come to us by
the ministry of these plant spirits.

In the winter, when the plant seems dead, these spirits
dwell dormant under ground ; but the warm suns of spring
thaw them, and renew their strength, and out they come
happy and strong as ever. Now it was so early in March,
that, if there had not been a most uncommonly warm season for a week or two past, there would not have been a
plant spirit stirring, and the new baby would have had to

go without the gifts and graces which they bring. As it was, there came slipping down on the moonbeam, first, old Mother Fern, all rolled up in a woolen shawl, with a woolen hood on her head, but with a face brimful of benevolence towards the new baby. Little Mistress Liverwort came trembling after her; for it was scarcely warm enough yet to justify her putting on her spring clothes, and she did it only at the urgent solicitations of Bluebird, who had been besieging her doors for a fortnight. And, finally, there was Pussy Willow, who prudently kept on her furs, and moved so velvet-footed that nobody would even suspect she was there; but they undrew the curtains to get a look at the new baby.

"Bless its heart!" said Mother Fern, peering down at it through her glasses. "It's as downy as any of us."

"I should think it might be a young bluebird," said Liverwort, looking down out of her gray hood; "it looks as much like one as anything. Come, what shall we give it? I'll give it blue eyes, — real violet-blue, — and if that is n't a good gift, I don't know what is."

"And I'll give her some of my thrift and prudence," said Mother Fern. "We Ferns have no blossoms to speak of, but we are a well-to-do family, as everybody knows, and can get our living on any soil where it pleases Heaven to put us; and so thrift shall be my gift for this little lady. Thrift will surely lead to riches and honor."

"I will give her a better thing than that," said Pussy Willow. "I grow under the windows here, and mean to adopt her. She shall be called little Pussy Willow, and I shall give her the gift of *always seeing the bright side of everything*. That gift will be more to her than beauty or riches or honors. It is not so much matter what color one's eyes are as what one sees with them. There is a bright side to everything, if people only knew it, and the best eyes are those which are able always to see this best side."

" I must say, Friend Pussy," said Mother Fern, " that you are a most sensibly spoken bush, for a bush of your age. You always did seem to me to have a most remarkable faculty in that line ; for I have remarked how you seize on the first ray of sunshine, and get your pussies out before any of us dare make a movement. Many a time I have said, ' Well, I guess Miss Pussy Willow 'll find herself mistaken in the weather this year ; ' but, taking one year with another, I think you have gained time by being always on hand, and believing in the pleasant weather."

" Well," said Pussy, " if I should hang back with my buds as our old Father Elm-tree does, I should miss a deal of pleasure, and people would miss a deal of pleasure from me. The children, dear souls ! I 'm always in a hurry to get out in the spring, because it pleases them. ' O here 's Pussy Willow come back ! ' they cry when they see me. ' Now the winter is over ! ' And no matter if there is a little dash of sleet or snow or frost after that, I stand it with a good heart, because I know it is summer that is coming, and not winter, and that things are certain to grow better, and not worse. I 'm not handsome, I know ; I 'm not elegant ; nobody thinks much of me ; and my only good points are my cheerfulness and my faith in good things to come ; so these are the gifts I bring to my little god-child."

With that Pussy Willow stooped and rubbed her downy cheek over the little downy cheek of the baby, and the tiny face smiled in its sleep as if it knew that something good was being done for it. But just then Nurse Toothacre, who had been snoring very regularly for some time, gave such a loud and sudden snort that it waked her up, and she sat bolt upright in bed.

"Was that a dog barking?" she exclaimed. "I thought I heard a dog."

Whisk! went all the little fairies up the ladder of moonshine; but Pussy Willow laughed softly as she softly patted her velvet tip against the window, and said, —

Good Night Dearie

" WELL ! " said the old nurse, " who would 'a' thought that 'ere baby would 'a' slept so ? — None o' your worry-cats, she ain't."

You will observe from this speech that good Nurse Toothacre had not had early advantages in forming her style of conversation ; in consequence of which her manner of expressing herself was not a thing to be recommended as a model for you young folks.   Well, now my dear young folks who have read the first chapter will agree that our baby has made a good beginning in life, and that the three fairies, Mother Fern, and the pretty Miss Hepatica, and Pussy Willow, have endowed her with rare gifts, such as beautiful blue eyes, a good healthy constitution, and the gift of seeing the bright side of everything.

This last gift was the greatest of all, as you will see if you think a little, because it is quite plain that it is not so much what people *have* that makes them happy, as what they think and feel about what they have.   If one little girl has an old hat of her sister's pressed over, and trimmed with some of her sister's last year's flowers, and likes it, and is delighted with it, she is really far better off than another little girl whose mother has bought for her three new hats trimmed each with different fine things, and none of which suit her, so that she declares she has n't a thing she can wear.

Little Pussy had great need to be gifted with this happy disposition, for she was not a rich man's daughter.   Her father was a hard-working farmer, who owed about five hundred dollars on his farm ; and it was his object, working day and night, to save up money enough to pay for this farm. She had six older brothers, — great, strong, stamping boys ; and her mother was a feeble, delicate woman, who had to do all the cooking, washing, ironing, making, and mending for all these men folk without any help from servants, — so you may believe she had small time to coddle and pet her baby. In fact, before Little Pussy Willow was four weeks old, she was lying in an old basket tied into a straw-bottomed rocking-chair, in the kitchen where her mother was busy about her work ; and all day long there she lay, with her thumb in her mouth, and her great, round blue eyes contentedly staring at the kitchen ceiling. Once in two or three hours her mother would take her up and nurse her a little, and pull her clothes down straight about her, and then Pussy would go off to sleep, and sleep an hour or two, and then wake up and stare at the kitchen ceiling as before, and sing and gurgle to herself in a quiet baby way, that was quite like the sound of the little brook behind the house.

When her father came home to his dinner, he would seize her in his great, strong, sun-browned hands, and toss her over his head, and her long-armed brothers would pass her from one to another, like a little shuttlecock, in a way that would have alarmed many another baby ; but Pussy took it all with the utmost composure, and laughed and crowed all the more, the ruder her nursing grew.

" I say, wife, what shall we call her ? " said Papa John ; " she 's a perfect March blossom, — come just as the pussy willows were out."

" Let 's call her Pussy Willow then," said Sam, the oldest boy ; and the rest laughed uproariously, and considered it a famous joke, — for when people work hard all day, and have a good digestion, it is not necessary that a thing should be very funny to make them laugh tremendously. In fine, whether the plant fairies secretly had a hand in it, or because Brother Sam was so fond of his conceit, the fact is that, though the baby was baptized in church by the name of Mary, she was ever afterwards called in the family "Pussy," and "Pussy Willow." Tom, the second boy, declared that her cheeks were soft and downy like the pussies, and when she was lying in her cradle, only two weeks old, he would sometimes tickle her cheeks with them to bring out that pretty baby smile which is as welcome on a little face as the first spring flower.

Pussy, having a tranquil mind and a good digestion, throve very fast. The old women of the neighborhood remarked that she began to "feel her feet" when she was only a month old, and if anybody gave her the least chance to show off this accomplishment, she would jump up and down till one's arms were tired of holding her; but when her father or brother or mother was weary of this exercise, and laid her flat on her back in the cradle, Pussy did not make up a square mouth and begin to cry, as many ill-advised babies do, but put her thumb into her mouth, like a sensible little damsel, and set herself to seeing what could be found to amuse her on the top of the kitchen wall. There she saw the blue flies coursing up and down, stopping once in a while to brush themselves briskly with the little clothes-brushes which nature has put on the end of each of their legs, when suddenly they would sweep round and round in circles, and then come down and settle on Pussy's face, and walk up and down over it, buzzing and talking with each other, first by her eyes, then by her nose, then over her forehead, as if the little face had been a flies' pleasure-garden, laid out expressly for them to amuse themselves in.

Pussy took it all in good part, though sometimes she winked very hard, and even took her thumb out of her mouth to make some blind little passes with her white baby fists doubled up, which would send the flies buzzing and careering again; but never a cry did she utter.

"Of all the good babies that ever I did see," said Nurse Toothacre, "I never see one ekil to this. Why, Marthy Primrose would n't know she had a baby in the house, if she had n't the washin' and dressin' and nussin' of her."

By and by little Pussy learned to creep on all-fours, and then she made long voyages over the clean-scoured kitchen floor, and had most beautiful times, because she could open the low cupboard doors and pull out all the things, and pick holes in all the paper parcels, and pull over pails of water, and then paddle in the clear silver flood that coursed its way along the kitchen in little rivulets. One day she found a paper of indigo in the low closet, with which she very busily rubbed her hands and face and her apron and the floor, so that when her mother came in from hanging out clothes she did not know her own baby, but thought she was a little blue goblin, and had to take her to the wash-tub and put her in like a dirty dress to get her looking like herself again.

Now as Martha Primrose was celebrated as one of the nicest housekeepers in the country, of course she could not allow such proceedings ; and as Pussy did not yet understand English, the only way she could keep her from them was to watch her and catch her away, when she saw her going about any piece of mischief. In consequence, Baby's life was a perfect series of disappointments. It often seemed to her that she was stopped in everything she undertook to do. First, she would scuttle across the floor to the kitchen fireplace and fill both little hands with ashes and black coals, just to see what they were made of ; and then there would be a loud outcry, and she would be made to throw them down, her apron would be shaken, and her hands washed, and the words, "No! no! naughty!" pronounced in very solemn tones over her. She would look up and laugh, and creep away, and bring up next by the dresser, where she would reach up for a pretty, nice dish of flour which she longed to pull over; and then the "No! no!" and "Naughty!" would sound again. Then Pussy would laugh again, and go into the back kitchen and begin paddling in a delightful pail of water, which was to her the dearest of all forbidden amusements, when suddenly she would be twitched up from behind, and "No! no! naughty baby!" once more sounded in her ear. Pussy heard this so much that it began to amuse her; and so, when her mother looked solemn and stern at her, she would shake her little head and look waggish, and try to imitate the "No! no!" as if it were something said for her diversion.

"You can't put her out," said Martha to her husband; "she's the best little thing; but it is wonderful the mischief she does. She just goes from one thing to another all day long."

The fact is, baby once got a pan of molasses pulled over on her head, and once fell, head first, into her mother's wash-tub, which luckily had not at the time very hot water in it; and once she pulled the tap out of her mother's cask of beer, and got herself pretty well blinded and soaked with the spurting liquid. But all these things did not disturb her serenity, and she took all the washings and dressings and scoldings that followed with such jolly good-humor that the usual amusement, when her father and brothers came home, was the recital of Pussy's adventures for the day; and Pussy, sitting on her father's knee and discovering herself to be the heroine of the story, would clap her hands and crow and laugh as loudly as any of them.

"She's got more laugh in her than a whole circus," said John Primrose. "I don't want no theatre nor no opera when I can have her;" — and her brothers, who used to be gone whole evenings over at a neighboring tavern, gradually took to staying at home to have a romp with little Pussy. When the hay about the old house was mown, they had capital times, tumbling and rolling with Pussy in the sweet grass, and covering her up and letting her scratch out again, and toss the hay about in her little fat hands, enchanted to find that there was one thing that she could play with and not be called " Naughty baby ! " or have " No ! no ! " called in her ear.

In my next chapter I will tell you all about what little Pussy had to play with, and what she did when she got older.

I CANNOT make my young folks understand just the value of the gift which fairies brought to Little Pussy Willow, unless I tell them about another little girl who did not have any such present, but had everything else.

Little Emily Proudie was born in a splendid house, with a white marble front, and a dozen marble steps leading up to the door. Before she was born there were all sorts of preparations to receive her, — whole drawers full of little dresses with worked waists, and of little caps trimmed with pink and blue rosettes, and cunning little sacks embroidered with silk and silver, and little bonnets, and little socks and little shoes, and sleeve-ties with coral clasps, and little silver and gold rattles, — in short, everything that all the rich aunts and uncles and cousins of a rich little baby could think of.

To be sure no plant-fairies came in at the window to look at her; but there were the fairies of the milliner's shop, and the jeweler's shop, and of all the shops and stores in New York, and they endowed the baby with no end of bright and beautiful things. She was to be handsome and rich, and always to have elegant clothes, and live in a palace, and have fine horses and carriages, and everything to eat and to drink that she could fancy, — and therefore everybody must think that this little girl would be happy.

But this one plain gift that the poor Little Pussy Willow brought was left out in all Emily's treasures. No good fairy ever gave her the gift of liking everything she had, and seeing the bright side of everything. If she had only had this gift, she might have been as much happier than our Little Pussy Willow as she had more things to be happy with; but as she did not have it, she grew up, notwithstanding all her treasures, to be a fretful, discontented little girl.

At the time I am speaking of, these two little girls are each of them to be seen in very different circumstances. It is now the seventh birthday of Little Pussy Willow; and you might think, perhaps, that she was going to have a holiday, or some birthday presents, or a birthday party. But no, it is not so. Pussy's mother is a poor hard-working woman, who never found any time to pet her children, though she loved them as much as any other mother. Besides, where she lived, nobody ever heard of such a thing as celebrating a child's birthday. Pussy never had had a present made to her in all her little life. She never had had a plaything, except the bright yellow dandelions in spring, or the pussies of the willow-bush, or the cat-tails which her brothers sometimes brought home in their pockets; and to-day, though it is her birthday, Pussy is sitting in a little chair, learning to sew on some patchwork, while her mother is kneading up bread in the kitchen beside her. There is a yellow mug standing on the table, with some pussy-willow sprigs in it, which have blossomed out early this spring, and which her father broke off for her before he went to his work; and Pussy sits pulling her needle through the gay squares of calico, and giving it a push with the little yellow brass thimble. Sometimes she stops a minute to speak to the little pussies, and touch their downy heads to her cheek, and sometimes she puts up her little mouth to kiss her mother, who comes to her with her hands all covered with flour; and then she tugs away again most industriously with her needle, till the small square is finished, and she says, "May I get down and play now?" And mamma says, "Wait a moment till I get my hands out of the bread." And mamma kneads and rolls the great white cushion in the bread-bowl, and turns it over and over, and rubs every bit and morsel of loose white flour into it, and kneads it smoothly in, and then, taking it up once more, throws it down in the bowl, a great, smooth, snowy hill of dough, in the middle of which she leaves one fist-print; and then she rubs her hands from the flour and paste, and washes them clean, and comes and takes up Pussy, and sets her down on the floor; and Pussy forthwith goes to a lower cupboard where are her treasures.

And what are they? They are the fragment of an old milk-pitcher, and the nose and handle of a tea-pot, and ever so many little bits of broken china, and one little old sleigh-bell which her grandfather gave her. There is a rag-doll made up on a clothes-pin, which Pussy every day washes, dresses, puts to bed, takes up, teaches to sew, and, in short, educates to the best of her little ability in the way in which she is herself being brought up. And there are several little strips of bright red and yellow calico which she prizes greatly, besides a handful of choice long curly shavings, which she got at a carpenter's bench when her mother took her up to the village.

Pussy is perfectly happy in these treasures, and has been sewing very industriously all the morning, that she may get to the dear closet where they are kept. Then for playmates she has only a great, grave, old, yellow dog named Bose, who, the minute he sees Pussy get down, comes soberly patting up to her, wagging his tail. And little Pussy gathers all her treasures in her short checked apron, and goes out under the great elm-tree to play with Bose; and she is now perfectly happy.

She makes a little house out of her bits of broken china, arranged in squares on the turf; she ties a limp sun-bonnet

on Bose's head, and makes believe that he is mother to
the clothes-pin rag-baby, and tells him he must rock it to
sleep; and Bose looks very serious and obedient, and sits
over the baby while Pussy pretends to yoke up oxen and
go off to the fields to work.

By and by Bose thinks this has lasted long enough, and
comes scampering after her, with the sun-bonnet very
much over one eye; and then he gets talked to, and
admonished, and led back to his duty. He gets very
tired of it sometimes; and Pussy has to vary the play by
letting him have a scamper with her down to the brook,
to watch the tiny little fish that whisk and dart among the
golden rings of sunlight under the bright brown waters.

Hour after hour passes, and Pussy grows happier every
minute; for the sun shines, and the sky is blue, and Bose
is capital company, and she has so many pretty playthings!

When Pussy lies down in her little crib at night, she
prays God to bless her dear father and mother, and her
dear brothers, and Bose, and dolly, and all the dear Little
Pussy Willows. The first part of the prayer her mother
taught her, — the last part she made up herself, out of her
own curly head and happy little heart, and she does not
doubt in the least that the good God hears the last as
much as the first.

Now this is the picture of what took place on little
Pussy's seventh birthday: but you must see what took
place on little Emily's seventh birthday, which was to be
kept with great pomp and splendor. From early morning
the door-bell was kept constantly ringing on account of the
presents that were being sent in to Emily. I could not
begin to tell you half of them. There was a great doll
from Paris, with clothes all made to take off and put on,
and a doll's bureau full of petticoats and drawers and
aprons and stockings and collars and cuffs and elegant
dresses for Miss Dolly; and there were little bandboxes

with ever so many little bonnets, and little parasols, and little card-cases, and nobody knows what, — all for Miss Dolly. Then there were bracelets and rings and pins for little Emily herself, and a gold drinking-cup set with diamonds, and every sort of plaything that any one could think of, till a whole room was filled with Emily's birthday presents.

Nevertheless, Emily was not happy. In fact, she was very unhappy; and the reason was that the pink silk dress she wanted to wear had not come home from the dressmaker's, and no other dress in the world would in the least do for her.

In vain mamma and two nurses talked and persuaded, and showed her her presents; she wanted exactly the only thing that could not be got, and nothing but that seemed of any value in her eyes. The whole house was in commotion about this dress, and messengers were kept running backward and forward to Madame Follet's; but it was almost night before it came, and neither Emily nor any of her friends could have any peace until then.

The fact is that the little girl had been so industriously petted ever since she was born, and had had so many playthings and presents, that there was not anything that could be given her which seemed half as pretty to her as two or three long clean, curly shavings seemed to Little Pussy Willow; and then, unfortunately, no good fairy had given her the gift of being easily pleased; so that, with everybody working and trying from morning to night to please her, little Emily was always in a fret or a worry about something. Her mother said that the dear child had such a fastidious taste! — that she was *so* sensitive! — but whatever the reason might be, Emily was never very happy. Instead of thinking of the things she *had*, and liking them, she was always fretting about something that she had not or could not get; and when the things she most longed for at last came into her hands, suddenly she found that she had ceased to want them.

Her seventh birthday ended with a children's ball, to which all the little children of her acquaintance were invited, and there was a band of music, and an exquisite supper and fireworks on the lawn near the house; and Emily appeared in the very pink silk dress she had set her heart on; but alas! she was not happy. For Madame Follet had not put on the flounces, as she promised, and the sash had no silver fringe. This melancholy discovery was made when it was entirely too late to help it, and poor Emily was in low spirits all the evening.

"She is too sensitive for this life," said her mamma, — "the sweet little angel!"

Emily sunk to sleep about midnight, hot, tired, feverish. She cried herself to sleep. Why? She could not tell. Can you?

AND now some of my little friends perhaps have a question to ask me. Is not a little girl more likely to be happy who is brought up in the simple and natural way in which Pussy Willow has grown up, than one who has had all that has been given to Emily Proudie?

I began by telling you that the *gift of being easily pleased* was what made the difference between the two little girls, — that it was a gift worth more than beauty, or riches, or anything else that could be thought of.

But I do think that a way of "bringing-up" like that in which poor little Emily was educated is the surest way to destroy this gift, even if a girl's birth fairies had given it to her. You know very well that, when you have been taking a lonely scramble among the rocks until long after your dinner-time, a plain crust of bread tastes so sweet to you that you wonder you ever have wanted cake or ginger-bread; and that sometimes, in like manner, when you have walked till you are hot and thirsty, you have dipped up the water out of some wild-wood spring, and drank it with an enjoyment such as the very best tea or coffee or lemonade never gave. That was because you were really hungry or really thirsty; and the pleasure you get from food and drink can never be known unless you become really hungry and thirsty.

But many poor little children are brought up in such a way that they never know what it is to have a real desire for anything. They are like a child stuffed with cake and sweetmeats from morning till night. Every wish is anticipated, and pleasures are crowded upon them so fast that they have none of the enjoyments of wishing, planning, and contriving which come to those who are left to seek their own pleasures and make their own way. The good God has so made us that the enjoyments which come to us through the use of our own faculties are a great deal more satisfactory than those which are brought to us by others. Many a little girl enjoys making a sand-pie out in the road far more than she would the most expensive playthings, because she trots about in making it, runs, laughs, works, gets herself into a healthy glow, and feels that she is doing something.

Poor little Emily Proudie never had that pleasure. From the time she was a baby, she has had constantly one, two, or three attendants, whose sole business it is to play with her and to contrive playthings and amusements for her, — and a very wearisome time they all have had of it. Yes, I do believe that if little Emily, without any more of a gift of being pleased than falls to the lot of all children, had been brought up exactly as Pussy Willow was, she would have been far happier than she is now.

There is another reason why Pussy Willow was growing up happy, and that is, that she was every day doing something that she felt was of some use. When she was so little that her head scarcely came above the table, she used to stand propped on a small stool and wash the breakfast cups and spoons, — and very proud she was of doing it. How she admired the bright bubbles which she could make in the clean, soapy water, and how proud she was of seeing the cups and spoons look so clear and bright as she rubbed them with her towel! — and then, getting down, she would trip across the kitchen with them, one or two at a time, and, rising on her little toes, by great good luck she could just get them on to the cupboard shelf; and then she would hang her towel on its nail, and empty her dishpan, and wipe off the table, and feel quite like a large woman in doing it.

When Pussy was ten years old, her mother one day hurt her arm by a fall, so that she had to wear it in a sling. This would not be an agreeable thing to happen to anybody's mamma; but Pussy's mother had no servants, and everything that was to be eaten in the house had to be made up by her one pair of hands, and she therefore felt quite troubled, as the house was far from neighbors, and there were a husband and four hungry young men to be fed.

In a city you can send out to a bakery; but in the country what is to be done?

"I really think you 'll have to harness and drive the old mare over to Aunt Judy's, and get her to come over," said Pussy's mother.

"That 's a trouble," said her father. "The hay is all ready to get in, and there will certainly be rain by afternoon. The horse cannot possibly be spared."

"Now, mother, just let me make bread," said Pussy, feeling very large. "I 've seen you do it, time and time again, and I know I could do it."

"Hurrah for Pussy!" said her brothers; — "she 's a trump. You let her try, — she 'll do it."

"Yes, yes," said her father. "I 'd rather have my little Pussy than a dozen Aunt Judys."

Pussy was wonderfully elated by this praise, and got one of her mother's aprons and tied it round her, — which, to say the truth, came quite down to her ankles, and made her feel very old and wise.

Her mother now told her that she might go into the buttery and sift eight quarts of flour into the bread-tray, and bring it out, and she would show her just how to wet it.

So away went Pussy; and right pleased was she to get

her little rosy hands into the flour. It was far more amusing than making believe make bread with sand, as she had often done when she and Bose were out playing together. So she patted and sifted, and soon came out lifting the bread-tray, and set it beside her mother.

"Now scatter in a handful of salt," said her mother.

Pussy did so.

"Now make a little hole in the middle, and measure three gills of yeast, and put that in the hole."

Pussy found this quite easy, because their tin quart-measure was marked around with rings for the gills; and so, when her yeast was up to the third ring, she poured it into the hole in the middle of the flour, and began stirring it with a spoon, till she had made a nice little foamy lake in the middle of her mountain of puffy white flour.

"And now for your wetting, Pussy," said her mother. "You want about a quart of hot water and a quart of good milk to begin with, and we'll see how you go on. But I'm a little afraid you're not strong enough to knead such a big batch."

"Oh, mother, I'm a large girl now," said Pussy, "and you've no idea how strong I am! I want to knead a real batch, just such as you do, and not a little play batch, — a baby's batch."

"Well, well, we'll try it," said her mother; "and I'll pour in your wetting." So she began to pour in, and Pussy plumped in both hands, and went at her work with a relish.

The flour stuck to her fingers; but she stirred about with vigor, and made her little hands fly so fast that her mother said they did the work of bigger ones. By and by the flour was all stiffly mixed, and now Pussy put out all her little strength, and bent over the tray, kneading and kneading, and turning and turning, till the paste began to look white and smooth.

"Oh mother, I like this! — it's the best fun I ever had," said Pussy. "How soft and smooth I am getting it! It's beginning to rise, I do believe, this very minute; I can feel it rising under my hands. I shall be so proud to show it to father and the boys! Mother, you'll always let me make the bread, won't you?"

"We'll see," said her mother. "Mind you knead in every bit of the flour. Don't leave any on the sides of the pan. Rub all those ragged patches together, and knead them in. You are getting it quite smooth."

In fine, Pussy, elated, took up the whole white round cushion of dough and turned it over in the tray, as she had seen her mother do, and left one very little fist-mark in the centre. "There now, Mrs. Bread, there you are," she said; "now I shall tuck you up warm and put you to sleep, till it's time to take you up and bake you." So Pussy covered her bread up warm with an old piece of quilt which her mother kept for this special purpose; then she washed her hands, and put away all the dishes she had been using, and swept up the flour she had dropped on her mother's clean, shining floor.

"And now, mother, shall I put on the dinner pot?" said Pussy, who felt herself growing in importance.

"Yes, you may put it on; and then you may go down cellar, and get a piece of beef and a piece of pork, and bring them up for dinner."

And away tripped Pussy down cellar, and soon appeared again with her pan full of provisions. After that she washed the potatoes and turnips, and very soon the dinner was on the stove, boiling.

"Now, Pussy," said her mother, "you can go and play down by the brook for an hour and a half."

"Mother," said Pussy, "I like working better than play."

"It is play to you now," said her mother; "but if you had to do these things every day, you might get tired."

Pussy thought not, — she was quite sure not. Nevertheless, she took her Dolly and Bose, and went down to the brook, and had a good time among the sweet-flags. But her mind kept running on her bread, and every once in a while she came running back to peep under the little quilt.

Yes, sure enough, there it was, rising as light and as nice as any Pussy's heart could desire. And how proud and important she felt!

"It was real lively yeast," said her mother. "I knew it would rise quickly."

Well, I need not tell my little readers the whole history of this wonderful batch of bread, — how in time Pussy got down the moulding-board, all herself, and put it on the kitchen table; and how she cut her loaves off, and rolled, and kneaded, and patted, and so coaxed them into the very nicest little white cushions that ever were put into buttered bake-pans. One small portion Pussy left to be divided into round delicate little biscuits; and it was good fun for her to cut and roll and shape these into the prettiest little pincushions, and put them in white, even rows into the pans, and prick two small holes in the top of each.

When all these evolutions had been performed, then came the baking; and very busy was Pussy putting in her pans, watching and turning and shifting them, so that each might get its proper portion of nice, sweet, golden-brown crust.

She burnt her fingers once or twice, but she did n't mind that when she drew her great beautiful loaves from the oven, and her mother tapped on them with her thimble and pronounced them done. Such a row of nice loaves, — all her own making! Pussy danced around the table where she had ranged them, and then, in the pride of her heart, called Bose to look at them.

Bose licked his chops, and looked as appreciative as a dog could, and, seeing that something was expected of him, barked aloud for joy.

That night Pussy's biscuits were served for supper, with the cold beef and pork, and Pussy was loudly praised on all sides.

"Wife, you'll take your ease now," said her father, "since you have such a little housekeeper sent to you."

Pussy was happier that night than if three servants had been busy dressing dolls for her all day.

"Mother," she said, soberly, when she lay down in her little bed that night, "I'm going to ask God to keep me humble."

"Why, my dear?"

"Because I feel tempted to be proud, — I can make such good bread!"

Pussy Willow was so happy and proud at her success in making bread, that she now felt a very grown-up woman indeed; and her idea of a grown-up woman was, as you will see, that of a person able and willing to do something to some useful purpose. Some of my readers may think that a little girl ten years of age could not knead up and bake a batch of bread like that which Pussy is described as doing; but they must remember that little girls who grow up in the healthy air of the mountains, and who have always lived a great part of their time in the open air, and have been trained to the use of their arms and hands from early infancy, become larger and stronger than those who have been nursed in cities, and who never have done anything but arrange dolls' baby-houses, and play at giving and receiving company.

Pussy was as strong a little mountaineer as you could wish to see; and now that her mother was laid up with a lame arm, Pussy daily gloried in her strength. "How lucky it is," she said to herself as she was dressing in the morning, "that I have got to be such a large girl! What mother would do without me, I'm sure I don't see. Well now, if I can make bread and biscuit, I'm sure I can make gingerbread and pies; and father and the boys will never miss anything. Oh, I'll not let grass grow under my feet."

This was in the dim gray of the morning, before another soul was awake in the house, when Pussy was up bright and early; for she had formed the design of getting up and

making breakfast ready, all of her own self, before anybody should be up to call her or ask her to do it. For
you must know it was Pussy's nature to like to run before
people's expectations. She took a great interest in surprising people, and doing more than they expected; and
she thought to herself, as she softly tiptoed down the
stairs: "Now I shall have the fire all made, and the tea-
kettle boiling, by the time that mother wakes. I know
she'll wake thinking 'I must go and call Pussy, and ask
her to get breakfast.' How surprised she'll be to find
Pussy up and dressed, the fire made, and the kettle boiling, and breakfast just ready to go on!"

So Pussy softly felt her way into the kitchen, where it
was hardly light as yet, and found the water-pail, and
then, opening the kitchen-door, she started for the little
spring back of the house for a pail of water. It had been
Pussy's work from her earliest years to bring water from
this spring to her mother, — at first in tiny little pails,
but gradually, as she grew older and bigger, in larger ones,
till now she could lift the full-sized water-pail, which she
had on her arm.

"So here you are, Mr. Robin," said Pussy, as she
stepped out of the door and heard a lively note struck up
from the willow-bush by the window. "You and I are
up early this morning, ar'n't we? Ha, ha, old Mr. Chipmunk, — is that you? Take care of yourself, or I shall
catch you. You are up getting breakfast for your family,
and I for mine. Mother is sick, and I'm housekeeper
now, Mr. Chip." So saying, Pussy splashed her pail
down among the fern-leaves that bordered the edges of the
spring, and laughed to see the bright, clear water ripple
into it; and having filled it, she drew it up all glittering
and dripping with diamond-bright drops, which fell back
again into the little spring.

"There's a girl for you!" said old Mother Fern, when

Pussy had turned her back on the spring. "That girl does credit to our teaching. Every feeling of her heart is as fresh and clear as spring-water, and she goes on doing good just as the brook runs in a bright, merry stream. That girl will never know what it is to be nervous or low-spirited, or have the dyspepsia, or any of the other troubles that come on the lazy daughters of men. And it all comes of the gifts that we wood-fairies have brought her. She takes everything by the smooth handle, and sees everything on the bright side, and enjoys her work a great deal more than most children do their play."

Meanwhile Pussy had gone in and kindled the fire in the stove, and set over the tea-kettle, and now was busy sifting some meal to make some corn-cakes for breakfast.

"I 've seen mother do this often enough," she said, "and I 'll surprise her by getting it all nicely into the oven without her saying a word about it." So she ran in all haste to the buttery, where stood a pan of milk which had turned deliciously sour, and shook and quivered as she moved it, like some kind of delicate white jelly with a golden coating of cream over it. A spoonful of soda soon made this white jelly a mass of foam, and then a teacupful of bright, amber-colored molasses was turned into it, and then it was beaten into a stiff mass with the sifted corn-meal, and poured into well-buttered pans to be baked. Pussy was really quite amused at all this process. She was delighted to find that the cake would actually foam under her hands as she had often seen it under her mother's, and when she shut the oven-doors on her experiment it was with a beating heart.

"I do believe, mother," said Pussy's father, opening one eye and giving a great stretch, — "I do believe Pussy is up before you."

"Good child!" said her mother, "she is making the fire for me. With a little instruction she will be able to make a corn-cake nicely."

Pussy's voice was now heard at the door. "Mother! mother! sha'n't I come in and help you dress?"—and a bright little face followed the voice, and peeped in at the crack of the door.

"Thank you, dear child; I was just thinking of coming to call you. I wanted you to make the fire for me."

"It's made, mother,—long ago."

"What a good girl! Well then, you may just get a pail of water and fill the tea-kettle."

"I got the water and filled the kettle half an hour ago, mother," said Pussy, "and you can't think how it's boiling! puffing away like a steamboat,—and I've put the coffee on to boil, and"—

"You have been a *very* good girl," said her mother, as Pussy was helping her into her gown. "You are such a nice handy little housekeeper that I think I can easily show you how to get the whole breakfast. Would n't you like to have me teach you how to mix the corn-cakes!"

Oh, then how Pussy laughed and crowed, as she led her mother into the kitchen, and, opening the oven-door, showed her corn-cakes rising as nicely as could be, and baking with a real lovely golden brown! And besides that there were slices of ham that she had cut and trimmed so neatly, lying all ready to be put into the frying-pan.

How Pussy enjoyed that breakfast! The cakes were as light and golden as her mother's best, and Pussy had all the glory of them, for she had made them all by herself. I don't think Miss Emily Proudie ever felt so delighted to walk out in a new hat and feather as did little Pussy to be able to get this breakfast for her mother, and to hear the praises of her father and brothers on everything she had made.

It would be amusing if the good fairies would let us ride on a bit of their fairy carpet through the air on this same bright morning, when Pussy was so gay and happy in her household cares, and set us down in the elegant chamber where little Emily was sleeping. Everything about the room shows such a study to please the sleeping child! The walls are hung with lovely pictures; the floor is carpeted with the most charming carpet; the sofas and chairs and lounges are all of the most elegant shapes, and spread out upon the sofa is a beautiful new walking-dress, which came home after little Emily went to bed last night, and which is spread out so as to catch her eye the first thing when she wakes in the morning. It is now past eight o'clock, and Pussy Willow has long since washed all the dishes, and arranged the kitchen, and done the morning work in the farmhouse, and has gone out with her little basket on her arm to dig roots, and pull young winter-green for beer; but all this while little Emily has been drowsily turning from side to side, and uneasily brushing off the busy flies that seem determined she shall not sleep any longer.

"Come now, Miss Emily! your mamma says you *must* wake up and see your pretty new dress," says Bridget, who has been in four times before, to try and wake the little sleeper. Emily sits up in bed at last, and calls for the new dress.

"So, she's got it done at last, — that hateful Madame Tulleruche! She always keeps me waiting so long that I am tired to death. But there! — she has gone and put that trimming on in folds, and I told her I wanted puffs. The dress is just ruined. Take it away, Bridget. I can't bear the sight of it. I *do* wonder what is the reason that *I* never can have anything done as other girls can. There's always something the matter with my things."

"Troth, Miss Emily, it's jist that ye's got too much of ivrything, and your stomach is kept turned all the time," said Bridget. "If ye had to work as I do for your new dresses, ye'd like 'em better, that's what ye would. I tell ye what would do ye more good than all the fine things ye 's got, and that same 's a continted mind."

"But how *can* I be contented," said Emily, "when nothing ever suits me? I 'm so particular, — mamma says so. I 'm so, and I can't help it, and nobody ever does do anything quite as I like it; and so I am unhappy all the time."

"And what if ye did something for somebody else, instead of having everybody else a-serving ye?" said Bridget. "I works from morning to night, and gets my two dollars a week, and sends the most part of it to me poor old mother in Ireland; and it keeps me jolly — praise be to God! — to think I 'm a-comfortin' her old age. Did ye ever think whether ye did anything for anybody?"

No; Emily never had thought of that. From the very first hour that her baby eyes had opened, she had seen all the world on their knees around her, trying to serve and please her. Neither her father nor mother ever spoke or acted as if they expected her to do the slightest service for them. On the contrary, they always spoke as if they must do everything for her; and Bridget's blunt talk now and then was the only intimation the little girl ever got that there was a way to be happy that she knew not of.

Our little friend Pussy went on in the way we have described, every day finding a new thing that she was able to do, and taking the greatest delight in doing it. Gradually her mother's arm recovered, — as it never would have done, had not the helpfulness of her little daughter enabled her to give it entire rest, — and she was in a situation to resume her family cares.

"What a blessing our little Pussy has been to us!" said her father to her mother, one night, as they were talking over their family affairs.

"Yes," said the mother; "that dear child is so unselfish, and so much more than willing to do for us, that I am fearful lest we shall make too much of her. I don't want to make a mere drudge of my daughter, and I think we must send her to school this summer. Pussy is a good reader, — I have always taught her a little every day, — and she writes little letters on a slate quite prettily for a child; but now I think we must send her over to the Academy, and let her go in with the primary class."

Now the Academy was two miles off; but all the family were used to being up and having breakfast over by seven o'clock in the morning; and then Pussy put on her sun-bonnet, and made a little bundle of her books, and tripped away cheerfully down the hard stony road, along the path of the bright brown brook, through a little piece of waving pine forest, next through some huckleberry pastures and patches of sweet fern-bushes, then through a long piece of rocky and shady forest, till she reached the Academy.

Little Emily Proudie also went to school, at one of the most elegant establishments on Fifth Avenue; and as she was esteemed to be entirely too delicate to walk, her father had provided for her a beautiful little coupé, cushioned inside with purple silk, and drawn by a white horse, with a driver in livery at her command. This was Emily's own carriage, and one would think that, when she had nothing to do but to get into it, she might have been always early at her school; but, unfortunately for her, this was never the case. Emily could not be induced, by the repeated calls of Bridget, to shake off her morning slumbers till at least half an hour after the time she ought to rise. Then she was so miserably undecided what to put on, and tried so many dresses before she could be suited, and was so dissatisfied with the way her hair was arranged, that she generally came to breakfast all in ill-humor, and only to find that they had got for her breakfast exactly the things that she didn't fancy. If there was an omelette and coffee and toast, then Emily wished that it had been chocolate and muffins; but if the cook the next morning, hoping to make a lucky hit, got chocolate and muffins, Emily had made up her mind in the mean time that the chocolate would give her a headache, and that she must have tea made; and with all these points to be attended to, there is no wonder that the little coupé, and the little white horse, and the driver in livery, were often kept waiting at the door long after the time when Emily ought to have been in her class-room.

Madame Ardenne often gently complained to Emily's mother, — very gently, because the Proudies were so rich and fashionable that she would have been in utter despair at the idea of offending them; but still the poor woman could not help trying to make Emily's mother understand that a scholar who always came into the class-room when the lesson was half over could not be expected to learn as fast as if she were there punctually, besides being a great annoyance to all the rest of the scholars.

Emily's mother always said that she was sorry it was so, but her dear child was of a most peculiar organization, — that it did not seem possible for her to wake at any regular hour in the morning, — and that really the dear child had a sensitiveness of nature that made it very difficult to know what to do with her.

In fact, young ladies who are brought up like little Emily, to have every earthly thing done for them, and to do no earthly thing for themselves, are often sorely tried when they come to school life, because there are certain things in education which all human beings must learn to do for themselves. Emily always had had a maid to wash her and dress her, and to do everything that a healthy little girl might do for herself; but no maid could learn to read for her, or write for her. Her mamma talked strongly of sending to Paris for a French dressing maid, to keep her various dresses in order; but even a French dressing-maid could not learn a French verb for her, or play on the piano for her. Consequently poor Emily's school life was full of grievous trials to her. Her lessons seemed doubly hard to her, because she had always been brought up to feel that she must be saved from every labor, and must yield before the slightest thing that looked like a difficulty.

Little Pussy, after her walk of two miles, would come into the Academy fresh and strong, at least a quarter of an hour before school, and have a good time talking with the other girls before the school began. Then she set about her lessons with the habit of conquering difficulties. If there was a hard sum in her lesson, Pussy went at it with a real spirit and interest. "Please don't tell me a word," she would say to her teacher: "I want to work it out myself. I'm sure I can do it." And the greater the difficulty, the more cheerful became her confidence. There was one sum, I remember, that Pussy worked upon for a week, — a sum that neither her father nor mother, nor any of her brothers, could do; but she would not allow her teacher to show her. She was resolutely determined to do it all alone by herself, and to find out the way for herself, — and at last she succeeded; and a very proud and happy Pussy she was when she did succeed.

My little girls, I want to tell you that there is a pleasure in vanquishing a difficulty, — in putting forth all the power and strength you have in you to do a really hard thing, — that is greater than all the pleasures of ease and indolence. The little girl who lies in bed every morning just half an hour later than her conscience tells her she ought to lie, thinks she is taking comfort in it, but she is mistaken. She is secretly dissatisfied with and ashamed of herself, and her conscience keeps up a sort of uneasy trouble, every morning; whereas, if she once formed the habit of springing up promptly at a certain hour, and taking a good morning bath, and dressing herself in season to have plenty of time to attend to all her morning duties, she would have a self-respect and self-confidence that it is very pleasant to feel.

Pussy's life in the Academy was a great enjoyment to her this summer. She felt it a great kindness in her mother to excuse her from all family duties, and take all the work upon herself, in order that she might have time to study; and so she studied with a right good will. Her cheerful temper made her a universal favorite. She seemed among her schoolfellows like a choice lot of sugar-plums or sweetmeats; everybody wanted a scrap or portion. One girl wanted Pussy to play with her; another made her promise to walk home with her; two or three wanted to engage her for recess; all Pussy's spare hours for days and days ahead were always engaged by her different friends. The girls said, "Pussy is such a dear girl! she is so bright!

she makes the time pass so pleasantly!" And Pussy in return liked everybody, and thought there never was so pleasant a school, or such a fortunate girl, as herself.

On Saturdays there was no school, and then Pussy would insist on going into the kitchen to help her mother.

"Now, my dear, you ought not to do it," her mother would say. "You ought to have Saturday to amuse yourself."

"Well, it amuses me to make the pies," Pussy would say. "I like to see how many I can turn out in a day. I don't ask better fun."

So went on the course of Pussy's education.

I HAVE told you how Pussy went to the Academy in summer, and what good times she had going through the fragrant sweet-fern pastures, and across the brown sparkling brooks, and through patches of woods green with moss and gay with scarlet wintergreen berries, — and what other good times she had studying and working out her sums, — and also how fond every one got of her.

Well, by and by autumn came, and the frost changed all the leaves on the mountains round the house to scarlet and orange and gold; and then the leaves began to fall, and the old north-wind came, and blew and whirled and scattered them through the air, till finally the trees stood bare. Then Pussy's father said, "It's time to make all ready for winter," — for he had been getting the cellar full of good things. Barrels of cider had been rolled in at the wide cellar-door, great bins had been filled with rosy apples and with brown-coated potatoes, and golden pumpkins and great crook-neck squashes had been piled up for Thanksgiving pies; and now it was time to shut the great doors, and to "bank up" with straw and leaves and earth all round the house, lest sharp-eyed Mr. Jack Frost should get in a finger or a toe, and so find a way into the treasures of the cellar. For a very sharp fellow is this Mr. Jack, and he always has his eyes open to see whether lazy people have left anything without proper care; and where he finds even a chink not stopped, he says, "Ha, ha! I guess I'll get in here;" — and in he goes, and then people may whistle for their apples and potatoes. But Pussy's folks were smart, careful people, and everything was snugly stowed and protected, you may be sure.

By and by the sun took to getting up later and later, setting a dreadfully bad example, it is to be confessed. It would be seven o'clock and after before he would show his red face above the bedclothes of clouds, away off in the southeast; and when he *did* manage to get up, he was so far off and so chilly in his demeanor, that people seemed scarcely a bit the better for him; and by half past four in the afternoon he was down in bed again, tucked up for the night, never caring what became of the world. And so the clouds were full of snow, as if a thousand white feather-beds had been ripped up over the world; and all the frisky winds came out of their dens, and great frolics they had, blowing and roaring and careering in the clouds, — now bellowing down between the mountains, as if they meant to tear the world to pieces, then piping high and shrill, first round one corner of the farmhouse, and then round the other, rattling the windows, bouncing against the doors, and then, with one united chorus, rumbling, tumbling down the great chimney, as if they had a mind to upset it. Oh, what a frisky, rough, jolly, unmannerly set of winds they were! By and by the snow drifted higher than the fences, and nothing was to be seen around the farmhouse but smooth waving hills and hollows of snow; and then came the rain and sleet, and froze them over with a slippery shining crust, that looked as if the earth was dressed for the winter in a silver coat of mail.

Now I suppose some of my little girls will say, "Pussy never can go two miles to the Academy through all the cold and snow and sleet." But Pussy *did*, for all that.

She laughed a gay laugh when her mother said it would be best to wait till spring before she went any more. " I wait till spring? What for? What do I care for cold and snow? I like them: I'm a real snow-bird, — my

blood races and bounds so in cold weather that I like
nothing better than being out. As to the days being
short, there are just as many hours in them as there were
before, and there's no need of my lying in bed because the
sun does." And so at half past five every morning you
might have heard Pussy bestirring herself in her room,
and afterwards in the kitchen, getting breakfast, and singing louder than the tea-kettle on the stove, as she drove
her morning's work before her; and by eight o'clock
Pussy's breakfast was over, and the breakfast-dishes
washed and put away, and Pussy gathered her books under
her arm, and took her little sled in her hand, and started
for school.

This sled her brothers had made for her in the evenings,
and it was as smart a little sled as ever you saw going.
It was painted red, and had "Snow-Bird" lettered on it
in black letters. Pussy was proud of its speed; and well
she might be, for when she came to the top of the long,
stony hill on which the house stood, she just got on to
her little sled, took her books in her lap, and away she
flew, — past the pastures, by the barn, across the plain
below, across the brook, — almost half a mile of her way
done in a minute; and then she would spring off and
laugh, and draw her sled to the next hill, and away she
would go again. The sled was a great help to Pussy, and
got her on her way famously; but then she had other
helps, for she was such a favorite in school that there was
always one boy or another who came to meet her, and
drew her on his sled at least half-way to school. There
were two or three boys that used to quarrel with each
other as to which should have the privilege of drawing
Pussy from the chestnut pasture to the school-house, and
he was reckoned the best fellow who got there first; while
more than once, after school, little Miss Pussy rode the
whole way home to her father's on the sled of some boy

who liked her blue eyes and felt the charm of her merry
laugh. You may be sure Pussy always found company,
and she used to say that she really could n't tell which she
liked best, summer or winter. In summer, to be sure,
there were the pretty flowers and the birds; but in winter
there were the sleds and sliding, and that was such fun!

In winter evenings, sometimes, when the moon shone
clear, whole parties of boys and girls would get an old
sleigh-bottom, and come to the farmhouse, and then Pussy
would get on her hood and mittens, and out they would
all go and get on the sleigh-bottom together. There were
Tom Evans and his sister Betsey, and Jim Styles, and
Almira and Susan Jenkins, and Bet Jenkins, and Mary
Stephens, and Jack Stephens, and nobody knows how
many more, all piled on together, and holding as tight as
they could; and away they would go, down the smooth,
white hill, and across the shining silvery plain, screaming
and laughing, like a streak of merriment; and the old
sober moon, as she looked down through the deep blue
sky, never said a word against it, or hushed them up, for
making too much noise.

Ah, it was splendid fun! and even when they stamped
their feet, and blew their hands for cold, not one of them
would hear of going in till nine o'clock; and then they all
got round the stove, and ate apples and cracked nuts for
half an hour more, and then went off home to be in bed
by ten o'clock, so that they might all be up early the next
day.

Another of the good times Pussy used to have was at
a candy frolic. When the weather was at the coldest, and
the frost so severe that everything really snapped, then
was the time to make candy. Then Pussy's mother
would put on a couple of quarts of molasses to boil in the
afternoon, while Pussy was at school, so that the candy
would be almost made by evening.

In the evening, when the supper-dishes were cleared off, you would hear them all trooping in, and a noisy, happy time they had of it, — trying the candy, pulling little bits of it out in tea-cups and plates and saucers, to see if it was done hard enough to pull. Finally the whole dark, smooth, ropy liquid was poured out from the kettle into a well-greased platter, and set out in a snow-bank to cool; and then all the hands were washed and greased, to begin the pulling.

Ah! then what sport, as each one took a share of the black-looking candy, and began pulling it out, and watching the gold threads come out as they worked and doubled and turned and twisted, till at last the candy grew bright amber-color, and then a creamy white, and, when finally hardened by setting it out again in the snow, would snap with a delicious, brittle crispness most delightful to see! How jolly were the whole party after this gay evening, as each wended his way home over the crisp sparkling snow, with a portion of candy-sticks, — and what talking there was in school next day, and what a going over of the jokes of last evening, — and how every latch of every door in all the houses round had molasses-candy on it for a week after, — are all things that my little readers who have ever given candy frolics will not need to have told them.

What I have said will be enough to show you that Pussy made a merry time of winter no less than summer.

LITTLE Pussy went on in the sort of life we have described two or three years longer, helping her mother at home, and going across the lots and through the woods to the distant Academy; and gradually she grew taller and larger, till one day her father woke up and said to her mother, "Wife, our Pussy is growing into a real handsome little woman."

Now Pussy heard the remark as she was moulding up some little biscuit in the next room, and she smiled to herself. "*Am* I pretty, I wonder?" she said to herself. So that evening she strolled down into the meadow, where the brook spread out in one place into a perfect little looking-glass, set in a green enameled frame of moss and violets and waving feathers of fern-leaves. Here she sat down on the bank, and began to consider herself in the water. Looking in, she saw a pair of eyes just the color of the blue violets which were fringing the bank, a pair of rosy cheeks, a fair, white forehead, and some long curls of brown hair. Pussy considered awhile, and then she gathered some violets and crowsfoot, and drooping meadow-grasses, and wove them into a garland, and put it on her head, and peeped into the brook again to see how it looked.

"She is pretty," said old Mother Fern to Miss Hepatica. "She is pretty, and she has come now to the time when she may as well know it. She will begin now to dress herself, and brush out her feathers, as the bluebirds and robins do in the spring-time."

Pussy walked home with the garland on her head, and at the door she met her father.

"Why, how now?" he said. "You look as your mother used to when I went a-courtin'. Girls always get the knack of fixin' up when their time comes."

And that night the father said to the mother, "I say, wife, you must get Pussy a new bonnet."

"I've been braiding the straw for one all winter," said the wife. "Last fall we picked and sorted the straw, and got the very nicest, and I have enough now done to make a nice straw hat. I will soon have it sewed, and then when you drive over to Elverton, you can get it pressed in Josiah's bonnet factory."

"And I'll buy her a ribbon myself," said the father.

"No, no, father; after all, it would be better to let me have the wagon and the old horse, and take her over to Worcester to choose for herself. Girls have their own notions."

"Well, perhaps that 'ere's the best way, mother. I tell you what, — that child has been a treasure to us, and I wouldn't stand for expense; get her a new gown too. I won't stand for money. If you have to spend ten dollars, I wouldn't mind it, to have her dressed up as handsome as any gal that sits in the singers' seats on Sunday."

What would little Emily Proudie have thought of a spring outfit that could be got for ten dollars? One of her dresses was trimmed with velvet that cost thirty dollars, and Emily cried when it was brought home because it was the wrong shade of color, and sent it back to Madame Tulleruche, to have all the velvet ripped off, and thirty dollars' worth of another shade put on. But what did she know or care how much it cost?

The next morning, after the worthy couple had arranged for Pussy's spring prospects, her father was so full of the subject that he could not forbear opening it to her at once.

So at breakfast he pulled forth a great leather pocket-book, out of which he took a new ten-dollar bill, which he laid on Pussy's plate.

"Why, father, what is this?" said Pussy.

"Well, I noticed last night how pretty you looked with your posies on, and I told your mother the time was come when you'd be a-wantin' folderols and such like, — as girls ought to have when they come to the right age; and, as you've been always a good daughter, and never thought of yourself, why, we must think for you; and so there 't is. Get yourself any bit of finery you want with it. I don't grudge it."

Now Pussy had never in her life had a dollar of her own before, and if, instead of ten dollars, it had been ten thousand, she could scarcely have been more delighted. She laughed and cried and jumped for joy, and she and her mother calculated over and over again how this large sum should be invested. Pussy insisted that half of it should be spent for mother; but mother very firmly insisted that every bit of it should go to Pussy's spring outfit.

"Let her have her way, child," said the father. "Don't you see that you are herself over again? She has her young days again in dressing you."

And so the straw braid was sewed into a little flat straw hat; and the straw was so white and delicate, and the braid so fine, that all the gossips round about said that the like of it had never been seen in those parts. And when she sent it over to the bonnet factory at Elverton, Josiah Stebbins — who was at the head of the factory, and was a cousin of Pussy's mother, and, some say, an old sweetheart too — he put the precious little hat through all the proper processes, and delivered it at last, safe and shining, to her, and would not take a cent in pay; so that there was Pussy's little fortune still untouched.

Then they had a glorious day, going over to Worcester, shopping. They had a friend in town with whom they could stay over night; and so, though it was a good twenty miles' drive, they did not mind it.

There they bought a white cambric dress, and a blue ribbon, and a wreath of lovely white daisies, mixed with meadow-grass, which the shopman said had been made in Paris. Pussy wondered in her heart how Paris milliners could know so exactly how meadow-flowers looked. The young man at first asked so much for the wreath that Pussy quite despaired of being able to get it; but when he saw the blue eyes fixed so longingly on it, and noticed the pretty light on her curls as she turned her head in the sunshine, somehow he began (like a great many other young men) to wish that a pretty girl could have her own way; so finally he fumbled at the lid of the box, and looked at the price-mark, and said that it was the last of the set, and that they were closing out the stock, and ended by letting her have it for just half the price he originally asked. So Pussy returned home the next day delighted, with what seemed to her a whole wardrobe of beautiful things.

Very fast flew her little fingers as she fixed the wreath of daisies and meadow-grass around the shining crown of the delicate straw hat, and then tied it with long strings of blue ribbon, and found, to her delight, that there was enough still remaining to make a sash to her white dress.

Her mother fitted the dress, and Pussy sewed it; and the next Sunday Pussy's father took her to church with a delighted heart. He was observed to keep wide awake all sermon-time, staring straight up into the front gallery, where Pussy sat in the singers' seats, with her pink cheeks, her blue eyes and blue ribbons, and nodding wreath of daisies and meadow-grass. He disturbed his wife's devotion several times while the choir were singing,

" While the lamp holds out to burn,
The vilest sinner may return,"

with his "Mother! mother!" (with a poke of the elbow.)

"What is it, father?"

"Do look up at her."

"I *have* looked."

"But, mother," (another poke,) "is n't she the prettiest girl you ever saw?"

"Father, dear, don't talk now."

"I declare," said the father, as they were driving home, "I don't grudge that 'ere ten dollars one grain."

AND so it became an established fact that our little Pussy Willow was very pretty to look at, as well as good for use. Now, for our part, we are not of the class of those who think it is no sort of matter how one looks if one is only good. Our kind Father in heaven has set us the example of making all his useful works ornamental. A peach-tree might have been made to bear good peaches without having any ornament about it; in fact, peaches might have been made just as they come into market, in rough bushel-baskets; but, instead of that, only see the beauty that is lavished on a peach-tree! There is no flowering shrub that one can get for one's front door-yard that is more beautiful. There is, first, the beauty of its long, narrow green leaf, which grows with so rich a luxuriance, and then the beauty of its lovely pink blossoms, and after that the charming velvet peach, colored so beautifully with a rosy bloom on one side. And .so, in the same manner, apple and pear-trees are in the spring of the year covered with the most delicate and delicious flowers. Now, as not more than one in a dozen of these thousands of blossoms ever sets for fruit, it is plain that our good Father meant them for ornament alone.

And so the impulse which makes men and women wish to ornament the houses they live in, and to wear delicate and beautiful clotliing, is quite in agreement with the will of our great Creator, who has made everything beautiful in its season.

So that when our little Pussy, on Sunday morning, felt such pleasure in tying on her pretty, fair straw hat, crowned with nodding daisies and meadow-grasses, she was just as good a little Christian as she was when she was getting breakfast and helping her mother about the daily work, or reciting her lesson in the Bible class at her Sunday school.

It is not wrong for you, my little girl who reads this, to wish to look pretty, any more than it is wrong to wish to be good; and it is not in the least true that it is of no sort of importance how you look if you are only good. It is true, though, that it is a great deal more really beautiful to be good than to have a pretty face, or be well dressed. Think this over by yourself, and see if you do not find it so. If you have two schoolmates, one of whom is very pretty and wears the prettiest of clothes, and the other of whom is plain, and wears very plain clothes, at first you like the pretty one the best. But if she is ill-tempered and cross, if she frowns and scolds and is disobliging, by and by she really begins to look homely to you. And if your plain friend is always bright and cheerful and good-tempered and ready to oblige you, you begin to think her quite pretty; she looks pretty to you because you love her.

Now the great trouble about girls and women is, not that they think too much of outside beauty, but that they do not think enough of inside beauty. If Pussy thought of nothing but how to dress herself, if her whole mind were taken up with thoughts about her clothes, she would be on the way to lose what is her best beauty, and her most lasting one, — that is, her unselfish and sweet disposition.

So there is not the least harm, also, in loving to be admired, — especially if you prefer the admiration of your own dear, true friends to that of strangers. There are some young girls who do not care how they look at home, who do not care that their fathers and mothers and brothers should see them with tumbled and torn dresses, and rough hair, while they will spend hours and hours in getting ready to shine in some party or ball. But our little Pussy was delighted to have her mother pleased, and her father happy, and to see that her brothers were proud of her. She looked at herself in the glass when she came home from church, and saw that she was very pretty, and thanked her Heavenly Father for it, and thought what a good girl she must try to be to those dear parents who loved her so dearly.

She felt as if ten dollars spent on her dress was almost an extravagant sum, but thought she would try to make it up by being very industrious and economical; and she began directly to be very busy, in secret, braiding straw to make her mother a bonnet that should be even finer and nicer than her own. She had learned so well that she could braid straw while she was reading or studying, and her little fingers were never idle, even while her mind was away on other things.

The love of beauty did not stop with her own dress. She began to consider what could be done to make their home attractive. There had been always a best room at the farmhouse, but it had been rather a bare place. Not one of the thousand little pretty things and knick-knacks which dress up modern parlors could they have at the farmhouse. The floor had not even a carpet, but was covered with clean white sand, crinkled with great art and care, so as to resemble the rippled sand on the sea-beach.

But Pussy set her eyes on this room, and resolved to make it pretty. First she persuaded her mother to let her open the windows and take away some heavy, dark paper curtains, so that the bright light of the sun might be let in. Then she searched the buffet, in the corner of the best room, and found there an old India china bowl that belonged to her mother's wedding tea-set, and this she set upon the table and kept constantly full of mignonette and other sweet flowers that perfumed the air of the room. Then she arranged mosses and ferns in various little fanciful plots upon various dishes and plates. Her brothers, seeing her object, lent her the aid of their strong arms, and dug up for her roots of plumy ferns, which they brought home all waving with their great fan-like leaves, and planted for her in the lower half of a cask which they sawed in two for the purpose. This was set in the fireplace, and then Pussy busied herself in covering the sides of the cask with green moss. The looking-glass she ornamented with wreaths of evergreen, intermingled with the long gray moss that grew on the boughs of pine-trees, and brightened by red berries. In short, after a while the little parlor looked like some of those quaint mossy bowers in the woods, where one loves to sit and enjoy the sunshine.

There were tall, climbing rose-bushes which grew up over the window and looked in with a hundred rosy, inquiring faces, all through the month of June; and by the time the roses had passed away, there were morning-glories planted at the roots of the bushes which kept up a constant succession of bright blossoms through the summer.

Pussy had induced her brother to make her a rough frame for a lounge, which she cushioned and stuffed, and then covered with a pretty, neat green chintz. A couple of rough boxes, cushioned and covered with the same material, made a pair of ottomans to match this lounge; and the room really began to wear quite an inviting appearance.

Pussy had persuaded her father to allow her the milk of one cow, which he cheerfully did, for he knew she was a deft little dairy-maid. Pussy was happy and busy enough taking charge of Clover, — for so her cow was called. She prepared a breakfast for her every morning with her own hands, and Clover would come up and stand with her head over the fence waiting for it. Pussy would stroke her head, and pat her, and talk to her, and tell her that she must try and be a good cow, and give her a plenty of milk to make butter of; and Clover would look at her attentively out of her great, clear, soft eyes, where you could see the shadow of the lashes just as you can see the rushes in a brook. The fact is, Pussy grew so fond of Clover that she spent a great deal of time petting her. Clover learned some of the arts of civilized life with great rapidity; she would eat cake and gingerbread and apples out of Pussy's hand, and Pussy would sometimes put a wreath of buttercups and daisies round her horns, and lead her by one horn to look at herself in the brook, and see how she liked herself. What Clover thought of all this she never mentioned; but she showed her regard for her young mistress in the best way that a cow could devise, by giving the most uncommon quantity of nice rich milk. And then Pussy's brothers went to work and built a milk-room out in the pasture directly over the brook, so that the little stream pattered directly through it; and here Pussy's pans of milk were set to raise their cream, and here was her seat when she used to churn and work her butter. Pussy's butter became quite celebrated in the neighborhood, and sold for an extra price, and Pussy counted the money with a glad heart. In six months she had saved enough to buy a neat little shelf of books to put in the parlor; and many and many a happy hour at home grew out of that shelf of books. No ornament of a house can compare with books; they are constant company in a room, even when you are not reading them.

Pussy used sometimes to take a book out and show it to Clover, and say, "Thank you for this, dear Clover," — all which Clover accepted in perfect serenity.

LITTLE PUSSY had now grown up to be quite a young woman. She was sixteen years old, tall of her age, and everybody said that, though she was n't handsome, she was a pretty girl. She looked so open-hearted and kind and obliging, — she was always so gay and chatty and full of good spirits, — so bright and active and busy, — that she was the very life and soul of all that was going on for miles around.

Little Emily Proudie was also sixteen, and everybody said she was one of the most perfectly elegant girls that walked the streets of New York. Everybody spoke of the fine style of her dress; and all that she wore, and all she said and did, were considered to be the height of fashion. Nevertheless, this poor Emily was wretchedly unhappy, — was getting every day pale and thin, and her heart beat so fast every time she went up stairs that all the household were frightened about her, and she was frightened herself. She spent hours in crying, she suffered from a depression of spirits that no money could buy any relief from, and her mother and aunts and grandmothers were all alarmed, and called in the doctors far and near, and had solemn consultations, and in fact, according to the family view, the whole course of society seemed to turn on Emily's health. They were willing to found a water-cure, — to hire a doctor on purpose, — to try homœopathy or hydropathy, or allopathy, or any other pathy that ever was heard of, — if their dear elegant Emily could only be restored.

"It is her sensitive nature that wears upon her," said her mamma. "She was never made for this world; she has an exquisiteness of perception which makes her feel even the creases in a rose-leaf."

"Stuff and folderol, my dear madam," said old Dr. Hardhack, when the mamma had told him this with tears in her eyes.

Now Dr. Hardhack was the nineteenth physician that had been called in to dear Emily, and just about this time it was quite the rage in the fashionable world to run after Dr. Hardhack, principally because he was a plain, hard-spoken old man, with manners so very different from the smooth politeness of ordinary doctors that people thought he must have an uncommon deal of power about him to dare to be so very free and easy in his language to grand people.

So this Dr. Hardhack surveyed the elegant Emily through his large glasses, and said, "Hum! — a fashionable potato-sprout! — grown in a cellar! — not a drop of red blood in her veins!"

"What odd ways he has, to be sure!" said the grand-mamma to the mamma; "but then it's the way he talks to everybody."

"My dear madam," said the Doctor to her mother, "you have tried to make a girl out of loaf-sugar and almond paste, and now you are distressed that she has not red blood in her veins, that her lungs gasp and flutter when she goes up stairs. Turn her out to grass, my dear madam; send her to old Mother Nature to nurse: stop her parties and her dancing and her music, and take off the corsets and strings round her lungs, and send her somewhere to a good honest farmhouse in the hills, and let her run barefoot in the morning dew, drink new milk from the cow, romp in a good wide barn, learn to hunt hens' eggs, — I'll warrant me you'll see another pair of cheeks in a year. Medicine won't do her any good; you may make an apothecary's shop of her stomach, and matters will be only the worse. Why, there isn't iron enough in her blood to make a cambric needle!"

"Iron in her blood!" said mamma; "I never heard the like."

"Yes, iron, — red particles, globules, or whatever you please to call them. Her blood is all water and lymph, and that is why her cheeks and lips look so like a cambric handkerchief, — why she pants and puffs if she goes up stairs. Her heart is well enough, if there were only blood to work in it; but it sucks and wheezes like a dry pump for want of vital fluid. She must have more blood, madam, and Nature must make it for her."

"We were thinking of going to Newport, Doctor."

"Yes, to Newport, to a ball every night, and a flurry of dressing and flirtation every morning. No such thing! Send her to a lonesome, unfashionable old farmhouse, where there was never a more exciting party than a quilting-frolic heard of. Let her learn the difference between huckleberries and blackberries, — learn where checkerberries grow thickest, and dig up sweet-flag root with her own hands, as country children do. It would do her good to plant a few hills of potatoes, and hoe them herself, as I once heard of a royal princess doing, because queens can afford to be sensible in bringing up their daughters."

Now Emily's mamma and grandmamma and aunts, and all the rest of them, concluded that Dr. Hardhack was a very funny, odd old fellow, and, as he was very despotic and arbitrary, they set about immediately inquiring for a nice, neat farmhouse where the Doctor's orders could be obeyed; and, curiously enough, they fixed on the very place where our Pussy lived; and so the two girls came together, and were introduced to each other, after having lived each sixteen years in this world of ours in such very different circumstances.

It was quite an event, I assure you, at the simple little farmhouse, when one day a handsome traveling-carriage drove up to the door, and a lady and gentleman alighted and inquired if they were willing to take summer boarders.

"Indeed," said Pussy's mother, "we have never done such a thing, or thought of it. I don't know what to say till I ask my husband."

"My daughter is a great invalid," said the lady, "and the Doctor has recommended country air for her."

"I'm afraid it would be too dull here to suit her," said Pussy's mother.

"That is the very thing the Doctor requires," said Emily's mother. "My daughter's nerves are too excitable, — she requires perfect quiet and repose."

"What is the matter with your daughter?" said Mary Primrose.

"Well, she is extremely delicate; she suffers from palpitations of the heart; she can't go up stairs, even, or make the smallest exertion, without bringing on dreadful turns of fluttering and faintness."

"I'm afraid," said Mrs. Primrose, "we should not be able to wait on her as she would need. We keep no servants."

"We would be willing to pay well for it," said Emily's mother. "Money is no object with us."

"Mother, do let her come," said Pussy, who had stolen in and stood at the back of her mother's chair. "I want her to get well, and I'll wait on her. I'm never tired, and could do twice as much as I do any day."

"What a healthy-looking daughter you have!" said Emily's mother, surveying her with a look of admiration.

"Well," said Pussy's mother, "if *she* thinks best, I think we will try to do it; for about everything on our place goes as she says, and she has the care of everything."

And so it was arranged that the next week the new boarder was to come.

AND so it was settled that our elegant young friend, Miss Emily Proudie, was to go and stay at the farmhouse with Pussy Willow. Dr. Hardhack came in to give his last directions, in the presence of grandmamma and the aunts and mamma, who all sat in an anxious circle.

"Do pray, dear Dr. Hardhack, tell us just how she must be dressed for that cold mountain region. Must she have high-necked, long-sleeved flannels?" said mamma.

"I will make her half a dozen at once," chimed in Aunt Maria.

"Not so fast," said Dr. Hardhack. "Let's see about this young lady," and with that Dr. Hardhack endeavored to introduce his forefinger under the belt of Miss Emily's dress.

Now the Doctor's forefinger being a stout one, and Miss Emily's belt ribbon being drawn very snugly round her, the belt ribbon gave a smart snap, and the Doctor drew out his finger with a jerk. "I thought so," he said. "I supposed that there wasn't much breathing room allowed behind there."

"Oh, I do assure you, Doctor, Emily never dresses tight," said her mother.

"No indeed!" said little Miss Emily. "I despise tight lacing. I never wear my clothes any more than just comfortable."

"Never saw a woman that did," said the Doctor. "The courage and constancy of the female sex in bearing inconveniences is so great, however, that that will be no test at all. Why, if you should catch a fellow, and gird his ribs in as Miss Emily wears hers all the time, he'd roar like a bull of Bashan. You wouldn't catch a man saying he felt 'comfortable' under such circumstances; but only persuade a girl that she looks stylish and fashionable with her waist drawn in, and you may screw and screw till the very life leaves her, and with her dying breath she will tell you that it is nothing more than 'comfortable.' So, my young lady, you don't catch me in that way. You must leave off belts and tight waists of all sorts for six months at least, and wear only loose sacks, or thingumbobs, — whatever you call 'em, — so that your lungs may have some chance to play, and fill with the vital air I'm going to send you to breathe up in the hills."

"But, Doctor, I don't believe I could hold myself up without corsets," said Miss Emily. "When I sit up in a loose dress, I feel so weak I hardly know what to do. I need the support of something around me."

"My good child, that is because all those nice strong muscles around your waist, which Nature gave you to hold you up, have been bound down and bandaged and flattened till they have no strength in them. Muscles are nourished and strengthened by having blood carried to them; if you squeeze a muscle down flat under a bandage, there is no room for blood to get into it and nourish it, and it grows weak and perishes.

"Now look there," said the Doctor, pointing with his cane to the waist of a bronze Venus which adorned the mantle-piece, — "look at that great wide waist, look at those full muscles over the ribs that moved that lady's breathing apparatus. Do you think a woman with a waist like that would be unable to get up stairs without fainting? That was the idea the old Greeks had of a Goddess, — a great, splendid woman, with plenty of room inside of her to breathe, and to kindle warm vital blood which should

go all over her with a glow of health and cheerfulness, —
not a wasp waist, coming to a point and ready to break in
two in the middle.

"Now just there, under Miss Emily's belt, is the place
where Nature is trying to manufacture all the blood which
is necessary to keep her brain, stomach, head, hands, and
feet in good condition, — and precious little room she gets
to do it in.   She is in fact so cooped up and hindered,
that the blood she makes is very little in quantity and
extremely poor in quality; and so she has lips as white as
a towel, cheeks like blanched celery, and headaches, and
indigestion, and palpitations of the heart, and cold hands,
and cold feet, and forty more things that people have when
there is not enough blood to keep their systems going.

"Why, look here," said the Doctor, whirling round and
seizing Miss Emily's sponge off the wash-stand, "your
lungs are something like this, and every time that you take
in a breath they ought to swell out to their full size, so
that the air that you take in shall purify your blood and
change it from black blood to red blood.   It's this change
in your lungs that makes the blood fit to nourish the
whole of the rest of your body.   Now see here," said the
Doctor, squeezing the sponge tight in his great hand, —
"here's what your corsets and your belt ribbons do, —
they keep the air-vessels of your lungs matted together
like this, so that the air and the blood can hardly get
together at all, and consequently it is impure.   Don't you
see ? "

"Well, Doctor," said Emily, who began to be frightened
at this, "do you suppose if I should dress as you tell me
for six months my blood would come right again ? "

"It would go a long way towards it, my little maid,"
said the Doctor.   "You fashionable girls are not good for
much, to be sure; but yet if a doctor gets a chance to save
one of you in the way of business, he can't help wishing

to do it. So, my dear, I just give you your choice. You can have a fine, nice, taper little body, with all sorts of pretty little waists and jackets and thingumies fitting without a wrinkle about it, and be pale and skinny, with an unhealthy complexion, low spirits, indigestion, and all that sort of thing; or you can have a good, broad, free waist, with good strong muscles like the Venus up there, and have red lips and cheeks, a good digestion, and cheerful spirits, and be able to run, frisk, jump, and take some comfort in life. Which would you prefer now?"

"Of course I would like to be well," said Emily; "and in the country up there nobody will see me, and it's no matter how I look."

"To be sure, it's no matter," chimed in Emily's mamma. "Only get your health, my dear, and afterwards we will see."

And so, a week afterwards, an elegant traveling-carriage drew up before the door of the house where Pussy's mother lived, and in the carriage were a great many bolsters and pillows, and all sorts of knick-knacks and conveniences, such as sick young ladies use, and little Emily was brought out of the carriage, looking very much like a wilted lily, and laid on the bed up stairs in a chamber that Pussy had been for some time busy in fitting up and adorning for her.

And now, while she is getting rested, we will tell you all about this same chamber. When Pussy first took it in hand it was as plain and dingy a little country room as ever you saw, and she was very much dismayed at the thought of putting a genteel New York young lady in it.

But Pussy one day drove to the neighboring town and sold her butter, and invested the money she got for it, — first in a very pretty delicate-tinted wall-paper and some white cotton, and some very pretty blue bordering. Then the next day she pressed one of her brothers into the ser-

vice, and cut and measured the wall-paper, and contrived
the breadths, and made the paste, and put it on the paper
as handily as if she had been brought up to the trade,
while her brother mounted on a table and put the strips
upon the wall, and Pussy stroked down each breadth with
a nice white cloth. Then they finished all by putting
round the ceiling a bordering of flowers, which gave it
quite an air. It took them a whole day to do it, but the
room looked wonderfully different after it was done.

Then Pussy got her brother to make cornices to the
windows, which she covered with bordering like that on
the walls, and then she made full white curtains, and bordered them with strips of the blue calico; she also made
a bedspread to match. There was a wide-armed old rocking-chair with a high back, that had rather a forlorn
appearance, as some of its slats were broken, and the paint
wholly rubbed off, but Pussy took it in hand, and padded
and stuffed it, and covered it with a white, blue-bordered
dress, till it is doubtful whether the chair would have
known itself if it could have looked in the glass.

Then she got her brother to saw out for her a piece of
rough board in an oblong octagon shape, and put four legs
to it; and out of this foundation she made the prettiest
toilet-table you can imagine. The top was stuffed like a
large cushion, and covered with white, and an ample flowing skirt of white, bordered with blue, like the bedspread
and window-curtains, completed the table. Over this
hung a looking-glass whose frame had become very much
tarnished by time, and so Pussy very wisely concealed it
by looping around it the folds of some thin white muslin
that had once been her mother's wedding-dress, but was
now too old and tender for any other usage than just to be
draped round a mirror. Pussy arranged it quite gracefully,
and fastened it at the top and sides with some smart bows
of blue ribbon, and it really looked quite as if a French
milliner had been at it.

Then beside this, there was a cunning little hour-glass stand, which she made for the head of the bed out of two old dilapidated spinning-wheels, and which, covered with white like the rest, made a handy little bit of furniture. Then Pussy had arranged vases of blue violets and apple-blossoms here and there, and put some of her prettiest books in the room, and hung up one or two pictures which she had framed very cleverly in rustic frames, and on the whole the room was made so sweet and inviting that, when Emily first looked around it, she said two or three times, "How nice! How very pretty it is! I think I shall like to be here."

Those words were enough to pay Pussy for all her trouble. "Oh, mother, I am *so* sorry for her!" she said, rushing down stairs; "and I'm so glad she likes it! To think of her being so weak, and I so strong, and we just of an age! I feel as if I could n't do too much for her."

And what the girls did together we will tell you by and by.

XII

WE left little Miss Emily Proudie lying like a broken lily, stretched out on the white bed that Pussy Willow had made for her, where, tired with her day's ride, she slept soundly.

Dr. Hardhack had been very positive in saying that neither her mother nor any of her aunts, nor indeed any attendant who had taken care of her in New York, should have anything to do with her in her new abode. "She is to break all old associations," he said, "and wake up to a new life. I can't answer for her health if you give her even a servant that she has had before. Engage some good, wholesome country-girl for a companion for her, and some good farmer's wife to overlook her, and turn her out into a nice, wide old barn, and let her lie on the hay, and keep company with the cows," he went on. "Nature will take care of her, — only give her a chance."

About five o'clock the next morning, Emily was wakened by a bustle in the house. What could be the matter? she thought, there was such a commotion on the stairs. It was, however, only the men folk of the household going down to their breakfast; and Pussy and her mother had been up long before, in time to get the corn-cake baked, and coffee made, and everything ready for them.

Then there began to come up into the windows such a sound of cackling and lowing and bleating, as the sheep and the cows and the oxen all began, in different tones, calling for their morning breakfast, and gossiping with one another about a new day. Emily lay in her bed, and

watched the pink light, making her white curtains look all
rose-color, and the sounds of birds and hens and cows and
sheep all mingled in her mind in a sort of drowsy, lulling
murmur, and she fell into a soft, refreshing doze, which
melted away into a deep sleep; and so she slept ever so
long. When she awoke again the sun was shining clear
and bright through her window-curtains, which had been
looped back with festoons of wild roses, that seemed so
fresh and beautiful that she could not help starting up to
look at them.

She perceived at once that while she had been sleeping
some one must have been in her room, for by the side of
her bed was a table covered with a white cloth, and on the
table was a tall, slender vase, full of fresh morning-glories,
blue and purple and rose-colored and dark violet, with
colors as intense and vivid as if they really had been morning clouds grown into flowers. "Oh, how beautiful!" she
exclaimed.

"I'm so glad you like them!" said a voice behind her;
and Pussy Willow stood there in a trim morning-wrapper,
with just the nicest white frill you ever saw around her
little throat.

"Oh, did you bring these flowers here?"

"Why, yes; I picked them for you with the dew on
them. I thought it a pity you should not see them before
the sun shut them up. They are ever so beautiful, but
they only last one morning."

"Is that so?" said Emily. "I never knew that."

"Certainly; but then we always have new ones. Some
mornings I have counted as many as sixty or seventy at
my milk-room window when I have been skimming the
cream."

"How very early you must get up!"

"Yes, about the time the bobolinks and robins do,"
said Pussy, cheerfully. "I want to get my work all done

early. But come now, shall I help you to dress?" — and Pussy brought water and towels to the bedside, and helped Emily with all her morning operations as handily as if she had been a maid all her life, till finally she seated her, arrayed in a neat white wrapper, in the rocking-chair.

"And now for your breakfast. I have got it all ready for you," — and Pussy tripped out, and in a few moments returned, bringing with her a tea-tray covered with a fine white cloth, which she placed upon the stand. "Now let's move your table up to you, and put your vase of flowers in the centre."

"Oh, what a pretty breakfast!" said Emily.

And so it was, and a good one too; for, first, there was a large saucer of strawberries, delightfully arranged on green vine-leaves; then there was a small glass pitcher full of the thickest and richest cream, that was just the color of a saffrano rose-leaf, if any of my little friends know what that is. Then there was the most charming little cake of golden butter you ever saw, stamped with a flower on it and arranged upon two large strawberry-leaves, that actually had a little round pearl of dew on each of their points. Pussy had taken great pains to preserve the dew-drops unbroken on those leaves; she called them her morning pearls. Then there were some white, tender little biscuits, and some nice round muffins of a bright yellow color, made of corn meal, by a very choice receipt on which Pussy prided herself. So on the whole, if you remember that Emily's chair stood before an open window where there was a beautiful view of ever so many green hills, waving with trees, and rolling their green crests, all sparkling and fresh with morning dew, you may not wonder that she felt a better appetite than for months before, and that she thought no breakfast had ever tasted so good to her.

"Do eat some with me," she said to Pussy, — for Emily

was a well-bred girl, and somehow did not like to seem to take all to herself.

"Oh, thank you," said Pussy, "but you see I had my breakfast hours ago."

"Why, what time do you get up?" said Emily, opening her eyes wide.

"Oh, about four o'clock."

"Four o'clock!" said Emily, drawing in her breath. "How dreadful!"

"I don't find it so," said Pussy, with a gay laugh. "If you only could see how beautiful everything is, — so fresh and cool and still!"

"Why, do you know," said Emily, "that when I heard people moving this morning, I thought it was some time in the night? I thought something must have happened."

"Nothing but what happens every morning," said Pussy, laughing. "I hope it did n't disturb you."

"Oh no; I fell into a very sound sleep after it. Why, it must have been two or three hours before I woke again. What do you find to do?"

"Oh, everything you can think of. I feed Clover, and milk her. You must get acquainted with Clover; she is just the gentlest, most intelligent little beast you ever saw, and I make a great pet of her. Mother laughs at the time I spend in getting her breakfast ready every morning, and says she believes I put eggs and sugar in her corn-cake. I don't quite do that; but then Clover expects something nice, and I love to give it to her. She has beautiful, great, soft eyes, and looks at me with such gratitude when I feed her! She would be glad to lick my hand; but her tongue is rather too rough. Poor Clover, she does n't know that! But you ought to see the milk she gives! By and by perhaps you would like to come down to my spring-house and see my pans of milk and cream."

"And do you really make butter?"

"Certainly; I made this that you are eating."

"What, this morning?"

"No, yesterday; but I stamped it this morning on purpose for your breakfast. It has a pansy on it, you see; Brother Jim cut my stamp for me, — he has quite a taste for such things."

"Dear me!" said Emily, "how much you must have to do! I think I must be quite a trouble to you, with all your engagements; I think Dr. Hardhack ought to have let me bring a maid."

"Oh, she would only be in the way," said Pussy; "you had a great deal better let me take care of you."

"But you must have so much to do" —

"Oh, my work for to-day is about all done; I have nothing to do really. The butter is made, and set away to cool, and the dinner all put up for the men to take to the field; and they won't come home till night. This is my time for sewing, and reading and writing, and doing all things in general. And so, now, when you feel like it, I'll show you about over the premises."

So the two girls put on their hats, and Pussy began to lead her frail young friend about with her.

First, they went down along by the side of the brook, at the bottom of the garden, to the spring-house. It seemed refreshingly cool, and the brook pattered its way through it with a gentle murmur. On either side was a wide shelf set full of pans of milk, on which the soft, yellow cream was rising, and there was a little rustic seat at one end.

"There is my seat," said Pussy, pointing it out. "Here's where I sit to work my butter, and do all sorts of things. It's always cool here, — even in the hottest days." Then Pussy showed Emily her churn, and the long row of bright tin pans that were sunning on a board on the outside.

All this was perfectly new to Emily; she had never in her life thought how or where butter was made, and it was quite a new interest to her to see all about it. "If only you didn't make it so very early," she said, "I should like to see you do it."

"It is right pretty work," said Pussy, "and it is a delight always new to see the little golden flakes of butter begin to come in the cream! Perhaps, by and by, when you grow stronger, you might get up early for one morning. You have no idea what beautiful things there are to be seen and heard early in the morning, that never come at any other time of day. But now let's go to the barn. Wouldn't you like me to take you to ride while it's cool? There is old Whitefoot left that the men are not using. I can have him whenever I please."

"But you say the men are all gone," said Emily.

"Oh, I'll harness him," said Pussy; "Whitefoot knows me, and will let me do anything I please with him. I do believe he'd buckle his own girths, and harness himself up to oblige me if he could, — poor Whitefoot!"

So saying, they came into the large, clean, sweet-smelling barn, now fragrant with the perfume of new hay. It had great wide doors on either side, and opened upon a most glorious picture of the mountains.

"Now," said Pussy, "you must need rest awhile, and I'm going to get you up into my more particular haunt, — up this ladder."

"Oh, dreadful! I couldn't go up there," said Emily, "it would set my heart beating so."

"Oh, never mind your heart," said Pussy; "just let me get my arm round your waist, and put your foot there," — and before Emily could remonstrate she found herself swung lightly up, and resting softly in a fragrant couch of hay.

"You didn't know how easy it was to get up here," said Pussy.

"No, to be sure I did n't," said Emily. "What a nice, queer old place, and how sweet the hay smells!"

"Now," said Pussy, "let me carry you to my boudoir, and put you on my sofa."

There was a great open door above, where the hay was pitched in, and opposite this door Pussy placed Miss Emily, with a mountain of sweet-smelling hay at her back, and a soft couch of it under her.

"There, now!" said Pussy, "you are accommodated like a duchess. Now, say if I have n't a glorious prospect from my boudoir. We can look quite up that great valley, and count all those cloudy blue old mountains, and see the clouds sailing about in the sky, and dropping their shadows here and there on the mountains. I have my books out here, and some work, and I sit here hours at a time. Perhaps you 'll like to come here days, with me, and read and sew."

Now, to tell the truth, Emily had never been fond of reading, and as for sewing, she had scarcely ever taken a needle in her hand; but she said nothing about this, and only asked to look at Pussy's books. There were Longfellow's "Evangeline," Bryant's Poems, Prescott's "Ferdinand and Isabella," and "Paul and Virginia" in French.

"So you read French," said Emily, in a tone of slight surprise.

"A little; I don't suppose I pronounce it well, for I never really heard a French person speak. Perhaps, by and by, when you are better, you will give me a few lessons."

Emily blushed, — for she remembered how very negligent of her studies she had been at school; but she answered, "I never was a very good scholar, but they used to say I had a very good accent; one cannot be years in a French school without acquiring that."

"And that is just what I need," said Pussy, "so it all

happens just right; and you will give me a lesson every day, won't you?"

"You are so kind to me," said Emily, "that I should be glad to do anything I can."

"Then it's all settled," said Pussy, exultingly. "We will come and sit here with our books, and breathe the fresh air, and be all still and quiet by ourselves, and I will read to you, — that is," she said, blushing, "if you like to be read to."

"Oh, you are very kind," said Emily; "I should like it of all things."

"And now," said Pussy, "if you would like a little drive before the heat of the day comes on, I'll just speak to Whitefoot."

"You're not really in earnest in saying you can harness him?" said Emily.

"To be sure I am; how should we women folk ever get about if I could n't? I can push out the wagon, and have him in in a twinkling."

And, sure enough, Miss Emily, looking through a crack, saw old Whitefoot come out of his stable at the call of his young mistress, and meekly bend his sober old head to her while she put on the harness, and backed him between the shafts of the carriage, and then proceeded to fasten and buckle the harness, till, finally, all was ready.

"Now let me bring you down," said Pussy.

"You seem to think I am only a bale of goods," said Emily, laughing.

"Well, you are not to exert yourself too much at first. Mother told me I must be very careful about you, because I am so strong, and not expect you could do anything like me at first."

"Well, I think I shall try to help myself down," said Emily; "it was only foolish nonsense that made me afraid. I can hold to that ladder as well as you, if I only choose."

"To be sure. It is the best way, because, if one feels that way, one can't fall."

Emily had never done so much for herself before, and she felt a new sensation in doing it, — a new feeling of power over herself; and she began to think how much better the lively, active, energetic life of her young friend was, than her own miserable, dawdling existence hitherto.

The two girls took a very pleasant drive that morning. First to mill, where Pussy left a bag of corn to be ground into meal, and where Emily saw, for the first time, the process of making flour. Emily admired the little cascade, with its foamy fall of dark water, that turned the old, black, dripping mill-wheel; she watched with somewhat awe-struck curiosity the great whirling stones that were going round and round, and the golden stream of meal that was falling from them. She noticed all along on the road that everybody knew Pussy, and had a smile and a word for her.

"Oh, here ye be!" said the old miller; "why, I'm glad to see ye; it's as good as sunshine any day to see you a-comin'." And in return, Pussy had inquiries for everybody's health, and for all their employments and interests.

So the first day passed in various little country scenes and employments, and when Emily came to go to bed at night, although she felt very tired, she found that she had thought a great deal less of her ailments and troubles that day than common. She had eaten her meals with a wonderful appetite, and, before she knew it, at night was sound asleep.

XIII

WELL, my dear girls who read this story, I want now just to ask you, seriously and soberly, which you would rather be, as far as our story has gone on, — little Miss Pussy Willow, or little Miss Emily Proudie.

Emily had, to be sure, twice or three times as much of all the nice things you ever heard of to make a girl happy as little Pussy Willow; she had more money, a larger and more beautiful house, more elegant clothes, more brilliant jewelry, — and yet of what use were these so long as she did not enjoy them?

And why did n't she enjoy them? My dear little girl, can you ever remember, on a Christmas or Thanksgiving day, eating so much candy, ice-cream, and other matters of that nature, that your mouth had a bitter taste in it, and you loathed the very sight of cake or preserves, or anything sweet? What earthly good did it do, when you felt in that way, for you to be seated at a table glittering with candy pyramids? You could not look at them without disgust.

Now all Emily's life had been a candy pyramid. Ever since she was a little girl, her eyes had been dazzled, and her hands filled with every pretty thing that father, mother, aunts, uncles, and grandmothers could get for her, so that she was all her time kept in this state of weariness by having too much. Then everything had always been done for her, so that she had none of the pleasures which the good God meant us to have in the use of our own powers and faculties. Pussy Willow enjoyed a great deal more a doll that she made herself, carving it out of a bit of white wood, painting its face, putting in beads for eyes, and otherwise bringing it into shape, than Emily did the whole army of her dolls, with all their splendid clothes. This was because our Heavenly Father made us so that we should find a pleasure in the exercise of the capacities he has given us.

So when the good fairies which I have told you about, who presided over Pussy's birth, gave her the gift of being pleased with all she had and with all she did, they knew what they were about, and they gave it to a girl that was going to grow up and take care of herself and others, and not to a girl that was going to grow up to have others always taking care of her.

But now here at sixteen are the two girls; and as they are sitting, this bright June morning, up in the barn-chamber, working and reading, I want you to look at them, and ask, What has Miss Emily gained by her luxurious life of wealth and ease, that Pussy Willow has not acquired in far greater perfection by her habits of self-helpfulness?

When the two girls stand up together, you may see that Pussy Willow is every whit as pretty and as genteel in her appearance as Emily. Because she has been an industrious country girl, and has always done the duty next her, you are not to suppose that she has grown up coarse and blowsy, or that she has rough, red hands, or big feet. Her complexion, it is true, is a healthy one; her skin, instead of being waxy-white, like a dead japonica, has a delicate shade of pink in its whiteness, and her cheeks have the vivid color of the sweet-pea, bright and clear and delicate; and she looks out of her wide clear blue eyes with frankness and courage at everything. She is every whit as much a lady in person and manners and mind as if she had been brought up in wealth and luxury. Then, as to education, Miss Emily soon found that in all real solid learning Pussy was far beyond her. A girl that is willing to walk two miles to school, summer and winter, for the sake of acquiring knowledge, is quite apt to study with energy. Pussy had gained her knowledge by using her own powers and faculties, studying, reading, thinking, asking questions. Emily had had her knowledge put into her, just as she had had her clothes made and put on her; she felt small interest in her studies, and the consequence was that she soon forgot them.

But this visit that she made in the country opened a new chapter in Emily's life. I told you, last month, that she had a new sensation when she was climbing down the ladder from the hay-mow. The sensation was that of using her own powers. She was actually so impressed with the superior energy of her little friend, that she felt as if she wanted to begin to do as she did; and, instead of being lifted like a cotton-bale, she put forth her own powers, and was surprised to find how nicely it felt.

The next day, after she had been driving about with Pussy in the old farm-wagon, and seeing her do all her errands, she said to her, "Do you know that I think that my principal disease hitherto has been laziness? I mean to get over it. I'm going to try and get up a little earlier every morning, and to do a little more every day, till at least I can take care of myself. I have determined that I won't always lie a dead weight on other people's hands. Let me go round with you, Pussy, and do every day just some little thing myself. I want to learn how you do everything as you do."

Of course, this good resolution could not be carried out in a day; but after Emily had been at the farm a month, you might have seen her, between five and six o'clock one beautiful morning, coming back with Pussy from the spring-house, where she had been helping to skim the cream, and awhile after she actually sent home, to her mother's astonishment, some little pats of butter that she had churned herself.

Her mother was amazed, and ran and told Dr. Hardhack. "I wish you would caution her, Doctor; I'm sure she's over-exerting herself."

"Never fear, my dear madam; it's only that there's more iron getting into her blood, — that's all. Let her alone, or — tell her to do it more yet!"

"But, Doctor, may not the thing be carried too far?"

"For gentility, you mean? Don't you remember Marie Antoinette made butter, and Louis was a miller out at Marly? Poor souls! it was all the comfort they got out of their regal life, that sometimes they might be allowed to use their own hands and heads like common mortals."

Now Emily's mother didn't remember all this, for she was not a woman of much reading; but the Doctor was so positive that Emily was in the right way, that she rested in peace. Emily grew happier than ever she had been in her life. She and her young friend were inseparable; they worked together, they read and studied together, they rode out together in the old farm-wagon. "I never felt so strong and well before," said Emily, "and I feel good for something."

There was in the neighborhood a poor young girl, who by a fall, years before, had been made a helpless cripple. Her mother was a hard-working woman, and often had to leave her daughter alone while she went out to scrub or wash to get money to support her. Pussy first took Emily to see this girl when she went to carry her some nice things which she had made for her. Emily became very much interested in the poor patient face and the gentle cheerfulness with which she bore her troubles.

"Now," she said, "every week I will make something and take to poor Susan; it will be a motive for me to learn how to do things," — and so she did. Sometimes she carried to her a nice little print of yellow butter arranged with fresh green leaves; sometimes it was a little mould of blanc-mange, and sometimes a jelly. She took to cutting and fitting and altering one of her own wrappers for Susan's use, and she found a pleasure in these new cares that astonished herself.

"You have no idea," she said, "how different life looks to me, now that I live a little for somebody besides myself. I had no idea that I could do so many things as I do, — it's such a surprise and pleasure to me to find that I can. Why have I always been such a fool as to suppose that I was happy in living such a lazy, useless life as I have lived?"

Emily wrote these thoughts to her mother. Now her mother was not in the least used to thinking, and new thoughts made a troublesome buzzing in her brain; so she carried her letters to Dr. Hardhack, and asked what he thought of them.

"Iron in her blood, my dear madam, — iron in her blood! Just what she needs. She'll come home a strong, bouncing girl, I hope."

"Oh, shocking!" cried her mother.

"Yes, *bouncing*," said Dr. Hardhack, who had a perverse and contrary desire to shock fine ladies. "Why shouldn't she bounce? A ball that won't bounce has no elasticity, and is good for nothing without a bat to bang it about. I shall give you back a live daughter in the fall instead of a half-dead one; and I expect you'll all scream, and stop your ears, and run under beds with fright because you never saw a live girl before."

"Isn't Dr. Hardhack *so* original?" said mamma to grandmamma.

"But then, you know, he's all the fashion now," said grandmamma.

XIV

Our little friend, Miss Emily Proudie, had on the
whole a very pleasant summer of it at the farm. By the
time that huckleberries were ripe, in August, she could
take her basket on her arm, and, in company with Pussy,
take long walks, and spend whole afternoons in the pastures, sitting down on the great wide cushions of white
foamy moss, such as you always find in huckleberry pastures, and picking pailfuls of the round, shining black
fruit. She never found herself tired and panting for
breath, as she used to in her city life; for there were no
bandages or strings around her lungs to confine her breathing, and in place of the hot, close air of city pavements
there were the spicy odors of the sweet-fern and the pine-
trees and the bayberry-bushes.

Then Pussy had brought her to be acquainted with all
the birds, so that she knew every one just as well as she
used to know her old calling acquaintance on Fifth Avenue.
There was frisky Master Catbird, who sang like every
other bird in the woods in turn, — five minutes like this
one, and the next five minutes like that one, — and ended
by laughing at them all, with as plain a laugh as ever a
bird could make. And there were the bobolinks, with
the white spots on their black wings, that fluttered and
said, "Chack, chack, chack!" as if they did n't know how
to sing a word, and then all of a sudden broke out into
a perfect bird babble of "Chee-chees" and "Twitter-twit-
ters," and said, "O limph, O limph, O limp-e-te! sweetmeats, sweetmeats!" and, "Veni si-no pi-le-cheer-ene!"

And then, too, there was the shy white-throated finch, that never sings unless it is perfectly sure of being all alone by itself in the deepest, shadiest little closet of an old pine-tree or a thick-leaved maple.

Pussy had taught Emily how to creep round among the bushes, holding her breath, and moving in perfect silence, till at last they would get directly under the tree where the shy little beauty was sitting; and then they would see her dress herself, and plume her feathers, and pour forth just six clear, measured musical notes, — a little plaintive, but so sweet that one who heard her once would want to hear again.

Pussy used to insist that the bird uttered just six words in the tune of one of her Sunday-school hymns, — "No war nor battle sound." By close listening, you might after a time be quite sure that the bird sung exactly these words in her green, still retirement.

Then there were a whole crowd more of meadow-larks, and finches, and yellow-birds, that used to sit on thistle-tops, and sing, and pick out the downy thistle-seeds, and snap them up, and send the little silvery plumes flying like fairy feathers through the summer air.

Emily used to suppose that there were no sights to look at in the country, where there was no theatre, and no opera, and no museum; but she soon found that she could see, every day, out in a common pasture-lot, things more beautiful and curious than any which could be gotten up to entertain people in the city.

On Sundays they used to ride two good miles over hill and dale to the village church, and there Pussy had her Sunday-school class of nice rosy boys and girls, whom she seemed so fond of, and who were always so glad to see her.

Many times the thought occurred to Emily, "How happy this girl is! Not a day of her life passes when she does not feel that she is bringing some good and useful thing to pass, feeling her own powers, and brightening the life of every one around her by the use of them. And I," Emily thought, "have lived all my life like some broken-winged bird or sick chicken, just to be taken care of, — always to receive, and never to give; always to be waited on, and never to wait on anybody."

With health and strength and cheerfulness came a sort of consciousness of power, and a scorn of doing nothing, in this young girl's mind. "Because I am rich, is that any reason why I should be lazy," she thought to herself, "and let my body and mind absolutely die out from sheer laziness? If I am not obliged to work to support myself, as Pussy is, still, ought I not to work for *others*, as she does? If I can afford to have all my clothes made, is that any reason why I should not learn to cut and fit and sew so as to help those who have not money? Besides," thought the sensible Miss Emily, "my papa may lose his money, and become poor. Now being poor is no evil to Pussy; she contrives to be just as happy, to look pretty, to dress well and neatly, and to make her home charming and agreeable, — all by using her own faculties to the utmost, instead of depending on others, and being a drag and a burden on them. I will try and do so too. To be sure it is late in the day for me, I have indulged laziness so long, — and I *am* lazy, that's a fact. But then " — And then Emily went on thinking over the explanation that she had heard Pussy give to her Sunday-school class, on the Sunday before, of the parable of the talents, and the uses different people made of them. "These talents," she thought, "are all our advantages for doing good; and I have had so many! I am like the man who just digged in the earth and buried his Lord's money in darkness; I have not done anything with my talents; I have not culti- vated my mind, though I have had every advantage for it;

I have not even perfectly acquired any accomplishment. I have not done anybody any good, and I have not even been happy myself. My talent has not only not been increased, but it has grown less; for I have lost my health, and come almost to the grave by foolish ways of dressing, by sitting up late nights, and living generally without any sensible worthy object. And now, if my Lord should come to reckon with me, what could I say about the use I have made of my talents?"

This was more serious thinking than our Miss Emily had ever done before, and it ended in a humble, hearty prayer to her Saviour to enable her for the future to lead a better life; and then she began to study as earnestly to learn how to do everything about a house as if she were in very deed a poor girl, and needed to know. She insisted on taking the care of her own room, and early in the morning you might have heard her stepping about her apartment in a thrifty way, throwing open her window, and beating up her pillows and bolster, and putting them to air. Then she would insist on helping Pussy wash the breakfast things, and she would get her to teach every step of the way to make bread and biscuit and butter, and all nice things. "It does me good, it amuses me, it gives me my health, and it makes me good for something," she said. "If ever I should have use for this knowledge, I shall be at no loss, and you don't know how much happier I am than when I did nothing."

"Now, Pussy dear," she used to add, "when I go back to New York this winter, you must come and visit me; for I cannot do without you."

"Oh!" Pussy would say, laughing, "you won't like me in New York. I do very well in the country, among the sweet-fern bushes and the bobolinks, but I should be quite *lost* in one of your New York palaces."

"No, but you *must* come and show New Yorkers what

a country girl can be. Why, Pussy, you are a great deal
better educated than I am, even in things where I have
had more advantages than you, just because you have had
to struggle for them; you have really set your heart on
them, and so have got them. Knowledge has just been
rubbed on to me upon the outside, while you have opened
your mind, and stretched out your arms to it, and taken it
in with all your heart."

Emily would not be denied, and Pussy's mother said
that she ought to have some little holiday, she had always
been such a good girl; and so it was arranged that she
should go back to New York with Emily when she went.

But Emily was in no hurry to go back, for, as autumn
came on, and the long fine days grew cooler, she found
that she could walk farther and farther, and spend more
and more time in the open air. She had great fun in
going chestnutting, out under the bright gold-colored chestnut-trees, where the prickly burrs opened and showered
down abundance of ripe, glossy nuts. Emily would sometimes come home long after dark, having spent a whole
afternoon in searching and tossing about the golden leaves,
and bearing her bag of chestnuts in triumph, — and so
hungry that good brown bread and milk tasted like the
most delicious luxury.

Then there were walnuts, and butternuts, and wild
forest grapes, and bright crimson barberries, all of which
the young maidens went forth to seek, and in pursuit of
which they garnered health and strength and happiness.

"Why, Dr. Hardhack," said Emily's mother, "I don't
see as we shall *ever* get our Emily home again. I keep
writing and writing, and still she says she isn't ready;
there is always something ahead."

"Let her alone, ma'am, let her alone," said the Doctor.
"Give Nature a chance more; you'll all be tumbling on
to her, and trying to undo all the good she's getting, as

soon as you get her home; so let her stay as long as possible."

"Oh, Dr. Hardhack, you are so queer!"

"Truth, ma'am!" said the Doctor. "You are perfectly longing to kill that child; it's all you can do to allow her a chance to breathe. But I insist upon it that she shall keep away from you as long as she has a mind to."

"Did you ever see such a queer old dear as Dr. Hardhack?" said Emily's mother. "He does say the oddest things!"

So in the next chapter we shall tell you about Pussy's adventures in New York.

XV

"WELL now, Dr. Hardhack, does n't our Emily look beautifully?" said Emily's mother and grandmother and aunt, all in one breath.

Emily had come home from her long abode in the country, and had brought her friend Pussy Willow with her; and they were sitting together now, a pair of about as rosy young females as one should wish to see of a summer day.

Dr. Hardhack turned round, and glared through his spectacles at Emily. "Pretty fair," he said; "pretty fair! A tolerable summer's work, that!" — and he gave a pinch to Emily's rosy cheek. "Firm fibre, that! real hard flesh, made of clover and morning dew, — none of your flabby, sidewalk, skinny construction."

"Well now, Doctor, we want you to tell us just what she may do, — just how much. I suppose you know, now she's got into a city, she can't dress exactly as she did up in the country."

"I see, I see," said Dr. Hardhack; "I *take* at once."

"You see," said Aunt Zarviah, "there is n't a thing of all her clothes that she can wear, having been all summer in those loose sacks, you know. She's sort o' *spread out*, you see."

"I should think so," said Dr. Hardhack. "Well, my advice is, that you begin gradually screwing her up; get her corsets ready, with plenty of whalebone and a good tough lace; but don't begin too hard, — just tighten a little every day, and by and by she 'll get back to where all her things will fit her exactly."

"But, Doctor, won't that injure her health?" said the mamma.

"Of course it will, but I fancy she 'll stand it for one winter; it won't quite kill her, and that 's all we doctors want. If it suits you all, it does me, I 'm sure. What should I do for my bread and butter, if all the girls of good families kept on living as these two have been living this summer? I really could n't afford it, in a professional point of view."

"Well, *I* have something to say on this point," said Emily. "I would n't lose my health again for anything that can be named."

"Oh, pooh, pooh! I 've heard a deal of talk of this sort before now. When patients are first up from a sickness, how prudent they mean to be!

' When the Devil was sick, the Devil a monk would be, —
When the Devil got well, the Devil a monk was he.' "

"Thank you, Doctor," said Miss Emily; "but I think *that* poetry does n't apply to *me*, if you please. I hope I 'm not of that family."

"Well, — but seriously, Doctor, you must tell us just how much it will do for Emily to do," said the mamma. "One does n't want to give up the world entirely, and yet one does n't want to lose one's health."

"I see," said the Doctor; "I appreciate the case entirely. Well, let her begin with the opera twice a week, and one German, kept up till daylight. In one week she will feel stronger than ever she did, and declare that nothing hurts her; then she can take two Germans, and then three, and so on. Fact is," said the Doctor, "of all the devices of modern society, none is so good for the medical practice as these Germans; my best cases are made out of 'em; they unite all the requisites for forming first-rate patients that keep on our hands for months and years, and are as good as an annuity to us. I 'm not a fool, madam. I must look ahead for my bread and butter next spring, you see."

"But, Doctor, I'm not going to Germans at all," said Emily, stoutly. "I know now what life is, and what health is worth, and I'm not going to waste it in that way. Besides, I'm going to try to live for something better."

"Live for something better!" said the Doctor. "What sort of talk is that for a young lady in the first New York society? What is there to live for better? I thought of it the other night when I was at a confirmation at Grace Church, and saw a whole bevy of pretty creatures, who all were engaging to 'fight manfully under Christ's banner,' and thought where they would be before spring. Whirling round all night in a low-necked dress is the kind of fighting they do; and then I'm called in as hospital surgeon to the dear disciples when they are carried off the field exhausted. I know all about it. You *can't*, of course, live for anything better. You couldn't, for the world, be called singular, and be thought to have odd notions, — could you? That would be too horrible.

"Now I knew a rich New York girl once who took to bad courses. She would go round visiting the poor, she would sit up with sick people, and there was no end to the remarks made about her. People clearly saw how wicked it was of her to risk her health in that way, — how late hours and bad air and fatigue would certainly undermine her health, — and she was quite cast out of the synagogue. You mustn't breathe bad air or over-exert yourself, unless you do so from a purely selfish motive; then it's all right and proper, — this is our New York gospel."

Pussy Willow's blue eyes were open very wide on the Doctor as he spoke, and there was a laugh in them, though she did not laugh otherwise. The Doctor caught the expression, and shook his cane at her.

"Oh, you need n't sit there looking mischievous, miss.
What do you know of life? You 're nothing but a country
girl, and you know no more of it than the bobolinks and
chip-squirrels do. You 'll soon learn to be ashamed of
your roses, and to think it 's pretty to have bad health.
I 'll bet a.copper that you 'll begin a course of corsets in
a fortnight, and by spring we shall send you back to your
milk-pails as white and withered as Miss Emily there.
It 's astonishing how fast we can run a girl down, taking
one thing with another, — the corsets, and the hot rooms
with plenty of gas escaping into them from leaky tubes,
and then operas and Germans for every night in the week.
Of course it 's a charity to give you a good stiff dose of it;
it 's hospitality, you see."

"Now, Doctor Hardhack, you dreadful man," said Emily, "you must stop this talk. I brought Pussy down here
on purpose to have somebody to help me to live better than
I have lived. We shall just take a peep or two at New
York sights, but we are not going into the gay world."

"Ta, ta, ta! don't tell me," said the Doctor, shaking
his cane playfully at her; "you won't be so unfair as to
cut me in that way. I shall hear of you yet, — you 'll
see;" and so the Doctor departed.

"What a droll man he is!" said Pussy.

"It 's just his way," said Emily's mother; "he 's always
running on in this strange way about everything. For my
part, I never know half what he means."

"It is tolerably plain what he means," said Emily.
"You must do exactly contrary to what he tells you, —
as I shall; so, aunty, don't trouble yourself to try to alter
my things, unless it be to let them all out, for I 'm going
to keep all the breathing-room I 've got, whether I have
a pretty waist or not. I 'd rather have color in my cheeks,
and a cheerful heart, than the smallest waist that ever was
squeezed together."

"Such a pity one couldn't have both!" said Aunt Zarviah. "Your cousin Jane was in here last week with her new bismarck silk, and it fits her so beautifully! Somebody said she looked as if she'd been melted and poured into it; there wasn't a crease or a wrinkle! It did look lovely!"

"Well, Aunt Zarviah, I must try some other way of looking lovely. Maybe, if I am always gay and happy, and in good spirits, and have a fresh bright face, it may make up for not looking as if I had been melted and poured into my clothes."

To do Emily justice, she showed a good deal of spirit in her New York life. She and Pussy agreed to continue together their course of reading and study for at least two hours a day; then they both took classes in a mission Sunday school, which was held in the Church of the Good Shepherd, and they took up their work in real good earnest.

"Now," said Emily, "I am not going to give my class just the odds and ends and parings of strength which I have left after I have spent almost all in amusing myself; but I mean to do just the other way, and spend the strength left from really useful things in amusing myself."

The girls kept a list of their classes, and used regularly every week to visit the families from which the children came. In the course of these visits they found much else to do. They saw much of the life of the poor; they saw paths daily opening before them in which the outlay of a little time and a little money enabled them to help some poor struggling family to keep up a respectable standing; they learned the real worth of both time and money; and the long walks they took in all weathers in the open air kept up their strength and vigor. They went occasionally of an evening to some of the best sights in New York, and they saw what was really worth seeing; but they did not make a winter's work of rushing from one amusement to another.

On the whole, the two girls, in spite of Doctor Hardhack, proved that a temperate, sober, healthy, useful life might be led even in the higher circles of New York.

Dr. Hardhack used to pretend to fly into a passion when he saw them, — shook his stick at them wrathfully, exclaiming, "What is to become of me if you go on so?" and threatening to denounce them. "It's a conspiracy against our bread and butter, the way these girls go on," he said. "I sha'n't have a shadow of a case in Miss Emily, and I'm an abused man."

So passed a pleasant winter, when one morning all New York waked up in arms. Emily's father brought home the newspaper, — there was a war; Emily's brother came rushing in all out of breath, — "The New York Seventh has got to be off in a twinkling. Girls, good-by."

You remember, my little readers, those first days of the last war. What a stir and commotion there was everywhere through all the families in the country! Fathers and brothers and lovers and husbands were marching off, and the women left at home were so wishing and longing to be able to do anything to help them!

That was the time when every man and woman that was good for anything wished that they were richer and wiser and stronger than they were, that they might be able to do more for their country.

Emily and her friend had hardly time to think, the thing had burst upon them so suddenly, and George Proudie was gone from them in an hour.

That day nobody in the house did anything but walk restlessly about the house and look aimlessly out of the windows, till the Seventh Regiment came down the street with banners flying and drums beating. Then the flags were waved from all the houses, and flowers were showered down, and people shouted and wept as they went by.

"Nobody knows whether we shall ever see George again," said Emily's mother, crying.

"Oh, why was I not a man?" said Emily. "Why could I not go with him?"

Emily's cheeks were flushed and her eyes bright, and she looked full a head taller than usual. She was waked up all through her heart and soul to feel the joy and glory of doing something, of living a strong, active, vigorous life; and she felt that to go out to suffer hardships, and brave dangers, and endure toil and self-denial for a noble object, had something in it happier than to live in ease and luxury.

"I am sick of all these things," she said to Pussy that night, when they were in their chamber.

The "things" she pointed at were a confused mass of French dresses, and her toilet covered with fancy jewelry. "I never knew before what a brave boy our George was," she added. "Do you know he told me that he was going to be in the thickest of all the fighting, and volunteer to go into every danger. Isn't it splendid of him?"

"Yes, indeed it is," said Pussy, with sparkling eyes. "I know my brothers have enlisted. Here is the letter mother writes about them. Three of them gone in one regiment, and only one left to help father! He wanted to go, but they felt it was the duty of one to stay, and so he stayed!"

The two girls lay awake half the night, wishing that they too could go for soldiers.

XVI

WELL, the war went on and on and on, and got to be a graver thing every day. What times those were, to be sure! Was n't everything for a while turned topsy-turvy? Those were days when all who had any capacity in them that was good for anything were sure to find it out and have it called into use. People who do great things and good things at such times do them because they have been laying up strength beforehand, and training themselves in body and mind. Then, when the time comes to use their faculties, they have them all ready, and know just where to find them.

Very soon came the news of battles and skirmishes, and then of precious blood shed. Then of battles that left ever so many of the noblest and most precious of our Northern soldiers wounded and bleeding. Cannot all of you remember how the mothers and daughters and sisters, all over the country, flew to their relief, — how societies were formed, and women worked day and night to send aid to the brave men who were fighting our battles on the field?

Then, had you been in New York, you must have seen the City Park lined along its edges with barracks thrown up to receive the wounded soldiers. Within were long lines of neat beds where the poor fellows lay. There you might have seen a pretty young girl, dressed in deep mourning, who came every day with her little basket on her arm, leaving at many a couch some token of her gentle presence and loving care. This is the girl that was once

the idle, selfish Emily Proudie. What is she now? To
the poor suffering men whom she visits every day she
seems like an angel; and as she passes among them she
leaves a bunch of flowers here, an interesting book or
pamphlet there. Sometimes there is a little bottle of
cologne, or a palm leaf fan, or a delicate, nicely hemmed
handkerchief, — luxuries for the sick-bed of which her
kind eye sees the need here and there. Occasionally she
will sit for an hour at a time by some poor feverish boy,
fanning away the flies, that he may sleep, and perhaps
singing a sweet hymn. Once she used to get vast credit
for singing French and Italian songs with a great many
shakes and trills in them, which it fatigued her very much
to learn, and which, when she got through with them,
people complimented her for as wonderfully well done.
Now she sang some simple airs from a soldier's tune-book;
and when her tender voice rose, it was in words like
these : —

"Sweet hour of prayer, sweet hour of prayer,
   That calls me from a world of care,
   And bids me at my Father's throne
   Make all my wants and wishes known."

Often, while she was singing, there would be such a
stillness all up and down the hospital that you might hear
a pin drop, and you might see hard, dark hands brushing
away tears quietly; and then the men would speak softly
of pious mothers, at whose knees they learned to pray long
years ago.

You remember the days when Emily had everybody in
the house at her feet, waiting on her, and yet was full of
disgust and weariness. In those days her back ached,
and her head ached, and everything constantly troubled
her; her dresses never were trimmed to suit her, and
everything went wrong with her from morning to night.

Now she is a different girl indeed. She wears a plain

mourning dress for her dear brother, who was one of the
first to lay down his life for his country; but her dress
costs her little thought and little care, because her heart is
full of sweeter and nobler things. Emily is living no
more for self, she is living for others; she has learned the
Saviour's beautiful lesson that it is more blessed to give
than to receive, and she finds it so. She uses every day
all the strength she has, resolutely and systematically, in
some good works of charity. Besides going to the hospital, she went often to the rooms of the Soldiers' Aid
Society to cut out work, and she took some home with
her, that every hour might be usefully employed. She
wrote letters for the poor fellows who were too feeble to
write for themselves, and told distant mothers and friends
how their beloved ones were doing. Many of Miss Emily's
letters are treasured in distant dwellings in the country,
where her face has never been seen, because they are all
the tidings that remain of some dear one forever lost to
earth.

Emily's mamma and aunts declared that the dear child
was doing too much, and actually wearing herself out; but
Emily found one great secret, and that was, when she had
used all her strength in good works, to look humbly to her
Father in secret for more,— and this strength always came.

"Are n't you afraid, Doctor, that Emily will wear herself out with visiting the hospitals and working for the
soldiers?" said anxious mamma.

The Doctor gave her a good look through his great round
spectacles.

"I think she 'll stand it," he said, "rather better than
she used to stand the opera and the German some winters
ago."

"And if I don't," said Emily, "I 'd rather wear out than
rust out. I have found out what life is good for now."

As to Pussy Willow, she had a brother who rose to be a

general, and had command of a whole State, and she went
to the South to keep house for him.   One of the largest
hospitals in the Southern Department was conducted under
her eye and care, and a most capital one it was.   She had
strength, the result of years of healthy energy, to give to the
service of her country.   She had experience in the use of
her hands, and could do everything in the neatest and
quickest way; and when a hundred desperately wounded
men are brought in at once to be relieved and made comfortable, nobody without experience can tell how important it is
to know how to do exactly the right thing in the least time.
The nights that Pussy has been up in her hospital kitchen,
making soup and gruel and coffee, when the wounded were
being brought in after a battle!   She moved so quickly
that she seemed to be everywhere; she directed everybody
and everything, and wherever anything seemed in danger
of going wrong, there she was in a trice, and set it right
again.

Nobody knows the amount of work done by fair, delicate
women in those days.   They did not turn aside from any
horror, they did not spare themselves any fatigue, they
called no service beneath them whereby they could relieve
a pain.   Among these heroines our Pussy was foremost.
Those blue eyes of hers became stars of hope to many a
poor fellow, and her ministering hands seemed to have the
very gift of healing in them.   She overlooked the stores
sent by the Sanitary Commission, and saw that they were
wisely kept and administered.   She wrote to the North for
whatever was wanting, and kept her patients well and carefully clothed, fed, tended, and nursed.   Many letters passed
between her and Emily in this labor of love, and many a
nice package of shirts and stockings came down to her from
Emily's Fifth Avenue sewing association.   So these two
girls were united in the service of their country.

And, in this war, it was the *women*, no less than the men,

that saved the country. If there had not been hundreds of thousands of brave women who did as Miss Emily and our Pussy did, thousands of dear and precious lives must have been wasted, and the war could not have come to so glorious an end.

Well, peace came at last. How glad we all were! And all our generals and colonels came North again, and laid aside their titles, and went to work at their farms and merchandise as quietly as though nothing had happened. But the people where Pussy lives still persist in calling her brother General, and his coat with the gold star on it is hung up with his sword in the little cottage where our story began.

As to Pussy, she has married lately, and gone to live in New York. She lives in a nice brown-stone house in Fifth Avenue, not far from Miss Emily, and the two girls are more intimate than ever. People do say that the General, Pussy's brother, is going to marry Miss Emily, and so they will, by and by, be sisters. I can't say certainly as to that; I only know that they are a great deal together; and on the whole, if my young folks will have it so, I guess we will finish up our story that way.

It is agreed that Pussy is always to spend her summers at the old homestead where she first saw the light, where the bright pussy-willow bush tassels out early in March under the chamber windows, and the old grandmotherly ferns, with their woolly nightcaps, peep out to see whether it will do to unroll and come up into this upper world.

Pussy is right, for the good fairies dwell in these quiet country places. Do you want to see one, my dear Charlotte or my blue-eyed Mary? Well, the next time you get a chance to look down into a clear spring, or a deep well all fringed with ferns, if the water is very still and clear, perhaps you will see one smiling and looking amiably at you.

Now remember to be a good girl, and live to help other

people. Begin by being, as Pussy was, a kind, helpful daughter to your mother, who has done more for you than you have any idea of ; and remember that your happiness consists in what you give and what you do, and not in what you receive and have done for you.

And now good-by.

THE MINISTER'S WATERMELONS

I

It was a proud day in my life when I first counted my-self as an academy boy in Highland Academy.

Highland was about as still and dreamy a little village as one could see among the White Mountains; but it was a grand, lively metropolis, compared to Blueberry, where my tender years were spent, and where I acquired sufficient primary knowledge to enable me to graduate into Highland Academy.

I remember now my emotions, as, seated on the top of the stage, with a very ancient and dilapidated hair trunk as the repository of my worldly goods, we came dashing into Highland in a glorious cloud of dust, which the setting radiance of the afternoon sun illuminated with splendor. "Here we go," thought I, as two dogs barked, and some roosting hens flew down and cackled, and a cat ran away from before us, and a flock of geese opened their beaks, and flapped their wings, and hissed, and the driver cracked his whip, and the clerks of the one country store, where the post-office was kept, came and stood out in the porch, while a half-dozen boys sat on a fence and waved their hats. "This is something like life," thought I, and my breast heaved, as I thought of the confined stillness of Blueberry, which was nine miles from any stage station.

The academy I surveyed with awe. It was quite as big as our meeting-house, and had a bell on it, which our meeting-house did not have. My heart fluttered and thumped when I was set down at Deacon Jones's. I was now, as my father and mother had reminded me, in a long talk the evening before, going to begin life for myself.

I ordered down my hair trunk and paid my fare with a high sense of responsibility. Deacon Jones stood on the doorstep, — a little, thin, wiry man, with a long, sharp nose, attired in a fluttering red calico dressing-gown. He was, at the moment, contemplatively chewing a long bit of straw, for which he appeared to have a relish.

When I gave him a letter from my father, and stood waiting, trunk in hand, he opened it with great crackling, wiped his spectacles a great many times, and read it over as if he found difficulty in making it out, and then, contemplating me through his spectacles, he drawled out, —

"Wal, I calculate we can take you. You'll have to go into No. 2. Miss Jones 'll show you the way. Miss Jones," he continued, turning round, with a flutter of the red double gown, "there aint but one boy in No. 2, is there?"

An anxious, hot-looking woman came out of some inner apartment, and, taking a hasty glance at me, said, "This way, if you please," and I followed, with my hair trunk on my shoulder, up an echoing pair of bare, painted stairs, into a large front room, the windows of which, on one side, opened upon two large maple-trees, and on the other upon a glorious blue vista of mountains.

There was one boy already there, and two more expected. Jimmy Seaforth, the present occupant, was a little, white-haired, blue-eyed, gentle-spoken fellow, who seemed to look up to me with a sort of apprehension as I came in. This rather flattered my self-importance, and forthwith a friendship was struck up between us, and we agreed to be bedfellows, whoever else might come to occupy the other bed.

I felt very grand as I took out my Latin books, and arranged them strikingly on the shelf, instructing Jimmy, all the while, and giving him the benefit, gratis, of the wisdom and sage counsel with which my father, and mother, and aunts had filled my head, on the grand and solemn occasion of my entering Highland Academy.

I examined him concerning his studies, gave him the benefit of my opinion in a most liberal manner, and promised to stand by him in case of any emergency. Jimmy was naturally of a timid, apprehensive disposition, and took to twining around me as naturally as a youthful bean-vine takes to a friendly bean-pole.

The next day we were examined and classed. I was to begin Virgil with three other boys and two girls. Myra Jones was one, and Lucy Sewell the other. Myra was large-boned, dark-complexioned, with a big, heavy waist; but Lucy Sewell was slender and golden-haired, with great blue eyes, and cheeks like a sweet pea. She was the minister's oldest daughter, and the very first sight of her filled me with the strangest mixture of pleasure and discomfort I had ever experienced. I remembered, with horror, that, in my haste in dressing that morning, I had put on a shirt-collar with a streak of smut upon it. "Who cares?" I thought as I stood before the looking-glass. But then I did not know that I was to sit side by side with Lucy in the Virgil class.

We all had to read and construe in turn, and this miserable bit of smut on my collar became so active in my imagination that I could hardly get my moods and tenses right, and I made one or two mistakes, which further covered me with confusion.

I knew the first book in Virgil almost by heart, and was burning to distinguish myself, but I was so harassed by this little fiend, that I was actually puzzled to translate one of the most familiar phrases. There was a movement and a flutter next me, as of dove's wings, and Lucy Sewell considerately knocked down a book, and, as she stooped to pick it up, she whispered the right phrase in my ear.

It set me straight. I recovered myself, grew more com-

posed, and went through with credit.   I looked up to thank
my good angel, but Lucy was blushing redder than I, with
her eyes fixed in most innocent ignorance on her Virgil.

Her portion of the lesson was construed charmingly; so
was Myra's; and Myra turned out to be a first-rate comrade,
and a real jolly girl — a fine bit of the good, hearty prose of
life; but Lucy was its poetry.

When school was out, I tried to express, in my best style,
my thanks for her kindness.

"Kindness, Mr. Somers!" she said; "not at all."

"Mr. Somers!" and by those pretty lips.   At home, in
Blueberry, I was only plain Bill Somers.   I felt taller and
grander at once; yet somehow I felt myself blushing like a
girl, but Miss Lucy was as quiet and cool as the white linen
collar round her throat.   The girl is always mistress of the
situation at that age.   Lucy, I found afterwards, was only a
month or two younger than myself, but full a year older, in
womanly gravity.

Nevertheless, she let me carry her Virgil and dictionary
for her, and walk beside her home, the most delighted of
individuals.

I went to my room, feeling grand and heroic; rushed to
the looking-glass, examined the state of my whiskers carefully, and remarked to Jimmy that the way the hair did
grow on my cheek and chin was astonishing!   It was really
necessary to shave every day; and Jimmy admired me
accordingly.   I studied my Virgil like a hero, overwhelmed
Jimmy with good advice and sage counsels till a late hour
that night, and went to sleep, feeling that

"Life is real, life is earnest."

I wrote home to my mother that week a letter filled with
the most profound moral reflections, which the dear woman
carried in her pocket, and read over at least a dozen times
a day.   On Sunday, I recorded punctually, for her edification,
the heads of Mr. Sewell's two sermons; and my behavior at

church was attentive and edifying in the extreme ; the more so that Lucy Sewell, all in white, and with a wonderful little bonnet garlanded with sweet peas, sat in the singers' seat, and I thought now and then gave me a friendly look, as I sat bending over my notes.   That first week was a glorified one, but alas —

Well, what of the alas ?

You shall hear.

For the first two weeks I had it all my own way in
No. 2, and fancied that I was getting to be quite a virtuous
hero. Jimmy looked up to me, and I explained his lessons
to him, and gave him all sorts of wise counsel, and I looked
up to Lucy, and Lucy was gracious to me.

I had taken my stand as one of the best scholars in
school, and the master gave me approving glances. The
minister cast benignant eyes on me, when I stood lounging
at his front gate under the sugar maples, of an evening, and
talked over it to Lucy. Sometimes he would look out of
his study window and say, " Come in, my son," and then
I came and sat on the front steps. It was so pleasant to
hear Lucy call me Mr. Somers, and ask my opinion about
the last poem of the day, and to hold grave discussions with
her on all sorts of subjects.

Punctually on Wednesday evening I called to walk with
her to the weekly evening lecture, sat by her side, and sung
out of the same hymn-book. I regarded myself as far
along in my pilgrimage of virtue, established in a sort of
Palace Beautiful, and Lucy figured in my eyes as the fair
damsel named Discretion, who kept the door. I did not
know how near to the Palace Beautiful of boys often lies
the Valley of Humiliation, but into this valley it was my
fortune to make a pretty rapid descent.

There were rumors that two more boys were expected in
No. 2 ; and one night, when I sauntered in from my evening stroll, I found Tom Danforth in possession.

" Why, is n't El Vinton here ? " he said. " I expected
to find him."

I had n't even heard of El Vinton, and said so.

" Not heard of him ! Why, he 's one of your Beacon Street mags," said Tom. " His father lives in a palace right opposite the Frog Pond, there on Beacon Street. El 's jolly ; he 's up to everything that 's going. We were in the Latin School together. I came here to chum with him."

" Why does n't he stay in the Latin School, then ? " said I, not well pleased with the idea of this Boston mag, as Tom called him.

" Well, El 's up to too many tricks, you see. The fact is, he 's been blowing a little too strong, and his governor is going to rusticate him. Sent him here because it is such a sweet little innocent place. El says he don't care a darn ; he can have jolly times anywhere."

And sure enough, that evening El came down in state and style on the top of the stage, and took possession in our quiet chamber with an abundance of racket.

" Hello, fellows ! Who 's here ? " he said, when he broke into the apartment. " You — what 's your name ? "

" Somers is my name," I said, endeavoring to maintain that mild dignity of demeanor which I had read about in story-books.

" My dear fellow, don't attempt that style," he said, as he seated himself on the table among my Latin books, and swung his feet in a free-and-easy manner. " Cultivate simplicity, my son, and tell your grandfather your name, like a good boy."

I could n't help laughing. Tom and Jimmy laughed, too, and I felt rather uncomfortable as I said, " Well, my name is William."

" Well, then, here we all are, — Tom, Bill, Jim, and your humble servant, El Vinton," he said ; " just a jolly room full. Now hand out the toothbrush mugs, or whatever drinking weapons you 've got, and let 's drink to better acquaintance. Tom, haul that hamper this way. Let's make friends with these natives. I'm abominably thirsty."

In a moment a bottle of claret was produced from a well-stuffed hamper, the top dexterously knocked off with a skillful blow by El Vinton, and we were discussing crackers, and cheese, and claret with our new friend.

Now, in my native village of Blueberry, I had signed a temperance pledge, and at first I had some faint scruples, and said that I never took wine, but the new ruler of the apartment put me down with, —

"Ah, now, my boy, don't come the moral dodge, — nothing but weak red ink, you know! I knew the grub here'd be abominable, and so I came stocked, — and share all round's my motto, — nothing that can intoxicate, of course," he added, with a wink at Tom Danforth.

Tom laughed, and seemed to think this was a capital joke.

Altogether we two innocent country boys seemed to be taken possession of by the new occupants of the room. Boys have the phrase " Coming it over one," and, like most phrases coined out of life, it expresses a real fact. Elliot Vinton " *came it over* " us both the very first evening, and settled himself as lord paramount in our apartment.

We certainly passed a very merry evening, and Elliot made himself most entertaining, recounting scenes and exploits of wild school-boy life in Boston, and Tom chorused the laugh always.

To be sure I could not help feeling, sometimes, that Elliot's jokes bore rather hard on poor folks. For example, he told, with great gusto, how they served an oysterman, one night, in Boston. In those days the oystermen used to cry the oysters through the streets of an evening. They commonly had a bag of shell oysters over their shoulder, and a pail full of opened oysters in their hand, so as to serve out either on demand of their customers.

"This was the way we fixed 'em," said Elliot. "Tom and a lot of fellows stood round a corner holding the ends of a stout line, with a strong codfish hook in it. I takes this in my hand and walks up to him just as he comes past the corner.

"'Hollo, mister,' says I, 'I want some of your oysters there in that air pail.' I had a little pail in my hand, as if I had come up to buy. At the same time I struck the cod-hook into his bag.

"Down came his bag on the sidewalk, while he stooped to open his pail. Whisk went the bag up the street.

"'Hollo! what's that?' says he; and he started off after it. But away went the bag round the corner. The minute his back was turned I caught the pail and was off round another corner. You ought to have seen how funny the old fellow looked. His old coat-tails flapped, and he flew round and round like a cat after her tail. He grabbed right and left — no bag, no pail — one gone round one corner, and one round the other before you could say Jack Robinson. Oh, it was funny!"

Now, when a set of boys are eating crackers, and drinking claret, and laughing, and the laugh once gets going, it is hard to stop it, and I laughed over the story with the rest, but with a sort of misgiving at my heart.

I felt as if I ought to say something, and finally I cleared my throat and said, "But after all it wasn't doing quite the fair thing, was it? Poor old fellow!"

"Oh, these oystermen get no end of money," he said, carelessly. "They build houses and own whole blocks. They can afford to give us boys a joke, now and then. Besides, I made it up to him. We bought oysters every night of him for six months."

"But that didn't pay him for those you stole," I said.

"Stole! We didn't steal. We only *hooked* them, my son," said Elliot, with a toss of his curls and a patronizing smile. "There 's all the difference in the world between hooking and stealing, my boy. Nobody ever calls such scrapes stealing !"

Elliot had such a condescending, knowing air of explaining things to us, and then his whiskers were full grown, and he had a decided mustache, and sported a gold watch, with an elegant chain, and altogether seemed so much a man of the world, that there is no wonder we let him lay down the law to us.

After the claret came a roll of cigars, and he handed one all round.

"I never smoke," said I.

"Time you did, then," he said, tilting back in his chair and lighting his cigar luxuriously. "Must be a first time for everything, my boy."

Jimmy looked up in an undecided way to me, and I played with my cigar carelessly, while Elliot and Tom were soon puffing magnificently.

"You 'll have to smoke in self-defense, my dear fellow," said Elliot, laughing. "You may as well have your own smoke as ours."

"Oh, I don't mind a cigar, now and then, just for company," said I, carelessly lighting mine.

Jimmy upon this lit his, and the room was soon blue with smoke. Now I had solemnly promised my mother not to smoke, and the thought of this promise came rather uneasily into my mind, but I said to myself, "A fellow does n't want to be a wet blanket — so just for this once !"

Pretty soon Jimmy began to look pale, and after a few uneasy minutes rushed to the chamber-window and began vomiting.

"Give him a stiffener, Tom," said Elliot ; and Tom drew out of the hamper a flask of brandy, and adroitly mixed a stiffener of brandy and water, which Elliot administered with a paternal air, making Jimmy lie down on the bed.

"Never mind, my boy, you're green," he said. "You'll get used to it after a little. Always make a fellow sick at first. Gracious me, how sick my first cigar made me! I think I was about your age. Here, set the windows open, and give him fresh air; and, Tom, you and I'll go down and finish in the street."

"Oh, you can't do that," said I; "it's contrary to the rules of the academy, and you'd be hauled up at once."

"Tom, this gets interesting," said El. "If there's any thing that gives a charm to life, it's a fight with these Dons. I half plagued their lives out in the Latin School."

"Well," said I, "Mr. Exeter is a pretty resolute fellow. It's a word and a blow with him, and if fellows don't keep up to the chalk mark, he just sends 'em off."

"All the jollier," said El, "but that sha'n't hinder my smoke the first evening. I ain't supposed to know the rules. To-morrow, you know, I shall find 'em out." And so saying, El and Tom sallied down into the little moonlit street, with their cigars in their mouths, walking grandly up and down with their hands in their pockets, while I sat, crestfallen and self-condemned, in the window, watching them.

As they came into the broad glare of the full moon, they met Lucy, leading by the hand her younger sister. I remember how pretty she looked, all in white, with her head of golden curls shining like a mist in the mysterious moonshine. I felt myself getting very hot and red, as I sat there in the window-seat, thinking how I had been spending my evening. There was my lesson unlearned, Jimmy groaning in bed with a raging headache, from the brandy and cigar, and I, who had thought myself so manly, and felt so sure of my principles, and had given him so much excellent advice, had gone down before the first touch of temptation!

The foolish fear of being thought green had upset all my good resolutions, and made me break all my promises. I could n't help seeing that the desire to appear manly had led me to do the most sneaking *un*manly thing in my life. My example had misled Jimmy, and I had lost his respect. In short, I could not help seeing that that one evening had made El Vinton master in our room. For if a man or boy is going to hold his own against another, he must begin in time. There's an old proverb, "If you say A, you must say B." If I had been going to keep my temperance pledge and my promise to my mother about smoking, then and there, on that first evening, was the time to have stood to it. The battle had come on and I had shown the white feather the very first moment.

The sight of Lucy made me feel all this the more, because in the short time of our acquaintance I had been very confidential, and told her all about my temperance pledge and my promise about tobacco, and she had said how much it increased her respect for me; and Lucy's respect was worth more to me even than my own. How I did despise myself! How mean and cowardly I seemed to myself!

El and Tom came back in high spirits.

"We passed a very nice P. G.," said El. "I wonder who she is."

"Her curls are stunning," said Tom.

"That was Miss Lucy Sewell you passed," said I. "She is the minister's daughter."

"She'll do, Tom," said El. "If I can find a decent team in this place, I'll trot her out some time this week."

The cup of my misery was full.

El Vinton proved to be a good scholar. The Boston Latin School generally turned out such, and El stood high, even there.

In truth, he was one of those bright, quick fellows for whom the ordinary lessons of school are not employment enough — who can keep at the head of their classes with but little outlay of time and thought — and so he soon took a high stand in his classes, with very little study. In fact, he did not scruple, in our room, to assume the airs of a gentleman of elegant leisure. He had a stock of novels, over which he lounged easily, while Jimmy and I were digging at our lessons with care-worn faces — and he contrived to do pretty much what he chose, spite of monitors, rules, and teachers.

He was a general favorite with the boys, and more so with the girls, who seemed to regard him as a sort of young nobleman in disguise.

There was, however, one exception. Lucy Sewell had a clear, cool, distant way of looking at him out of her blue eyes, that was quite surprising to him.

" Hang that girl ! " he said, one day, as he stood at his glass; " she don't seem to appreciate me. Well, I must give her a drive, and have a little private conversation with her."

And El posted off to the only livery stable in town to get up what he called a decent turnout. This was two or three days after the evening I have described.

I can't tell anybody what a wretched, subjugated, kept-down kind of life I was leading. The fear of El Vinton's ridicule. and a sort of anxious sense of what he would think of what I said and did, embarrassed me day and night.

Then I was uncomfortable with Lucy, because I felt as if I had forfeited all pretensions to her respect; and when with her I was constantly wondering what she would think of me, if she knew just how miserably weak I had been.

Added to all this, I was wretched to think El Vinton was going to take her to ride. It seemed so manly and grand to have all the money one wanted, and be able to go to livery-stables and order turnouts, and here was I with not a nine-pence for spending-money! I thought I had money enough the two weeks before El came, but now things looked quite changed to my view. A week ago, to escort Lucy to the Wednesday evening lecture seemed to be all I could ask, but now I saw a wider sphere of desire opening before me ; and when El Vinton came driving up street that afternoon, bowing, and kissing his hand to the girls as he passed, in his showy buggy, with a fast horse, I felt bitter repinings.

" Well," he said, as he came in that evening, " I 've got a decentish affair, considering the place, and now I shall go and engage my girl for to-morrow." So, after an elaborate arrangement of necktie, he started over to the minister's to make his call.

He was gone about half an hour, and then came back in a very ill humor.

" What time are you going to-morrow ? " said Tom.

" She won't go at all," said El.

" What 's the matter ? "

" Oh, she says her father don't approve of her riding out with young gentlemen."

" What an old tyrant ! " said Tom. " I say, El, she might meet you accidentally, and he know nothing about it."

"Well, that's just what I proposed to her," said El. "I wish you could have seen her! Why, the girl actually seemed to take it as an insult! She stood up so straight, that really I thought her feet were going off the carpet, and said she was astonished that I should propose such a thing. She's a real prig, that girl is; a regular stiff, green-spectacled school-ma'am."

"That sounds like sour grapes," said I, immensely delighted with the result of the transaction, and thinking more of Lucy than ever.

"Well," said El, shaking his shoulders, "I'll go and ask one of those Seymour girls. One of them shook her handkerchief out of the window at me when I drove by this afternoon. The loss will be her own — I'm sure *I* don't care. If she don't want to ride, I don't know why I should want to take her."

It is the way of our selfish sex, I suppose, but it is a fact, nevertheless, that nothing makes a girl's good opinion more precious in our eyes, than to hear that she has been snubbing some other fellow. That which anybody may have, we set small value on, but the girl who makes distinctions, if she happens to be gracious to us, is forthwith a peg higher in our esteem. I had supposed, of course, that El Vinton's dashing air, and his many advantages of person, wealth, and position, would carry all before them, and I must say I was surprised at his receiving this repulse from Lucy.

It was Wednesday evening, and I called to ask her to go to the lecture. Yes, she would go — and down she came in the distracting little white bonnet, with the wreath of sweet peas upon it, and we walked off to lecture in the most edifying manner. I expatiated on our new roommate, and tried to draw out Lucy's opinion of him.

"To be frank with you, Mr. Somers, I do not like Mr. Vinton," she said.

"How charming of her!" was the immediate language of my heart; but I said, "Why, he is just the person I supposed you would be quite carried away with."

"Then you know very little of me or my taste," said Lucy. "I have heard a good deal of this El Vinton, and think it is rather a misfortune that he has been sent to our academy. He is a rich, fast, drinking, smoking boy, just the one to lead young boys astray."

"He's a real jolly fellow," said I, feeling in honor bound to say something.

"I dare say he is," she said, "but I think he is a dangerous companion. Then that little Jimmy Seaforth, in your room! He is a delicate boy, and his mother is constantly anxious about him. She told father all about it. His father died a drunkard, and his mother is very anxious lest he should form any bad habits. So she sent him here because Mr. Exeter is so particular with his boys, to keep dangerous influences out of their way. If it were not that *you* were in the same room with him I should feel troubled about Jimmy, but you will keep him straight, I know."

This conversation took place as we were walking home from lecture. This commendation from Lucy fell like a pound of lead on my heart. I felt like a miserable, degraded sneak, as I walked by her side in silence. I was appalled, too, by what she told me of Jimmy, for during the fortnight following El Vinton's arrival Jimmy had seemed quite enkindled with the ambition to learn to smoke, and was in the habit of keeping off the qualmish feelings thus brought on by the aforementioned stiffeners of brandy and water.

The conviction that I had helped to lead him astray, by not standing my ground that first night, now became unpleasantly strong in my mind. What a fool I had been! Why did I not *at first* declare my temperance principles, and my promise to my mother. A little firmness then might have cost me an effort, but it would have made my after-way easy. Now I was every day miserably conscious of being under a sort of slavery. I did not smoke very often. I excused myself, when invited, on various pleas. It did not agree with me. It confused my head. It hurt my eyes, and so on. In the same manner I sometimes took a sip of El's wine, but generally apologized for declining it.

All this did no good. It was no testimony to principle, one way nor the other. But what frightened me to think of was that Jimmy seemed to be developing a real taste, both for tobacco and for drink. How horrid, I thought, if there should be a serpent lying coiled up at the bottom of the poor boy's heart, which these things should rouse and strengthen, till it should strangle him !

All this dimly came before my mind as I walked silently by Lucy's side, but I had not courage to tell her the whole story. I thought once or twice I would do it; but it is very hard when you see that people evidently have a very high esteem for you, to begin deliberately to pull yourself down in their eyes. I think Lucy must have wondered what made me so absent and silent, for in the conflict of my mind I often quite forgot to talk.

" What in the world has come over you ? " said Lucy to me, finally, after I had been standing looking gloomily over the gate after she had passed through it that night, and turned, as her custom was, for a little farewell chat in the moonlight. " I was thinking of Jimmy," said I.

" I knew you would feel it," she said, with enthusiasm. " I know Jimmy's mother, and last week I wrote her how fortunate it was that he had you for a room-mate."

I could have kicked myself, in the utterness of my self-contempt, and I abruptly bade Lucy good-evening, and turned away.

THINGS went on in this way for some weeks. Boys, and men, too, sometimes, by a single step, and that step taken in a sudden hurry of inconsideration, get into a net-work of false positions, in which they are very uneasy and unhappy, but live along, from day to day, seeing no way out.

This was my case. I was in false relations with Lucy, feeling that she thought altogether too well of me, but did not have the courage to undeceive her.

I was in false relations with Jimmy, having assumed the part of a true friend to him, and now wanting the steadiness and firmness necessary to save him from the dangerous courses into which he was entering.

El Vinton's whirl of animal spirits, his wit and fun, kept a sort of vortex round him, into which it appeared impossible to get a serious consideration. The slightest attempt in me to say a word of the kind was shouted down by the general laugh of the room.

My conscience was so stirred by what Lucy had said to me, that I tried, as far as I was concerned personally, to keep out of the smoking, and drinking, and violation of school rules that went on in our room, and for that I was voted a wet blanket, a muff, and sometimes El would ask me if I intended to report them to Mr. Exeter, or the parson.

The thing came to a crisis in an attack on the minister's watermelon patch, as I am about to relate.

For two or three days El Vinton and Tom and Jimmy had seemed to have some plan on foot from which I was excluded. There was a great deal of chaffing and laughing among them, and passing of catch-words from one to another; and it was evident that something was going on which was not to be communicated to me.

One evening, just at twilight, El proposed that we should all go in swimming together in a neighboring pond. The evening was delightful — it had been a hot August day — the full moon was just rising, and would light our way home. El Vinton put his arm in mine, and made himself unusually gracious and agreeable. In fact, he usually did that, and if he had not possessed that easy, jolly kind of way, I think I should not have borne as I did the sort of dictation he exercised over us all.

He rattled, and chattered, and talked all the way to the pond, and we had a glorious swim. By the time we started to return home, it was broad, clear moonlight, clear enough to see to read by.

We came along cross-lots, swishing through the high, dewy meadow-grass, and I gathered, as I went, handfuls of bright, spicy wild roses and golden lilies, as a bouquet for Lucy. Suddenly we came to the minister's watermelon patch, and I was going to propose that we should make a circuit round it, to avoid tramping the vines, when El Vinton, putting one hand on the top rail, swung himself over, saying,—

" Now for it, boys! Here's a dessert for us ! "

The boys followed him, and forthwith began, in the bright moonlight, sounding the melons.

" Take care, fellows ! " said El. " I'm the judge of ripeness. Don't cut till I give verdict."

" Boys," said I, " what are you doing ? "

" Oh, you 'll see if you live long enough," said El, coolly cutting off one or two fine melons, and taking them to a retired spot under a large tree. " This way, Tom, with that one. Jimmy, don't you cut any; let me cut them."

"But," said I, "boys, this is too bad. This is Mr. Sewell's patch — the minister."

"All the better," said El. "Just as if we did n't know that. I would n't have taken Deacon Sharpe's, for I know they would give us a stomach-ache; but Mr. Sewell's are your real Christian melons — won't hurt anybody."

The boys all laughed as they sat down under the tree, and El began cutting up a great, ripe, red melon. I stood irresolute.

"Perhaps you had better run and tell of us," said El.

"I think it 's a shame for you to say that, El Vinton," said I. "You know it 's unjust."

"Well, so 't is," he said, with a frank, dashing air. "I know, Bill, that you are as good-hearted a fellow as breathes, and any one that says you are a sneak or a spy, I 'll fight him. So sit down with us."

"But seriously," said I, sitting down, "I must expostulate."

"Well, wet your whistle first," said El, cutting a great fresh piece, and holding it up to my mouth.

Now, if you imagine a thirsty boy, on a hot August night, with a cool, trickling slice of watermelon held right to his lips, you will, perhaps, see how it was that I ate my slice of watermelon before I was well aware what I did.

"Goes down pretty well, don't it?" said El, stroking my back. "You see there 's nothing like your real orthodox, pious melons. Why, I don't doubt that there 's grace grown into these melons that will set us a long way on in saintship."

There was a general laugh at this sally, and I laughed, too, but still said, in an uneasy voice,—

"After all, El, it is n't handsome to take the minister's melons in this way."

"Bless you!" said El, "it is n't the melons we care for, it 's the fun. Let 's see. These melons are worth, say half a dollar apiece ; that 's a liberal estimate. Well, suppose we eat six of them ; that 's three dollars ! What 's three dollars ? " he said, with a magnificent slap of his pocket. " Now I, for one, am ready to plank down five dollars, this minute, as my part of a subscription to get Sewell a concordance, or a cyclopædia, or set of Shakespeare, or any such thing as folks give to ministers ; but I want my fun out of him, you see. I want my melons in this pastoral way, just when I feel like eating 'em,— and enough of them, — and so here goes a roarer," giving a smart slash of his knife across the third melon.

And so, on and on we went, never knowing that Abner Stearns, the parson's hired man, had his eye at a hole in the shrubbery, and was taking an exact account of us. Long before we left the fields, Abner had made his way across the lots, and detailed to Mr. Sewell the whole that he had seen and heard.

" There 's one on 'em, — that are Bill Somers, — *he* seemed rather to go agin it, but they would n't hear to it, and kind o' roped him in among 'em," said Abner. " And now, Mr. Sewell, if you say so, I can jest go up with you to Mr. Exeter, with this ere story, 'cause I got a good look at every one on 'em, and knows exactly who they be, and I can testify on 'em slick as a whistle. That air Vinton boy, from Boston, he 's the head o' the hull. I haint never had no great opinion o' him. He 's up to every kind o' shine, and jest the one to rope in other boys."

" Well, Abner," said Mr. Sewell, " I have my own plan about this affair, and you must promise me not to say a single word about it to any human being, not even to your wife."

" That 's pretty well put in, too," said Abner, " for if I told Cinthy, she 'd want to tell Dolly Ann, and Dolly Ann, she 'd want to tell Dolly, and 't would be all over town afore night."

"Precisely so," said the minister, "but my plan requires absolute silence. I can't manage without."

"Go ahead, Parson Sewell," said Abner, "I'll be dumb as a catfish," and Abner went home, wondering what the minister's plan was.

"Lucy," said Mr. Sewell, coming out of his study, "I think we had four nice, ripe melons put down cellar this morning, did n't we?"

"Yes, papa."

"Well, I'm going to invite the boys over to the opposite house to a little melon supper. I'll bring up the melons, and you set out a table, and I'll go over and invite them."

Now, as Lucy had particularly friendly feelings towards, at least, one boy in the lot, she set about her hospitality with alacrity.

We were coming up the street in the full, broad moonlight.

"I tell you," said El, "I'm about as full as I can wag. It's wonderful how watermelons can fill a fellow up. I feel as I used to after a Thanksgiving dinner."

"So do I," said Tom. "I could n't really get down another morsel."

At this moment, as we turned the corner to our boarding-house, Mr. Sewell stood out plain before us, in the moonlight.

"Good-evening, young gentlemen," he said, in a bland, polite tone. "I've been looking for you."

Our hearts all thumped, I fancy, a little quicker than before, but Mr. Sewell was so calm and polite, it could not be that he suspected where we had been.

"I've been looking for you," said Mr. Sewell, "just to ask you to step in a few moments and eat watermelons with us. We have a splendid lot of nice, ripe watermelons, and I thought you could help us to put some of them away."

I saw El give Tom Danforth a look of despair; but of
course there was nothing to be done but seem highly delighted and honored, and we followed Mr. Sewell into the
house and to a table piled with ripe melons, for which,
wearied and cloyed as we were, we had to feign a boy's fresh
appetite.

Mr. Sewell was pressing. He cut and carved without
mercy — would not hear an apology, piled up our plates
with new slices before we had half demolished the old ones,
while we munched away with the courage of despair.

Lucy was there, doing her part of the hospitality in the
prettiest and most graceful manner possible.

I had reasons of my own why the feast seemed almost to
choke me. I had eaten very little of the melons in the
lot, but the sense of the meanness of my conduct oppressed
me. I could not bear to meet Lucy's eyes — and Mr.
Sewell's politeness was dreadful to me. I rather fancy that
there never was a set of boys who groaned more in spirit
over a delicious banquet than we over those melons. It
was in vain we made excuses; feigned modesty, delicacy;
said, "No, I thank you," and so on. The hospitality was
so pressing, and our guilty consciences made us so afraid of
being suspected, that we nearly killed ourselves in the
effort. But at last we had to stop short of what was provided for us.

There was a sort of subdued twinkle in Mr. Sewell's eye,
as he bade us good-night, that struck me singularly. It
was like a sudden flash of lightning on a dark night. I
felt perfectly sure that somehow he knew all about us.
I felt my cheeks flame up to my hair, and my misery was
at its climax.

When we stumbled home the boys were alternately laughing and groaning, and declaring that the parson had caught
them; but I stumbled into bed, blind and despairing. Oh,
the misery of utter shame and self-contempt! I really

wished I had never been born; I wished I had never come
to Highland Academy; never known Lucy or Mr. Sewell;
wished that El Vinton had kept a thousand miles away;
and, finally, it occurred to me to wish the right wish which
lay at the bottom of all, — that I had had sense and man-
liness enough, weeks ago, to begin with my room-mates as
I knew I ought to go on, and not get into the miserable
tangle which had ended in this disgrace!

I did not sleep a wink that night, and next morning,
at five o'clock, I was up, and seeing Mr. Sewell out in his
garden, I resolved to go to him and make a clean breast
of it.

I went and told him I wanted to see him alone, and went
with him into his study and told him what a miserable,
silly fool I had been for the few weeks past.

"I tell you, Mr. Sewell, because I won't play the hypocrite any longer," I said. "Lucy thinks a great deal too
well of me; and you have been a great deal too kind to
me; and I thought I might as well let you see just how
mistaken you had been in me, and what a mean, miserable
humbug I am."

"Oh no, not quite a humbug," said Mr. Sewell, smiling.
"Courage, my boy. You've made a clean breast of it, and
now you've got down to firm ground, I think. It's just
as well to get through this kind of experience while you
are a boy, if you are one of those that can learn anything
by experience."

"But now I don't know what to do," said I. "I am
wrong all round; and seem to have lost the power of doing
right."

"Well, you have made it pretty hard to do right," he
said; "but if you've pluck enough now, to face about, and
to tell your room-mates just what you have told me, —
that you have been going wrong, but that you are determined now to do right, and having told them so, if you

will keep to it with steadiness for a week or two, you may get back the ground that you never ought to have lost in the first place. It's tremendously hard to face about when you have been yielding, but it can be done."

"It shall be done," said I; and I took my hat up and walked over to our room, and got the boys together and made my speech to them. I blamed nobody but myself. I told them I had acted like a sneak; and that I didn't wonder they had no respect for me, but I told them I meant to be done acting like a sneak, and be a man; that I should, for the future, keep from drinking and smoking, and breaking school rules, and that if they would join me, well and good, but if they didn't, it should make no difference.

Mr. Sewell that same day sent for El Vinton and Jimmy, and had a talk with them, and matters in our room began to wear quite another appearance.

"I tell you, fellows," said El Vinton, "it was rather bully of the parson not to blow on us. Exeter would have turned us out of school in less than no time. And Sewell gave me some precious good counsel," he added; "and on the whole, I don't know but I'll make an experiment of the ways of virtue."

I had a penitential confession to make to Lucy, but she took it like an angel. The fact was, she seemed determined to make the best of me — a course in which she has persevered ever since.

Mrs. William Somers having just looked over this manuscript, is of opinion that I have said too much about Lucy; but I am not.

The moral of my tale I leave every boy to make out for himself.

A DOG'S MISSION

CHAPTER I

THE OLD HOUSE AND THE OLD WOMAN

"THE old house" of the city of Hindford stood upon a fashionable avenue, with city pavements in front and elegant brick mansions on either side.

It was a sort of ancient phenomenon, standing there amid smart modern houses, on a gay and bustling street; for it was an old brown wooden farm-house, of the kind that our ancestors used to build in days of primitive simplicity a hundred years ago. It was a two-story house in front, but the long roof sloped down behind, till a child might easily jump from it on to the ground.

It had never been painted; its shingles were here and there green with patches of moss. Certain enterprising shrubs had seeded themselves in the eave-troughs, and formed a fantastic nodding fringe along the edges, that made the old house look as queer as antiquated nodding finery makes an old face.

The clapboards here and there were curled with age and starting from the timbers; the lintel of the door had sunk so that the door-posts stood awry; the door-steps were broken and sunken like old grave-stones, and green with dank clinging moss.

Of course there were in front, as must be about every old New England house, the inseparable lilac trees; but these had grown to weird and preternatural proportions, looking into the chamber windows, and even here and there brushing the herbage of the eave-troughs.   Their stems below were gnarled and wreathed, and covered with bright yellow lichen, making their whole air as quaint and witch-like as the rest of the surroundings.

A narrow strip of front door-yard was inclosed by a demoralized old picket-fence ; the gate swung unevenly on its hinges, and like everything else about the ancient dwelling, looked forlorn and dreary.

The house, as we have said, stood on one of the fine driving avenues of Hindford, and elegant carriages and prancing horses went by it every day ; and everybody said, —

" What a queer old witch-like house !   How strange that it should be on this street !   Who lives there ? "

The answer was, " Oh, that 's the old Avery place.   It can't be sold till old Miss Zarviah Avery dies ; she has the life-right, and she won't live anywhere else."

In fact this old Avery house was the decaying relic of a farm that had once lain quite out in the country near the town of Hindford, but the city had grown and traveled and thrown out its long arms here and there, and drawn into its embrace suburb after suburb, cutting streets and avenues through what was once farm and woodland, and so this old brown farm-house was left a stranded wreck of the old village life, standing by itself, and seeming to frown with a sullen amazement on a street of modern fine houses.

Miss Zarviah Avery was a human wreck like the house. Her village cronies had sold out, or moved off, or died ; her family, all but one brother, were dead ; nobody came to see her, and she visited nobody.

She was punctual in her seat in the neighboring church every Sunday, and sat always conspicuously on the front seat in the weekly prayer-meeting, where her phenomenal bonnets, her old-fashioned dress, and high, shaking voice, as she intoned the hymns, moved the mirth of that younger generation, who think all the world is a show for their amusement.

She also was a punctual though silent attendant of the weekly female prayer-meeting. It was said Miss Zarviah never had uttered her voice among the sisters but once, when, in a faded old green calash and a shrunken washed-out merino shawl, she uttered an emphatic testimony against the vanity of dress and the temptations to worldliness in this regard.

The old inhabitants of Hindford said that Miss Zarviah came of a very respectable family. Her father, Squire Avery, was a deacon in the church, selectman in the village, and a thriving, well-to-do farmer, but the family had dropped away one by one, and she was left, like the last fluttering leaf of the gaunt catalpa in her door-yard, desolate and without a kindred leaf to speak to.

When both parents died Miss Zarviah was left guardian of a younger brother about ten years of age, who with herself was joint heir to the estate. Now Miss Zarviah loved her brother with all her heart, but, unluckily, she felt it her duty to show her love in ways that make a boy specially uncomfortable.

She was always checking and reproving him, and setting his sins in order before him. These were many. He came in without wiping his shoes ; he hung his hat on the wrong nail, or did n't hang it anywhere ; he slopped water when he went to help himself to it ; he whistled ; he drummed ; he brought home and domesticated a puppy who was seven-fold more mischievous than he was.

He was always taming rabbits and squirrels and birds, who all made litter and dirt. Above all, he whittled from morning till night everywhere.

His clothes were in a chronic state of dilapidation, — hat, trousers, stockings, shoes, all giving out before his endless activity.

Poor Miss Zarviah was in despair, and told him so in varied phrases almost every hour of the twenty-four till he began to have an uneasy sense of being a sinner all the time, simply for being a boy. He was secretly of the opinion that his sister hated him, — a point where he did her the greatest injustice.

When he was fourteen years old he fell out of a boat in one of his fishing expeditions, wet himself to the skin, and had in consequence one of those good old-fashioned " runs " of fever, that used to be the support of village doctors, and Miss Zarviah nursed him with unfailing care and tenderness, and used to rehearse to her friends how for ten days and nights she never had her clothes off, nor got a regular night's rest.

So her boy was nursed back from the very borders of the grave, but as soon as he was up and well, he began again to be a sinner, and Miss Zarviah to tell him so.

There is an age when the waves of manhood pour in on the boy like the tides in the Bay of Fundy. He does not know himself what to do with himself, and nobody else knows, either ; and it is exactly at this point that many a fine fellow has been ruined for want of faith and patience and hope in those who have the care of him.

When Eben Avery was seventeen, he flung away from the homestead and his sister at the end of a bitter discussion, in which many sharp and true things had been said on both sides, and away he went to California, seeking his fortune.

He never wrote. He had committed the oversight of his share of the property to a faithful old lawyer, a friend of his father, through whom Miss Zarviah heard only that he was living and doing well, — and so she was left alone.

But there was a sore spot in her old heart. A conscientious person should beware of getting into a passion, for every sharp word one speaks comes back and lodges like a

sliver in one's own heart; and such slivers hurt us worse
than they ever can any one else.

It was true she was now mistress of the house, with not
a soul to disarrange any of her matters. She could clean
and shut up rooms, and nobody opened them. There was
no litter, no dirt anywhere, for there was nobody to make
any. She and her house were as clean and orderly as she
wanted to be; nobody whittled; nobody whistled; there
were no footsteps to track the floors; no tramping up and
down stairs.

The old clock ticked away hour after hour, the only sound
to be heard in the ancient dwelling. Miss Avery had a sort
of shivering, unspoken sense of lonesomeness. The waters
of life were freezing around her, and the circle unfrozen narrowed every year, as one crony and acquaintance after another dropped out of life and came no more.

Still, from year to year, she opened and aired chambers
that nobody ever slept in, and at stated intervals routed
everything out and conducted a severe house-cleaning where
no dirt had been made. As for her own personal quarters,
they had narrowed themselves down into one room, which
was to her bedroom, kitchen, and sitting-room.

The old family "keeping-room" was shut up and kept in
an immaculately clean state, with its bright brass andirons,
with a bright brass candlestick on each end of the mantel-
piece. One day in a week she scrubbed the white floor on
her hands and knees, as also the table and dresser in like
manner. All her tins were brightened, and everything made
resplendent, and she sat down to her knitting victorious.

One would have said that she had nothing to do but to
rest on her laurels, but alas! perfection is not for mortals.

The dust from the avenue before the house, kept lively
by whirling carriages, would filter through the cracks of the
old mansion, and rest on tables and chairs in a manner to
keep her combativeness on the stretch.

Then rats and mice bred, mustered, and multiplied in the house. Certain cockroaches, too, had invaded the ancient dwelling, and set up housekeeping in its old cracks and crannies. In vain Miss Avery scolded, scrubbed, scoured; they throve and multiplied and grew impudently bold.

But the dust and the cockroaches, and the rats and the mice, were nothing to another trial of Miss Zarviah's life,—*the boys!*

Back of her fence ran a little alley that abounded with some of the noisiest and most graceless little wretches in Hindford. These boys were in the habit of swarming over her fence and through her yard as a shorter cut to the avenue.

This, which was at first a matter of mere convenience, became amusing to the boys when Miss Zarviah, broom in hand, and with her mouth filled with objurgations, chased them and ordered them out of her yard, and threatened them with the police.

Then the matter became exciting, and the fun of making old Witch Avery mad, cutting through her yard and over her fence, and hearing her scold when safely lodged behind it, was a stimulating form of recreation to these graceless little wretches, and great were the glee of the boys and the energetic rage of Miss Zarviah on one of these occasions, which is the subject of our next chapter.

Such was Miss Zarviah, such her troubles and tribulations, when our story opens.

CHAPTER II

IT was a dreary, dripping November night, just between daylight and dusk. Miss Zarviah had hung on her lonely tea-kettle, and was proceeding with her arrangements for an evening meal, when, Whoop! hurrah! hallo! and a sound of a yelping dog and of pattering footsteps came through her yard.

Instantly she seized the broom, and ran and opened the back door. Something that looked like a draggled bundle of rags swept by her into the house with a rattling noise, and fled into the room and under her bed.

"Now, you wretches, if you don't get out this minute, I'll—"

Vigorous blows of the broom finished the sentence. The little imps danced and shouted, but retreated towards the fence.

"We want our dog. He's run into your old house!" shouted the boldest.

"You sha'n't have your dog! and if you don't clear out, I'll call the watch!" and Miss Avery seconded her words with well-directed thwacks and thumps, which sent the whole posse in a giggling cataract over the fence, behind which rose such parting salutes as these:

"Who cares for you, old Witch Avery?"

"We'll come in for all you!"

"Catch us if you can! Where's your policeman?" and away they went.

Miss Avery went in and shut the door.

She came back into her room and hung up her broom. She felt on the whole that she had gained a victory, — the enemy had lost the dog and she had got him.   That was some comfort, and instantly her whole nature rose in determination that they never should have him again.

She looked under her bed, and there, crouching in the far corner, the fire-light gleamed upon a pair of great mournful eyes, and a subdued whine came from the obscurity.

Miss Avery never had been fond of dogs, but this dog she had resolved to protect, and all her combativeness was on his side.

"Come here, doggie!" she said; "good doggie!"   So she tried to call him out.

But the tones were rather dry, and wanting in native cordiality, and doggie only crouched farther in his corner, and gave another piteous whine.

Miss Zarviah moved the bed, and walking straight into the dark corner, reached down and took him.

The poor wretch was drabbled with mud, and an old tin kettle, which had been tied to his tail, rattled dubiously as she lifted him.

"Well, did I ever!" exclaimed Miss Zarviah, and she brought him out to the fire-light, and setting him down, put on her spectacles, took her scissors and cut the string.

The pail fell off, and the creature looked up at her with his great sad eyes, and licked her hand humbly.

"Well, I do declare! you poor cre'tur!" said Miss Zarviah.

The dog was quivering and trembling with wet, cold, and fright, but seemed to understand that Miss Zarviah meant well by him; he tried to wag his bedraggled tail, and then raising himself on his hind legs, he made vigorous gestures of supplication with his two fore-paws.   Evidently this was an accomplishment which had been taught him in more prosperous days, and which he now brought forth as a means of conciliation.

It had its effect on Miss Zarviah.

"Well, I will," she said; "poor doggie! I won't let any one catch you again; but you must be washed clean."

And Miss Zarviah brought a small tub which she filled tenderly and carefully, adding warm water from her tea-kettle, and testing it with her hand as if for a baby. Then she produced soap and towels, and set to work vigorously.

She washed and scrubbed till the dog seemed really to half melt away, and be no bigger than a good-sized cat. Then she wiped him dry, wrapped him in an old flannel petticoat, tucked him up in a basket, and set him in the warmest corner to dry, while she proceeded to get her supper.

Her protégé stopped shivering, gave a sound of satisfaction as he nestled himself in the warm flannel, and followed her with his great bright eyes as she arranged her supper.

Miss Avery was methodical in all her ways, and this night was the precise night of the week when she always made milk toast, and so milk toast she proceeded to make.

She shook down a glowing clear bed of coals; she cut a couple of slices of very nice bread; she put a skillet of milk down to heat, and proceeded to toast her bread on the end of a long fork. The large bright eyes in the flannel surveyed these proceedings with much apparent interest.

When the milk was poured into the skillet, there was a stir in the basket, and the occupant struggled to get a good view of her progress.

"The cre'tur really seems to know that there are victuals getting ready," said Miss Zarviah; "no doubt he's hungry;" and with this thought she cut another half slice.

When the dipped toast was made, and the tea drawn, and the little round stand set out before the fire, and Miss Avery sat down to enjoy her tea, there was another commotion in the flannel.

Miss Avery looked; the dog was standing up in his basket, gazing very intelligently at the tea-table.

"Lie down, doggie," she said, "you shall have your supper by and by."

But doggie did not lie down, but got out of his basket, and gave himself a shake and a lick here and there, and having repaired to the best of his ability the defects in his toilet, he came and sat down by Miss Zarviah, and rising on his hind legs, made as before supplicating gestures with his fore-paws.

The mouthful of dipped toast that was going to Miss Zarviah's mouth was arrested, and she held it to him.

He took it off her fork and swallowed it with evident appreciation.

"Well, did I ever!" said Miss Avery. "No, I never did; why, the cre'tur all but talks! Well, well," she said, "you shall have your supper right away," and she cut up his half-slice of toast, and put a liberal allowance of milk over it, and set it down before him, and he fell to work at it with gratifying earnestness.

Miss Avery certainly enjoyed seeing the way that half-slice of toast was disposed of more than she did the corresponding morsel which she was eating herself.

"What, more?" she said, cheerfully, as, after the half-slice had disappeared, the great, bright, silent eyes looked up at her; and immediately the saucer was replenished with another portion nicely cut-up, which speedily went the way of the former; and thus sociably she and her protégé finished the supper.

CHAPTER III

"WELL, of all things! Who would have thought it?" mused Miss Avery, as, supper being over, she leaned back in her chair and took a dispassionate survey of her new acquisition.

He was now quite dry, and his soft flossy hair of a fine silver color would, if Miss Avery had known anything of such matters, have proclaimed him a dog of blood and breeding; one of those sagacious little Scotch terriers that are pets in high places.

But Miss Avery only knew that he was a *dog* who, by a strange "Providence," as she called it, had become *her* dog, and now she was meditating what to call him.

Her mind reverted to the days long since, when Eben brought home the puppy that made such trouble, and called him Trip.

"Poor Eben!" she said, "I reely was hard on him. I wish now I had been more patient with Trip — just for his sake. Well, well, we do things that we can't take back, if we want to ever so much," and Miss Avery gave a sigh to those old days, and concluded to call her adopted pet Trip.

She tried the name on him, and he looked bright and wise, and started at it to go after her as she moved about the room, setting up dishes and sweeping the hearth.

If ever a dog could express eager, quivering, joyful devotion, it was Trip; and his assent to being called by this name

was so unequivocal that Miss Avery flattered herself she
had hit upon the very cognomen he had always gone by.

Miss Avery swept up the hearth, mended her fire, and took
out her knitting-work.   Trip, who had no knitting-work of
his own, looked ardent interest in and approbation of all her
movements.

It was a new sensation to Miss Zarviah to be looked upon
with such admiration and devotion as were evident in Trip's
great soft eyes.   He seemed so every way companionable
that she could not help talking to him.

"Did the wicked boys plague you?" she said, in a sympathizing tone.   "Well, they sha'n't any more; I'll take
care of you."

The effect of these words was most unexpected.   Trip
jumped up and rested his paws against Miss Avery's knees
a moment, and then, as if taking a sudden resolution, he
sprang into her lap boldly, and began kissing her face with
eager dog-caresses.

"Oh! oh!   Why, Trip-*pee*!   Why! *why*!   Good dog!
Don't! don't!" said Miss Avery, as much flustered as if it
was a suitor that was declaring his regard for her.   "There,
there! get down, Trip."

But Trip had no idea of getting down; he only quirled
himself round, and established himself composedly in the
hollow of her lap.

"Did I ever!" said Miss Avery; "he's determined to
sit in my lap; well, if you will, you will," and Trip nestled
down, closed his eyes, and seemed inclined to take a nap in
this comfortable situation.

Outside the wind whistled drearily; the rain dripped
from the eaves with a dull, lonely thud; but inside the fire
purred and snapped and crackled, and the knitting-needle
clicked, and Miss Avery said to herself, —

"Well, how much company a cre'tur is!" and she
looked down at Trip with patronizing complacency.

Miss Avery had not had so pleasant an evening within her recollection.

It seemed wonderful to her that she, who had always despised dogs and opposed their way, should be sitting now with one in her lap, and enjoying his being there. Certainly, there must be a Providence in it, said Miss Avery.

When the clock struck nine, Miss Avery knit into her seam-needle, and rolled up her knitting-work, and then, in company with Trip, proceeded to fasten and bolt all the doors, and to take a tour of survey through all the house, and look under every bed and in every closet, lest a robber might have slipped in and hidden himself.

Trip entered into this survey in high spirits, scampering before her, racing into corners, smelling complacently at rat-holes, and giving here and there a lively bark, for Trip had rat-catching blood in his veins, and felt his foot upon his native heath in an old rat-haunted house.

He ran under beds with cheerful alacrity, and saved Miss Avery's creaking joints the trouble.

When they entered the pantry there was a sudden scuffle and squeak, and Trip stood growling and glorious, his soft eyes blazing, shaking a rat in his teeth.

It was all over with Mr. Rat in a minute ; but Trip barked and leaped and shook the victim over, and thrice he slew the slain.

" Well, I declare, you are a good dog ; there's that rat that has been plaguing me night after night ! " and Miss Avery glorified and fondled Trip to his heart's content, and was more than ever convinced that he was "a Providence."

CHAPTER IV

HE MAKES HIMSELF AGREEABLE

WHEN they were a little settled down from this excitement, Miss Avery raked up the fire, and proceeded to array herself for the night, putting on a portentous night-cap that so altered her appearance that Trip at first ran away and barked, and was only to be reconciled when she stroked and talked to him.

Then she arranged his basket in the warm corner, put him in it, and told him to lie down and be a good doggie, and, having extinguished her candle, turned in to her bed.

She felt a sweet serenity and composure in having her protégé so nicely disposed of, and shut her eyes, and was dropping off to sleep, when a tick of paws on the floor aroused her.

Trip had got out of his basket, and was standing by her bedside looking up wistfully.

"Why, Trip, Trippy! what's the matter? Go lie down, Trip!"

A whine, and a begging gesture of the fore-paws.

"Trippy, go lie down; there's a good dog."

Instead of this, Trip gave a spring, and jumped upon the foot of the bed, with evident indications that he wanted to sleep there.

She was astonished at his presumption, and rising, she took him firmly in her arms, and, carrying him back to his basket, said, as she laid him down, —

" There, Trip, that is a nice warm bed in a warm corner,

and you must lie down and be still." And she patted him
down, and drew the flannel over him.

Trip made no more remarks for that time, but lay quite
still in his basket; and Miss Avery, complacently reflect-
ing how easy it was to train dogs in the way they should
go, resigned herself to her slumbers.

Soon as a fine high piping through the nose announced
that Miss Avery was sound asleep, Master Trip ticked
quietly across the floor, jumped upon the bed, and settled
himself in a comfortable little ball at her feet.

The next morning early, Miss Avery, feeling a remarkable warmth in the region of her feet, looked down and saw
the foot-warmer that had established himself there.

The moment she moved, Trip frisked to the top of the
bed, and kissed her face, and seemed so delighted and
overjoyed to see her awake that she had not the heart to
scold him.

" The cre'tur 's ben used to sleeping on somebody's bed,"
she said, " and he was lonesome, poor fellow! Well,
Trippy, you 've kept my feet beautiful and warm, any-
how."

Miss Avery now began to reflect on the responsibilities
she had assumed. Trip was certainly a lively, entertaining
companion, and he had warmed quite a place in her half-
frozen heart; but he was evidently a thoughtless, frisky,
heedless fellow, that would be sure to fall into the enemy's
hands again if she did n't look after him.

So, the first thing after breakfast, she did what she had
so long vainly threatened to do, went to the policeman who
had charge of her beat, — a good-natured man, who went
to the same church with her, — and detailed to him with
some warmth her persecutions from the boys of the neighboring alley; whereupon he took down their names, and
assured Miss Avery that he would look after them; and
then she went to a carpenter near by, and, as a consequence

of this interview, her backyard before night was adorned
along the top with a row of sharp, lively spikes, set points
uppermost, so as to render it entirely ineligible as a mode
of entrance or egress.   So she began to feel herself forti-
fied and defended in the possession of her new treasure.

After a week of seclusion, to make sure that Trip would
not run away, Miss Avery took him with her whenever she
went to market to look out her daily meals, to the stores,
and along the constitutional walks which she maintained
for the benefit of her health.

But Sundays and prayer-meeting evenings were seasons
of heavy affliction to him.   Trip wanted to go to church
like a good Christian.

Twice he scandalized Miss Avery by jumping out of a
window, and surreptitiously following her to church, appearing before her pew door with a joyous and confident
air, as much as to say, " Why, you forgot to take me ! "
and Miss Avery, to her great mortification, was obliged to
take him out, with boys and children looking on and titter-
ing in a distressing manner.

Once, too, he got into prayer-meeting, nestling so discreetly and quietly under her skirts that she never saw him
till the services were over.   Then he was wild with delight
at his success, and barked in a most disreputable manner
all the way home.

Trip was always scurrying off after cats, or hens, or other
dogs, in their daily promenades, to her poignant anxiety
and affliction.

At last, while whirling across a crossing to speak to another dog who was running with a carriage, he got tumbled
under the wheel, and broke one of his fore-paws, and came
back to Miss Avery crying and limping on three legs.

If Miss Avery could have been told a year before of the
patience, the loving kindness, with which she was to nurse
a dog through indiscretions like these, she would almost

have said, with the Scriptural character, " Is thy servant a
dog to do this ? "

But the fact was, that Trip seemed only to win the more
on her heart for having broken his paw.

Miss Avery bandaged it and wet it with camphor, held
him in her lap, let him sleep on her bed ; and two or three
times in the night, when he cried, got up to wet his bandage,
and to console and comfort him.

Poor Miss Avery ! No more alone in the world, for
there was this little silver-colored thing with dark eyes that
adored her, worshiped her, depended on her, and that she
thought and cared for and loved in return.

So wore the winter away ; but in the spring, when the
new leaves came out on the trees, a new leaf was turned
in Miss Avery's history.

CHAPTER V

BLUE EYES COMES TO SEE HIM

"PLEASE, ma'am, may I come in and see your dog?"

These words were spoken on a bright June day, when the lilacs were abloom in front of the old house. Miss Avery stood out on the stone flagging at the back side of her house doing some washing, and Trip was present helping her.

The words were piped up in a clear little voice that seemed to come from fairy land. Miss Avery was at first dazed and astonished, and turned round to look for the speaker.

A pair of great blue eyes were looking up at her out of a cloud of curly hair. A little cambric sunbonnet hung loosely back on the shoulders of a small maiden who seemed to have risen out of the flagstones.

"Eh! What? What do you say?" said Miss Avery.

"I said, 'Please let me see your Carlo, ma'am,'" said the little girl, making movements towards Trip.

"His name is n't Carlo; it 's Trip," said Miss Avery, shortly.

"Oh, is it? I thought it was Carlo. May n't I play with him, please, ma'am?"

Trip, meanwhile, had run to the little girl, and was investigating her character, applying his nose seriously to her shoes and dress, and, apparently satisfied, jumped up and fawned upon her.

"He 's just like a dog I had once that we called Carlo,"

said the little voice. "That's the reason I wanted to see him."

"But he is *my dog*, child," said Miss Avery, with a withering frown, "and I don't want anybody to come toling him away."

"Oh," said Blue Eyes, in the most conciliatory tones, "I know he's your dog. I didn't mean to say that he *was* my Carlo, only that he was *like* my Carlo, and that was why I wanted to play with him. I love dogs. I won't tole him away, and I won't make any trouble, not a bit. I just want to stroke him and play with him a little, he's such a dear little doggie ; and see, he loves me," and Trip, springing up, kissed the little face with tumultuous caresses.

"Well, well, child, there's no harm in your stroking him as I know of, but you mustn't try to get him away," said Miss Avery, but half pleased with the intimacy that she saw was beginning.

"Oh, I shan't, indeed I shan't ; you can see. I'll just play with him here a few minutes, — it's our recess now, and I can't stay long, — and I'll be very careful not to trouble you. He looks so much like my Carlo that I lost. He run away last fall, and we never could find him."

Now Miss Avery felt a severe twinge of conscience. She was, in fact, the most ultra-conscientious person in all that respected the right of property.

She couldn't help the uncomfortable reflection, "What if this were in fact somebody else's dog ?"

It was a question she did not wish to have opened for discussion.

She did not mean to believe any thing of that kind, and was determined to make good her right in him.

But she compromised with her conscience in thinking she would let the little girl come and enjoy his society under her own auspices.

So when the child said, —

"I guess it's time to go back to school now, but if you'll let me, I'll come next recess," Miss Avery responded graciously, —

"If you'll be a good little girl and not make any trouble, you may come and play with the dog whenever you like."

"Oh, thank you, ma'am. I'll try to be as good; I'll be very quiet, and do just as you tell me," and the little puss gave a parting kiss and hug to Trip, and then made a courtesy to Miss Avery, and ran off to her school.

"It isn't — it can't — it *shan't* be her dog," said Miss Avery to herself. "I saved his life; he'd have been dead before now if it hadn't been for me. Who has the best right, a little careless chit like that, that never ought to be trusted with a cre'tur, or one that knows how to take care of 'em! Besides, Trip *loves* me: he wants to stay with me, and cre'turs have some rights; they know who they want to stay with, and they ought to stay where they are taken care of. Trip is happy here, and he ought to stay here."

Thus Miss Avery reasoned while stirring about her housework, sweeping, dusting, and scouring on the immaculate keeping-room.

"You love me, don't you, Trip?" she often asked, stopping for a moment in her work, and Trip frisked and jumped and licked her face and hands, and in every possible inflection of dog dialect professed his undying fealty and devotion.

"What nonsense! What a fool I am to worry," she said; "jest for that little chit who don't know one dog from another. Suppose she did have a dog run away. Does that prove that this is the dog? Of course not. The city is full of dogs; one dog looks just like another. Besides, her dog was named Carlo, and this one was named

Trip.   I knew his name was Trip ; he knew his name the
first time I called it.   Don't tell *me !* " and Miss Avery
shook her head threateningly at an imaginary opponent,
and as she had an old red handkerchief tied over it with
flapping ends, her head-shaking appeared really formidable
and convincing.   Trip barked at her once or twice, she
looked so very belligerent.

CHAPTER VI

THE WOMAN WHO HATES DOGS

Now little Blue Eyes had the fullest conviction in her wise young heart that this was her own dog — her lost Carlo. Her father had bought for her in New York a little silky silver-colored Scotch terrier, and given fifty dollars for him, on purpose that Blue Eyes might have him for a playmate and confidential friend while her mother and he were gone.

But, unfortunately, Mrs. Symons, in whose house and under whose care the little one was placed, was one of those good women who hate dogs of every degree. She never would have one in the house if she could help it, and Carlo was sedulously kept outside of the house at all times, except when his little mistress was at home. If he happened to stray into the parlor or dining-room, the good lady seemed to feel that the place had been polluted, — his hair, she declared, would come off on the sofa or chairs, or he would be sure to do some mysterious mischief, and so he was broomed out ignominiously as soon as Bright Eyes' back was turned.

Carlo naturally did n't like this state of things. He became despondent and timorous, and would make frequent excursions into the street in the forlorn hope of looking for his young mistress. In one of these excursions he fell into the hands of the rabble of boys that infested Miss Avery's back lane, and for six months had been lost to the sight, though dear to the memory, of poor little Blue Eyes.

So, the first day she had seen him at Miss Avery's, she

went home and announced that she had found Carlo. The
news was received with very active opposition on the part
of Mrs. Symons.

" Why, no, child ! you can't have found Carlo ! How do
you know ? There are dozens of dogs of that sort. Carlo
has been gone these six months, and for my part I am glad
of it; he was nothing but a plague."

" Well, at any rate, Miss Avery says I may come and see
him, and play with him at her house," said Blue Eyes, " and
that's better than having him here, because Miss Avery
likes him, and is kind to him."

" What! that old cross Miss Avery ? "

" She isn't cross; she's just as good as she can be to
Carlo. She calls him 'Trip,' she thinks everything of him,
and she says I may come to see him as often as I 've a mind
to ; and I shall go and see him every day, and all Saturday
afternoon," said the little one, resolutely, as she went up-
stairs.

" Wife," said Mr. Symons, who had been listening to this
talk from the next room, " did she say it was Miss Avery
she was visiting ? "

" Yes ; " said his helpmeet.

" Well, let her go there. But what is the attraction ?
Not Miss Avery's personal charms, I 'm sure."

" No ; it 's a little dog that the child thinks is like hers
that ran away. For my part, I think like enough it *is* hers.
But I 'd rather Miss Avery would keep it than have it back
in the house here. I hate dogs, and I was glad when it ran
away. But just to think that the child should go right to
the house of her own aunt ! "

Now Mr. Symons was the friendly lawyer to whom Eben
Avery had committed the management of his property. The
little girl had been left with him this summer, while the
parents were away attending to some necessary business.
In the fall they were to come back, and then there was to
be an attempt at a final settlement of the Avery estate.

Eben Avery had become a stout, cheery, well-to-do man of forty, had come back from California, and was desirous now to return to Hindford and build a house on the old place.

Miss Avery's life-right in the ancient ruinous dwelling was all that stood in the way of the plan, and Mr. Symons had long been searching for acceptable words wherewith to break to her the news of her brother's return, and of his plans.

He had mentally surveyed her as a fortress to be carried, and had not known where to effect an entrance. When, therefore, he heard what the little one had done, he put his hands in his pockets, and gave a contented whistle.

"Well," he said, "the old woman's such a crotchety, crabbed old thing, I did n't know how to go to work with her; and there was no saying whether she 'd take to Eben, or whether she 'd rake up the old grudge. There 's never knowing what folks will do in their family quarrels. But there 's a soft streak in the old lady, it appears. Better let Patty Coram work on her. She 'll bring her round, if anybody can. Of course, she don't know whose child it is?"

"Oh no; I don't think she does."

"Well, tell Patty Coram not to tell her. There 's never any saying with these crotchety people. It might spoil all the fun if she knew whose daughter she was. She 'd get going over the old story of the quarrel between her and Eben, and maybe it would set her against the girl."

So Mrs. Symons warned the little one, with many a head-shake, that old Miss Avery was very queer indeed, and she better not tell her name to her — it might make the old lady cross, and she would n't let her come; but that if she were careful she might go and see Carlo as often as she liked. And Mrs. Symons congratulated herself that the dreadful dog was thus taken care of in a way to both satisfy his young mistress and keep him out of her own way.

CHAPTER VII

THE next day the little girl came again, and this time the interview was accorded in the house.

It was bright June weather, and the "keeping-room" windows were open, and the smell of lilacs came pleasantly in, and Miss Avery sat with her sewing. "Oh, how pleasant it is here," said Blue Eyes. "I'm *so* glad you let me come. I do *love* Trip so, and Trip is glad to see me, ain't you, Trip?"

Trip responded to this with his usual effusion, expending so many caresses on the little face that Miss Avery began to feel a twinge of jealousy.

"What is your name, little girl?" she said.

"Oh, I've got lots of names. Papa calls me Pussy and Daisy; and Mr. Symons calls me Patty Coram, and Aunty Symons calls me Pet, and I don't know which is my name."

"Do you live with Mr. Symons?"

"Yes, I'm staying with them now till my papa and mamma come; they're gone a journey now, and Aunt Symons takes care of me while they're gone, and I go to school to the school-house on this street,—that's where I go to school,—and it's so near I can come in at recess; but it's time to go now," said the little maid, running for her bonnet. "Please, Miss Avery, may I come here to-morrow afternoon? To-morrow is Saturday, and I can stay a good long while."

Miss Avery looked intently into the great, wide, earnest blue eyes that were looking up from her knee,—it was as if a blue violet were talking to her,— and the little rosy mouth quivered with earnestness.

She said, " Yes, my dear," in a voice softer than she was in the habit of using. The little one, with an impulsive movement, threw her arms round her neck and kissed her.

" Oh," said Miss Avery, half-pleased, half-shocked, " you should n't kiss such an old thing as I am."

" Yes I should, because you are good to me," said Blue Eyes, as she kissed her again, and then tripped lightly away.

Miss Avery sat in a sort of maze. Those kisses had roused a commotion in her dry old heart.

" What a dear little thing it is ! " she said. " Strange she should want to kiss me,— my poor old withered face ! Well, if she 's coming to-morrow —"

Miss Avery here rose and went to her pantry. As if inspired by a new thought, she changed her dress immediately, and put on one devoted to cooking, and went to work with flour and sugar and spices to compound some cakes such as she remembered Eben used to love. She sifted, she grated, she pounded, she beat eggs, to Trip's great amazement.

" Yes, Trippy," she said, " you and I are going to have company to-morrow, and we must get ready, Trippy, must n't we ? "

Trip responded vigorously to the suggestion, and flew about in a very active manner to express his pleasure in the proceedings.

Miss Avery cleared her fire, and put down her tin baker, and soon the cakes rose clear and light, and browned to her heart's content.

" I 'll frost them," she said, meditatively. " Children always like frosting. Oh, if I had only some caraway sugar-plums to put on top ! Oh, you Trip, if you were good for anything, I could send you over to get some caraways."

But as Trip, with all his activity, could not compass this errand, Miss Avery changed her dress again, and went across to a confectioner's, and bought an ounce of caraway sugar-plums of divers colors most brilliant to behold, wherewith, on her return, she adorned the frosting of her little cakes.

Then Miss Avery remembered an upper drawer in which there was a china image of a little white lamb standing in a very green china hedge of very pink and blue flowers, and this lamb she now drew out of his hiding-place.

It was given to her when she was a little girl, and as she looked at it, her thoughts traveled back to the days when she was no higher than this little one, and when Saturday afternoon was a paradise of untold brightness for her.

She set it on the mantel-piece between the candlesticks, and in front of the snuffer-tray.

Then she proceeded to cover a ball of old ravelings with some bright flannels, and fasten a long cord to it, for the little girl and Trip to play with together ; and just to try its effects, she threw it time and again, and laughed to see Trip scamper after it.

"Why, what a fool I am ! " she said, when she had consumed about half an hour playing with Trip.

Miss Avery was beginning to feel young again.

CHAPTER VIII

A BRIGHT SATURDAY AFTERNOON

THE keeping-room wore quite a festive air. Some purple and white lilacs in an old china vase adorned the table, and Miss Avery, conscious of stores of attractions in her cupboard, had been waiting impatiently for her little visitor, when she heard a knock at the front door, and it was a race between her and Trip which should get to it first.

Trip's joyful barks filled the house, while Miss Avery pulled and jerked the old front door, which, being rheumatic and unused to opening, hung obstinately back, and at last flew open with a bounce that was like to upset them both.

"There, now!" said the little one. "It's Saturday afternoon, and I can stay till sundown; ain't you glad?" she asked, looking up at Miss Avery with great, clear, wide blue eyes.

"To be sure I am," said Miss Avery, heartily, as she hung up the little bonnet; and then, taking down the china lamb from the mantel, she said, "See there! that's what I used to play with when I was a little girl; you shall play with it when you come to see me."

"Oh, how beautiful! May I take it?" said the child.

"Yes," said Miss Avery; and stooping shyly towards her, as she handed the toy, she said, —

"Have n't you got another kiss for me?"

"Oh, dear, yes," said the little one, throwing her arms round her neck. "I've got twenty kisses for you; for I really love you, 'cause you are so good."

"No, no, I'm not good," said Miss Avery, with a half-sigh; "I'm a poor, homely, cross old woman."

"No, you're not; you're not cross a bit. Nobody shall say you are cross, shall they, Trippy? Trip knows how good you are, don't he, Trippy?" And Trip barked an energetic testimony of Miss Avery's goodness.

Miss Avery felt the sweet flattery of a child's love with a new and strange delight, and all the lines of her face softened and lighted up, so that she looked almost handsome.

The small visitor now chattered on like a little brook over stones, running here and there, and asking questions about everything she saw.

"What funny chamber stairs!" she said, as she peeped into the entry; "they look just like pieces of pie. Can Trippy and I go and see what is up there?"

"Oh, yes; I'll show you," said Miss Avery; and she took the little girl and Trip the round of the chambers above.

One of them was kept with a special nicety. The window curtains were spotless and white, the bed was neatly made; there was a writing-table with books and papers on it.

"This was my brother's room," said Miss Avery.

"Where is he?" said the little one, innocently.

"I don't know," said Miss Avery, and her countenance fell.

The little one picked up a book on the table, and opened it, and read on the fly-leaf, —

"EBEN AVERY."

"Why, that's my papa's name!" she said; "his name's Eben Avery."

Miss Avery turned pale and sat down in a chair, putting her hand to her head. The room seemed to go round for a moment; but in a moment more she commanded herself, and said, —

"Your papa's name Eben Avery? Where is he?"

"He's traveling now. I don't know where he and mamma are, but he's coming here by and by. We used to live way, way, *way* off, out in California; but papa is coming to live here in Hindford."

"Oh, you dear child! you dear child!" said Miss Avery, catching her in her arms with a sort of dry sob. "Why, I'm your own aunty! Your father was my brother Eben. This used to be his room when he was a boy. Thank the Lord I see you!" she said.

"Well, there now! I knew you must be my aunty," said the little one cheerily, "you are so good to me; you are my ownty downty aunty, and I shall love you always;" and this was confirmed by a shower of kisses.

"Yes, yes," said Miss Avery. "I wasn't good to your poor father; I was cross to him. I didn't mean to be cross, but I was; but I'll never be cross to you, my darling. I'll make it all up to you."

"I don't believe you ever was cross to papa or anybody else," said the child sturdily.

"Yes, I was; but I've been very sorry ever since, and I hope he won't lay it up against me," said Miss Avery, humbly.

"Oh, indeed, papa will love you, I know! Papa is always good to everybody; and as full of fun! he's always making people laugh and have good times."

"He never told you what a cross old sister I was?"

"Oh, indeed, he didn't! he said how you used to sit up with him and nurse him when he was sick."

"Did he remember that? Well, I did love Eben, though I didn't always act like it."

"I'm ever so glad," remarked Blue Eyes, "that you *are* my aunty, 'cause now you'll come and live with us. You and I and Trip, — we'll live together; won't it be fun?"

Miss Avery laughed, — she had n't felt so gleeful for
years, —and then, when she had opened all her drawers
and all her cupboards, and showed everything she had in
the house, and answered questions without end, the happy
party came down again and produced Trip's ball, and soon
she and little Blue Eyes and Trip were engaged in a real
romp, and the old house rang with peals of laughter and
barks, and there was such scampering and pattering and
skurrying about as had n't been known for years. Miss
Avery got her hair loosened and her cheeks red, and laughed
till she had to sit down and hold her sides.

When tired of this fun, Miss Avery recovered her dignity,
and set herself seriously to getting tea, in which business
Blue Eyes and Trip assisted according to their ability.

The little round table was set in the keeping-room, and
some nice biscuits were baked in the baker before the fire,
and tea was made, and finally, as a crowning glory, the plate
of frosted cakes, gay with many-colored sugar-plums, was
put on the table.

Miss Avery was not disappointed in the sensation they
produced. The little one clapped her hands, and laughed
and admired, and Trip barked, and altogether they had a
merry time of it.

They sat down at table, with Trip between them deco-
rously mounted on his cushion, and Miss Avery said grace,
and Trip looked as sober and devout as if he had two legs
instead of four, a feat which Blue Eyes warmly commended.

"Trip knows just how to behave at table, don't he?" she
said; "that's because you've taught him, aunty."

"Yes, Trip is a good dog," said Miss Avery; "you see he
waits till I fix his supper for him."

It was a joyous tea-party, and full justice was done to the
cakes, and Miss Avery went back into long histories of the
old days when Eben was a boy, and the house stood on a
farm far out from the city, and they used to have hens and

chickens, and pigs and ducks, and all sorts of nice things. Miss Avery seemed to grow young again as she told the story.

"Now, dear, what is your name?" she said; "you never really told me your name."

"Well, my real name is Margaret; but they call me lots of other things, — Daisy, and Dot, and Puss, and Mr. Symons calls me Patty Coram and Chatterbox; he's a funny man, Mr. Symons is."

"Margaret — I knew it — it's mother's name," said Miss Avery. "Dear, your grandmother was a good woman — you are named after her — I hope you'll be like her."

When the sun sank low, the child started for home with two cakes, that she could not eat, stuffed in her small pocket.

There were kisses exchanged, and promises to come again. As she trotted gayly off, Miss Avery gazed after her till the last of her little pink dress faded in the distance.

"Thank the Lord! thank the Lord!" she said. "He has been good to me."

CHAPTER IX

A JOYFUL SUNDAY

Miss Avery woke next morning with a vague sense of some sudden good fortune, and gradually the events of the day before came over her.

She was no more alone in the world, with nobody to love and nobody loving. She rejoiced in her little niece as one that findeth great spoil.

She stepped about alertly getting her breakfast; she went up stairs and set open the windows of Eben's room. The purple and white lilacs looked in inquisitively as to say, —

"What now?"

"He'll come here; Eben will come back now. Well, he'll see I've kept his room for him," said Miss Avery, as she smoothed a wrinkle on the bed and flecked a little dust from the table.

The first bells were ringing for church; to her they seemed joy-bells; and Miss Avery dressed herself to go out with a light heart. Trip ran to her quivering with eagerness. Miss Avery's heart was touched for him.

"Trippy, you poor doggie! I'm sorry, but I can't take you to church," she said, as he stood wagging his tail, and looking eagerly at her. "It's Sunday, Trippy, and you can't go to church with me, though you are a great deal more up to your light than some who do go."

Miss Avery explained this over to Trippy, but it didn't seem to convince him; and when she left the house, he stood on his hind legs at the window barking frantically.

Miss Avery's mind in sermon-time wandered to her little niece. She saw her blue eyes, and felt her caresses and kisses, and her heart was glad within her; and she caught herself in sermon-time projecting how she would make some "crullers," and sift sugar over them for the child's delectation when she came to see her old aunty.

"I'm afraid I shall make an idol of that child," she said to herself when she found where her thoughts had been wandering.

When she got home Trippy was outrageous in his joy.

"It's worth going out for, to have any cre'tur so glad to see one," she said. "Ah, Trippy! you was a Providence. If it had not been for you, Trippy, she would n't 'a' ben here, Trippy! Trippy! you've ben a real blessing to me. Now to-morrow she'll come again, the dear little thing!"

The next day Miss Avery looked eagerly at the old clock, and counted the minutes to recess-time, but no little Blue Eyes came. She wondered and waited in vain.

The solemn old clock ticked and struck, and Miss Avery strained her ears for the sound of the little footsteps. Never had the house seemed so lonely; but no little footsteps came.

"Why, I could n't have believed I'd 'a' missed her so," said Miss Avery to Trip, and Trip looked as if he thought so, too. "Well, she'll be here to-morrow, anyway," she said, as she lay down to sleep at night.

CHAPTER X

BUT to-morrow came and told the same story, — no little girl. Miss Avery lay awake at night wondering and wishing she knew ; but when the third day passed, and she did not come, Miss Avery put on her bonnet and marched up to Mr. Symons's, and knocked at the front door, and inquired for Mrs. Symons.

That good lady, a little fat easy woman, appeared, for some cause, agitated and worried.

Miss Avery was a very square, direct, exact sort of a person, in her dealings, and never wasted words, so she came to the point directly.

"Good-morning, Mrs. Symons," she said. "I came to inquire for my brother's little girl."

"Oh," said Mrs. Symons, "then you know? Well, I declare! I told Mr. Symons you *ought* to know; but dear me! I don't know what we shall all do. She's taken down with scarlet fever — got it at school, I s'pose — taken Monday morning — I expect she sat by some child that had it in school or Sunday-school ; any rate she's got it, and we don't know where to look for a nurse."

Miss Avery here interposed briefly, —

"*I* will come and nurse her. It's *my* place. I will take care of her."

"Oh, you will ? Well, if you feel able. I ain't used to sickness, you see, and I " —

"I *am* used to sickness," said Miss Avery, briefly, "and

if I undertake a thing, I *do it*. I'll just go home and take my things and lock up the house and be here in an hour. I shall have to bring my little Trip with me. I can't leave him alone in the house ; but he never makes any trouble, and she's fond of him, and loves to have him round."

"Well," said Mrs. Symons, "we'll do the best we can."

"And I shall do the best *I* can," said Miss Avery, resolutely.

And in a few hours she was established at the bedside of her little patient, with her old-fashioned watch on the stand, and her gargles and medicines all arranged in order, with a soft pair of list shoes upon her feet, the very image of regularity, neatness, and order.

The little one woke from a heavy sleep, opened her eyes and smiled.

"*You* here, aunty ? " she said, and she reached her arms up to her ; and Aunt Avery stooped down and kissed her once and again.

"I'm *so* glad you've come ! " said the child. " My throat hurts me so, and I'm *so* hot ! "

"I came to help you, darling. I'll take care of you till you are well again."

The child dozed off in a heavy stupor. After a while, Miss Avery put a spoonful of the rose-leaf gargle in her mouth, and she woke again, and looked earnestly at Miss Avery.

"I'd like to go to heaven *sometime*," she broke out ; " but I don't want to go now. I want to see papa and mamma again."

"Yes indeed, darling ; I trust you will," said Miss Avery, who felt her heart sink within her at the very suggestion.

" Have you brought Trip ? " faintly whispered the child.

"Oh yes ; here he is," said Miss Avery. And sure

enough, Trip, standing on his hind legs, was gazing on his little playmate, with his great soft eyes full of sympathy. She smiled faintly, and reached her little hand. He licked it, and she laughed. "It tickles," she said. "Let him stay where I can see him," she added; and so Trip had his cushion put in a chair by her bedside, where he conducted himself in a sympathizing and Christian manner, restraining his natural impetuosity, and behaving with the utmost quietness.

Now and then he would step gently and softly on the bed, and steal up and put his cold nose to the little hot face; and then she woke from her feverish stupor, and said, "Dear Trippy, is that you?"

"The cre'tur knows something is the matter as well as I do," said Miss Avery.

Something was the matter, and a very grave something; for the disease was of a virulent type, and for days and nights it was uncertain how it would go with the child. Miss Avery was every moment at her post.

She had all her life been combating dust, dirt, disorder, rats, and flies; but now she was in a more awful combat, — fighting hand-to-hand with *death !*

One night the symptoms grew worse. The hands and feet of the little sufferer became cold as ice, and the doctor said that if there was no rallying she could not live till morning.

Miss Avery was grimly resolute and watchful, and incessant in her care, but there was a dreadful sinking in her heart.

"I can't — I *can't* spare her, — oh, I *can't !* " she said; and then there came into her head a verse she sung every week at prayer-meeting: —

> "The dearest idol I have known,
>   Whate'er that idol be,
> Help me to tear it from thy throne,
>   And worship only thee."

"Oh, I can't — I *can't* say that !" she said. She turned in a sort of blind way, and opened a Bible and read, —

" *My daughter is even now dead, but come and lay thine hand on her, and she shall live.*"

She fell on her knees, rested her head on the bed, and cried out, —

" O Jesus, help me — help me ! I *can't* give her up !" It was a paroxysm, a rush of the whole soul ; and a moment after, the words passed through her mind, as if a gentle voice had spoken them, —

"I will come and heal her."

She rose again, with a strange new sense of relief and trust. It was as if she had indeed touched the hem of His garment.

She bent over the child, and felt her hands ; they were warmer ; a little moisture stood on her forehead ; she looked better. The tide of life had passed the lowest ebb, and was beginning to flow back, and by morning there was a decided improvement. " Well, Miss Avery, you 've fought it out bravely," said the doctor, when he felt the child's pulse in the morning. " I think we shall keep her. The crisis is over, and, with good nursing like yours, we shall have her on her feet in a week."

CHAPTER XI

THE telegram that was to have summoned Eben Avery to the bedside of his little daughter missed him, coming one hour after he had left the place of address. It was not till the danger was over, and recovery fairly established, that he heard of the child's state. Then he and his wife hurried to Hindford.

Miss Avery was sitting in the well-ordered room, with her little patient in her lap.

For the first time the child had been dressed that day in her ordinary clothes, and was reposing after the fatigue in those fond, faithful old arms that had borne her through her sickness.

" Here she is ! " said a voice outside the chamber door, and immediately a stout, cheery, middle-aged man had his arms round both of them, and was kissing both indiscriminately.

" Eben ! Eben ! " " Sister ! " " Papa ! " " Mamma ! " were the sounds that rose all together, and then a pretty little woman claimed her share, and kissed both Miss Avery and the child.

It was a confused, laughing, crying, joyful sort of meeting, and Trip barked distractedly, not knowing what to make of it.

"There, now, let's sit down and be quiet," said Eben Avery. "We mustn't make such a racket among us. Come, Sister Zarviah, let me take her a minute." And

Miss Avery put the little one into his arms, and her face for the moment was radiant with its expression of tender feeling.

"There, Eben," she said, "I've kept her for you; now you'll forgive my being cross to you."

"Forgive you, my dear old soul! Why, that's a pretty story! What have I to forgive? Were n't you always the most painstaking creature that ever was? and I was enough to tire the patience of Job himself. My wife, there, will tell you what a fiery trial I am."

"O papa, you are not!" said the little one.

"Shut up, Pussy; you must n't talk! You'll get a relapse, or something. We ought not to have come in on you so suddenly; but there! it's just like me. I could n't help it. I'm the same noisy, careless fellow."

"Dear sister," said the beautiful lady, her eyes filling with tears, "I don't know what I can ever say to thank you!"

"Oh, don't say anything," said Miss Avery. "I did it because I wanted to. I loved her. She's the dearest little thing! and the Lord's given her back. I felt when she was so low — that — if she died, I should die, too!"

"Well, well," said Eben, "you shan't either of you die now! and we'll all live together in peace, and plenty, and prosperity."

The last scene in our story is a Thanksgiving dinner at the old Avery house.

There were present at table Mr. Eben Avery and his wife, our little Blue Eyes, Miss Avery, and Trip, — Trip, with a fine new collar, with a little silver bell upon it. Miss Avery presided, attired in a new black India satin which Eben had brought to her from California, and a thread-lace cap which Eben's wife had trimmed with her own fair hands.

"Now this seems like old times," said Eben, looking cheerily round. "Nobody like you, Sister Zarviah, for getting up a Thanksgiving dinner!"

Miss Avery confessed that she had given her mind to this one, and that she was relieved that the turkey had "browned just right." Perfection in one thing, at least, had been reached.

"And now, Zarviah, since this is the last of the old Avery house, let's have a rousing good time in it," said Eben. "Give Trip all the turkey he wants, and Pussy all the pie, and let me talk nonsense much as I've a mind to."

"Yes," said Miss Avery; "Trip ought to have his share of our Thanksgiving, for he's been a good Providence to me. I was getting crusty and cross, and frozen up, and didn't care for anybody till Trip got me to caring for him."

"And then, auntie, I came after Trip, and you got to loving *me*, did n't you, auntie?"

"That I did," said Miss Avery, heartily.

"I tell you what, wife," said Eben, "I'm going to build the finest house in Hindford on this very spot, and I'm going to build Zarviah's room just to suit her, with all sorts of cupboards and closets and squirrel-holes for her to put all her precious things in, and she shall have a keeping-room with all the old things in it that are here; and we'll keep the old lilacs to look in at the chamber windows, and Zarviah won't know but what she's living in the old house, only there'll be no leaks, and no rats, and no cockroaches; and Zarviah shall have it all her own way in her part of the house."

"Well, I shall stay in auntie's part; I know I shall like it best. She always lets me do just what I want to."

"There, Zarviah, you'll just spoil that child," said Eben.

"She can't be spoiled," said Miss Avery, sententiously.

"At any rate," said the little lady, "Trip and I know we shall have good times with auntie, don't we, Trippy?" Trip barked his assent; and so ends the story of a dog's mission.

LITTLE Miss Lulu was tired of all her dolls, — and she had a good many dolls to be tired of. There was the big china doll with blue eyes and light flaxen hair; and there was the pink wax doll with a curly golden wig; and there was the little china doll dressed like a boy, and the black china doll with a red petticoat that waited on the white lady dolls; and there was the doll that could open and shut its eyes, and the doll that could say "Mamma;" in fact, there were about a dozen more that I cannot now enumerate, but Lulu had become tired of them all. "I want a real *live* doll," she said.

So one day her mamma brought her home a pet. It was a little Spitz puppy named Muff. His hair was long and silvery white, he had bright black eyes, and the prettiest pink tongue in the world, and was about the jolliest little dog that could be bought for any money. He was called Muff because he looked, when set down upon the carpet, very much like a little white muff running about on four little white stumpy legs; and the moment he was put down in the parlor he trotted about smelling at everything he could find. He smelt of the curtains, of the chairs, of the ottomans, and ran his nose all along the side of the room, which is a dog's way of taking an observation.

Lulu was delighted. This was a pet worth having. Her dolls, she thought, were stupid. They never did anything; they never moved unless she moved them; the doll that could open and shut its eyes never did open or shut them except just while Lulu pulled the wire, and Lulu got tired of pulling the wire. But no sooner was Mr. Muff set down on his four paws in the corner than he began such a whisk and scamper that it made lively times for Lulu. Round and round he ran, snuffing at this thing and at that, and barking with a short, quick snap, like the letting off of a pistol.

"Mercy on us!" said Lulu's mamma, "what shall we do if that dog is going to bark so? It goes through my head like a knife. Lulu, if you are going to have Muff for your dog, you must teach him not to bark."

"Oh, yes, indeed, mamma," said Lulu, "I'll teach him;" and so she sat down on the ottoman and took Muff in her lap to instruct him how to behave.

Muff had been racing, so that his little pink tongue hung like a ribbon out of his mouth, and Miss Lulu proceeded to fan him in order to cool him, as she said, —

"Now, Muffie dear, you must remember you are *my* dog now, and I must teach you exactly how to behave. You must n't bark out loud in the parlors, Muffie; do you hear?"

Just then the door-bell rang, and down jumped Muffie, and "whack, whack, whack" went his sharp little bark.

It was Miss Marabout and Miss Tulleport come in all their best flowers and feathers and silk dresses to call on mamma.

In vain did Lulu try to stop Muff; she could not catch him. He ran "whack, whack, whacking," now here and now there, under Miss Marabout's silk trail and over Miss Tulleport's new satin, and made such a din and confusion that nobody could hear anybody else speak.

"Jennie, you must take that dog and shut him up in the nursery," said mamma; and away Muff was carried in deep disgrace, barking like a pocket-pistol all the way.

"O dear me, Muffie, what a bad dog you are!" said little Miss Lulu, who came trailing up-stairs after him, "to bark so just after I talked to you so nicely, and told you just how to behave."

Well, that was not the worst scrape that Muff got his young mistress into. He was, to tell the truth, the most mischievous little wretch that ever wore dog-skin. What do you think of this? One day it was decided that Lulu was to go with a whole party of children to a picnic in the country. Her mamma had just finished for her a smart little cambric dress to wear on the occasion, and when Lulu went to bed it was laid out on a chair that she might put it on in the morning.

But, alas! in the morning there was no dress to be seen, and after great searching and wondering it was found under the bed in Mr. Muff's possession. Muff was shaking it about in his mouth, and had torn and mangled it so that it was not fit to be seen. In fact, he had chewed up and swallowed half the front breadth, so that there was no possibility of mending it.

Lulu wept bitterly over the spoiled dress, and all the more that it was spoiled by her new favorite. It was agreed that Muff should be put into solitary confinement while she went to the picnic. So Muff was locked into a closet, and Lulu went off with her tears dried, and an old dress in place of the new one she had expected to wear.

Arrived on the picnic ground, who should appear, fresh and noisy, but Master Muff? He had jumped out of the closet window and followed his mistress, determined to see some of the fun.

This is only one specimen of the mischief that Muff was always doing. He used to run away with Lulu's shoes and stockings, and chew them to a paste; he used to tear her ribbons to shreds, and, when nothing else came to hand, would attack the books and newspapers, shaking and worrying them till they were all in tatters.

Every day Maggie or Susan came down to mamma with

some new story of Muff's naughty doings. He had torn the window-curtains, he had chewed off a corner of a sheet, he had scratched and pawed off the fringe from the ottoman. "What *shall* we do with the creature?" said mamma. "I 'm sure I never would have bought him had I known what a trouble he would be."

"He will have to be sent away if he don't mind," said papa.

But the moment papa spoke of sending Muff away, Lulu's great blue eyes filled with tears, and her lips trembled, and she seemed so broken-hearted that papa said, "Well, well, we 'll try him a little longer."

Then how hard Lulu tried to make Muffie comprehend the situation! She would take him into her lap and preach to him gravely: "Now you see, Muffie, I love you, and I don't want you sent off; but if you go on so they will send you 'way, 'way off, where you 'll never, *never* see me any more. Would n't that make you feel bad, Muffie?"

Muffie would sit with his head very much on one side, and his tongue like a pink streamer hanging out of his mouth, and listen with a waggish air to all his mistress's instructions, showing just about as much feeling as some little boys and girls do when their mammas tell them of what may happen to them when they grow up if they do not heed their counsel.

"The fact is," Muff seemed to say, "I have always been a pretty lucky dog, and I don't believe anything very bad will happen to me."

Muff liked very much to trot about with his little mistress when she went out for a walk. Then he would cock his ears and tail, and pad along as important as possible. He would run and bark at every cat and dog or hen and chicken in his way, and seemed delighted to keep everything about him in a flutter.

People scolded a great deal, and some even threatened to

shoot him; but when little Lulu came in sight with her blue eyes and golden hair they concluded to let him go for her sake.

Muff wanted very much to go to church Sundays. He went everywhere else with Lulu, and why he was shut up to private meditation on Sundays was a thing he could not understand. So he would watch his opportunity and slip out of a door or window, and trot off to church, and to Lulu's astonishment appear suddenly in the broad aisle. Once he even went up and sat in the chancel as grave and innocent as possible. Lulu's heart was in her mouth when the sexton put him out, and she had to leave church to go home with him.

"How often must I tell you, Muffie, church is n't for dogs?" she said, when she got him safe home. "You may go everywhere else with me, but you must n't go to church!"

Muffie could not speak, but his eyes said, "Why must n't I?" as plainly as the thing could be spoken.

However, on reflection, Muff thought he had found out a way to manage the matter. He waited till everybody was in church one Sunday, and then jumped out of the pantry window and trotted off to meeting. He took possession of a deserted slip near the door, and, mounting the seat, sat up as grave as a judge, and seemed resolved to show that a dog could act like a good Christian.

For a while all went on very well, and nobody noticed that he was there; but at last a great bluebottle fly whizzed down into his face, when "whack" came out Muff's short bark. Everybody looked round, and Muff barked again; then Lulu got up and ran down the aisle just as the sexton seized him.

"Oh, please don't do anything to him!" said Lulu. "You know he's only a dog; I try to teach him so hard, but he won't learn."

The sexton smiled on the little maiden, and she took her pet home.

"Muffie, Muffie, what trouble you do make me!" she said; "but yet I love you, and I would n't have you sent off for the world."

Since then little Lulu has grown a bigger girl, and Muff has grown an older and a soberer dog. He no longer chews up her shoes and stockings, and he has learned to spend Sundays in private reflection, but he never will learn not to bark. Little by little, however, people have become used to his noise, and like him in spite of it.

THE DAISY'S FIRST WINTER

SOMEWHERE in a garden of this earth, which the dear Lord has planted with many flowers of gladness, grew a fresh, bright little daisy.

The first this little daisy knew, she found herself growing in green pastures and beside the still waters where the Heavenly Shepherd was leading his sheep. And very beautiful did life look to her, as her bright little eyes, with their crimson lashes, opened and looked down into the deep crystal waters of the brook below, where the sunshine made every hour more sparkles, more rings of light, and more brilliant glances and changes of color, than all the jewelers in the world could imitate. She knew intimately all the yellow-birds and meadow-larks and bobolinks and blackbirds, that sang, piped, whistled, or chattered among the bushes and trees in the pasture, and she was a prime favorite with them all.

Multitudes of beautiful flowers grew up in the water, or on the moist edges of the brook. There were green arrowheads, which in their time gave forth their white blossoms with a little gold ball in the centre of each; and the pickerel-weed, with its thick, sharp, green leaf, and its sturdy spike of blue blossoms; and the tall meadow-grass, with its graceful green tassels hanging down and making wavy reflections in the water; and there was the silver-weed, whose leaves as they dipped in the brook seemed to be of molten silver, and whose tall heads of fringy white blossoms sent forth a grateful perfume in the air; and there, too, were the pink and white azalias, full of sweetness and beauty, and close along in the green mosses of the banks grew blue and white violets, and bloodroot, with its silvery stars of blossom ; and the purple hepatica, with its quaint hairy leaves ; and the slender wind-flower on its thread-like stem ; and the crowfoot, with its dark bronze leaf and its half-shut flower, looking like the outside of a pink sea-shell.

These beautiful blooming things did not all blossom at once, but had their graceful changes ; and there was always a pleasant flutter of expectation among them, — either a sending forth of leaves, or a making of buds, or a bursting out into blossoms ; and when the blossoms passed away, there was a thoughtful, careful maturing of seeds, all packed away so snugly in their little coffers and caskets of seed-pods, which were of every quaint and dainty shape that ever could be fancied for a lady's jewel-box. Over-head there grew a wide-spreading apple-tree, which in the month of June became a gigantic bouquet, holding up to the sun a million silvery opening flowers, and a million pink-tipped buds ; and the little winds would come to play in its branches, and take the pink shells of the blossoms for their tiny air-boats, in which they would go floating round among the flowers, or sail on voyages of discovery down the stream ; and when the time of its blossom was gone, the bountiful tree from year to year had matured fruits of golden ripeness which cheered the hearts of men.

Little Daisy's life was only one varied delight from day to day. She had a hundred playmates among the light-winged winds, that came to her every hour to tell her what was going on all over the green pasture, and to bring her sweet perfumed messages from the violets and anemones of even the more distant regions.

There was not a ring of sunlight that danced in the golden network at the bottom of the brook that did not bring a thrill of gladness to her heart ; not a tiny fish glided in his crystal paths, or played and frolicked under the water-lily shadows, that was not a well-known friend of hers, and whose pleasures she did not share. At night she held conferences with the dew-drops that stepped about among the flowers in their bright pearl slippers, and washed their leaves and faces before they went to rest. Nice little nurses and dressing-maids these dews! and they kept tender guard all night over the flowers, watching and blinking wakefully to see that all was safe; but when the sun arose, each of them spread a pair of little rainbow wings, and was gone.

To be sure, there were some reverses in her lot. Sometimes a great surly, ill-looking cloud would appear in the sky, like a cross schoolmaster, and sweep up all the sunbeams, and call in a gruff voice to the little winds, her playfellows, to come away from their nonsense; and then he would send a great strong wind down on them all, with a frightful noise, and roar, and sweep all the little flowers flat to the earth; and there would be a great rush and pattering of rain-drops, and bellowing of thunders, and sharp forked lightnings would quiver through the air as if the green pastures certainly were to be torn to pieces; but in about half an hour it would be all over, — the sunbeams would all dance out from their hiding-places, just as good as if nothing had happened, and the little winds would come laughing back, and each little flower would lift itself up, and the winds would help them to shake off the wet and plume themselves as jauntily as if nothing had gone amiss. Daisy had the greatest pride and joy in her own pink blossoms, of which there seemed to be an inexhaustible store; for, as fast as one dropped its leaves, another was ready to open its eyes, and there were buds of every size, waiting still to come on, even down to little green cushions of buds that lay hidden away in the middle of the leaves down close to the root. "How favored I am!"

said Daisy; "I never stop blossoming. The anemones and the liverwort and the bloodroot have their time, but then they stop and have only leaves, while I go on blooming perpetually; how nice it is to be made as I am!"

"But you must remember," said a great rough Burdock to her, — "you must remember that your winter must come at last, when all this fine blossoming will have to be done with."

"What do you mean?" said Daisy, in a tone of pride, eyeing her rough neighbor with a glance of disgust. "You are a rough, ugly old thing, and that's why you are cross. Pretty people like me can afford to be good-natured."

"Ah, well," said Dame Burdock, "you'll see. It's a pretty thing if a young chit just out from seed this year should be impertinent to me, who have seen twenty winters, — yes, and been through them well, too!"

"Tell me, Bobolink," said Daisy, "is there any truth in what this horrid Burdock has been saying? What does she mean by winter?"

"I don't know, — not I," said Bobolink, as he turned a dozen somersets in the air, and then perched himself airily on a thistle-head, singing, —

> "I don't know, and I don't care;
> It's mighty pleasant to fly up there,
> And it's mighty pleasant to light down here,
> And all I know is chip, chip, cheer."

"Say, Humming-bird, do you know anything about winter?"

"Winter? I never saw one," said Humming-bird; "we have wings, and follow summer round the world, and where she is, there go we."

"Meadow-lark, Meadow-lark, have you ever heard of winter?" said Daisy.

Meadow-lark was sure he never remembered one. "What is winter?" he said, looking confused.

" Butterfly, Butterfly," said Daisy, " come, tell me, will there be winter, and what is winter ? "

But the Butterfly laughed, and danced up and down, and said, " What is Daisy talking about ? I never heard of winter. Winter ? ha ! ha ! What is it ? "

" Then it 's only one of Burdock's spiteful sayings," said Daisy. " Just because she is n't pretty, she wants to spoil my pleasure too. Say, dear lovely tree that shades me so sweetly, is there such a thing as winter ? "

And the tree said, with a sigh through its leaves, " Yes, daughter, there will be winter ; but fear not, for the Good Shepherd makes both summer and winter, and each is good in its time. Enjoy the summer and fear not."

The months rolled by. The violets had long ago stopped blooming, their leaves were turning yellow, but they had beautiful green seed-caskets, full of rows of little pearls, which next year should come up in blue violets. The dog-toothed violet and the eye-bright had gone under ground, so that no more was seen of them, and Daisy wondered whither they could be gone. But she had new acquaint-ances far more brilliant, and she forgot the others. The brook-side seemed all on fire with golden-rod, and the bright yellow was relieved by the rich purple tints of the asters, while the blue fringed gentian held up its cups, that seemed as if they might have been cut out of the sky, — and still Daisy had abundance of leaves and blossoms, and felt strong and well at the root. Then the apple-tree cast down to the ground its fragrant burden of golden apples, and men came and carried them away.

By and by there came keen, cutting winds, and driving storms of sleet and hail ; and then at night it would be so cold, so cold ! and one after another the leaves and flowers fell stiff and frozen, and grew black, and turned to decay. The leaves loosened and fell from the apple-tree, and sailed away by thousands down the brook ; the butterflies lay dead with the flowers, but all the birds had gone singing away to the sunny south, following the summer into other lands.

"Tell me, dear tree," said Daisy, "is this winter that is coming?"

"It is winter, darling," said the tree; "but fear not. The Good Shepherd makes winter as well as summer."

"I still hold my blossoms," said Daisy, — for Daisy was a hardy little thing.

But the frosts came harder and harder every night, and first they froze her blossoms, and then they froze her leaves, and finally all, all were gone, — there was nothing left but the poor little root, with the folded leaves of the future held in its bosom.

"Ah, dear tree!" said Daisy, "is not this dreadful!"

"Be patient, darling," said the tree. "I have seen many, many winters; but the Good Shepherd loses never a seed, never a root, never a flower: they will all come again."

By and by came colder days and colder, and the brook froze to its little heart and stopped; and then there came bitter, driving storms, and the snow lay wreathed over Daisy's head; but still from the bare branches of the apple-tree came a voice of cheer. "Courage, darling, and patience! Not a flower shall be lost: winter is only for a season."

"It is so dreary!" murmured Daisy, deep in her bosom.

"It will be short: the spring will come again," said the tree.

And at last the spring did come; and the snow melted and ran away down the brook, and the sun shone out warm, and fresh green leaves jumped and sprang out of every dry twig of the apple-tree. And one bright, rejoicing day, little Daisy opened her eyes, and lo! there were all her friends once more; — there were the eye-brights and the violets and the anemones and the liverwort, — only ever so many

more of them than there were last year, because each little
pearl of a seed had been nursed and moistened by the snows
of winter, and had come up as a little plant to have its own
flowers. The birds all came back, and began building their
nests, and everything was brighter and fairer than before ;
and Daisy felt strong at heart, because she had been through
a winter, and learned not to fear it. She looked up into
the apple-tree. "Will there be more winters, dear tree ? "
she said.

"Darling, there will ; but fear not. Enjoy the present
hour, and leave future winters to Him who makes them.
Thou hast come through these sad hours, because the Shepherd remembered thee. He loseth never a flower out of his
pasture, but calleth them all by name : and the snow will
never drive so cold, or the wind beat so hard, as to hurt one
of his flowers. And look ! of all the flowers of last year,
what one is melted away in the snow, or forgotten in the
number of green things ? Every blade of grass is counted,
and puts up its little head in the right time ; so never fear,
Daisy, for thou shalt blossom stronger and brighter for the
winter."

"But why must there be winter ? " said Daisy.

" I never ask why," said the tree.   " My business is to
blossom and bear apples. Summer comes, and I am joyful ;
winter comes, and I am patient. But, darling, there is another garden where thou and I shall be transplanted one
day, where there shall be winter no more. There is coming
a new earth ; and not one flower or leaf of these green pastures shall be wanting there, but come as surely as last
year's flowers come back this spring ! "

OUR CHARLEY

WHEN the blaze of the wood fire flickers up and down in our snug evening parlor, there dances upon the wall a little shadow with a pug nose, a domestic household shadow — a busy shadow — a little restless specimen of perpetual motion, and the owner thereof is " Our Charley."

Now, we should not write about him and his ways, if he were strictly a peculiar and individual existence of our own home circle ; but it is not so. " Our Charley " exists in a thousand, nay, a million families ; he has existed in millions in all time back : his name is variously rendered in all the tongues of the earth ; nay, there are a thousand synonyms for him in English — for certainly " our Willie," or " our Harry," or " our Georgie," belongs to the same snub-nosed, rosy-cheeked, restless shadow-maker. So in France, he is " Léonce," or " Pierre," as well as " Charles ; " in Italy, he is " Carlino " or " Francesco ; " in Germany, " Max," " Carl ," or " Wilhelm ; " and in China, he is little " Ling-Fung," with a long silk tail on the back of his head,— but the same household sprite among them all : in short, we take " our Charley " in a generic sense, and we mean to treat of him as a little copy of a grown man — enacting in a shadowy ballet by the fireside all that men act in earnest in after-life. He is a looking-glass for grown people, in which they may see how certain things become them — in which they may sometimes even see streaks and gleamings of something wiser than all the harsh conflict of life teaches them.

"Our Charley" is generally considered by the world as an idle little dog, whose pursuits, being very unimportant, may be put off or put by for every and any body ; but the world, as usual, is very much mistaken. No man is more pressed with business, and needs more prudence, energy, tact, and courage to carry out his schemes, in face of all the opposing circumstances that grown people constantly throw in his way.

Has he not ships to build and to sail ? and has he not vast engineerings to make ponds and docks in every puddle or brook, where they shall anchor ? Is not his pocket stuffed with materials for sails and cordage ? And yet, like a man of the world as he is, all this does not content him, but he must own railroad stock too. If he lives where a steam whistle has vibrated, it has awakened an unquiet yearning within him, and some day he harnesses all the chairs into a train, and makes a locomotive of your work-table and a steam whistle of himself. He inspects toy-shop windows, gets up flirtations with benevolent shopmen ; and when he gets his mouth close to papa's ear, reveals to him how Mr. So-and-so has a locomotive that will wind up and go alone — so cheap too — can't papa get it for him ? And so papa (all papas do) goes soberly down and buys it, though he knows it will be broken in a week.

Then what raptures ! The dear locomotive ! the darling black chimney sleeps under his pillow that he may feel of it in the night, and be sure when he first wakes that the joy is not evaporated. He bores everybody to death with it as artlessly as grown people do with their hobbies. But at last the ardor runs out. His darling is found to have faults. He picks it to pieces to make it work better ; finds too late that he can't put it together again ; and so he casts it aside, and makes a locomotive out of a broken wheel-barrow and some barrel staves.

Do you, my brother, or grown-up sister, ever do anything

like this ? Do your friendships and loves ever go the course
of our Charley's toys ? First, enthusiasm ; second, satiety ;
third, discontent ; then picking to pieces ; then dropping
and losing? How many idols are in your box of by-gone
playthings ? And may it not be as well to suggest to you,
when you find flaws in your next one, to inquire before you
pick to pieces whether you can put together again, or
whether what you call defect is not a part of its nature ?
A tin locomotive won't draw a string of parlor chairs, by
any possible alteration, but it may be very pretty for all
that it was made for. Charley and you might both learn
something from this.

Charley's business career, as we have before intimated,
has its trials. It is hard for him to find time for it ; so
many impertinent interruptions. For instance, there are
four hours of school, taken out of the best part of the day ;
four mortal hours, in which he might make ships, or build
dams, or run railroad cars, he is obliged to leave all his affairs, often in very precarious situations, and go through the
useless ceremony of reading and spelling. When he comes
home, the house-maid has swept his foremast into the fire,
and mamma has put his top-sails into the rag-bag, and all
his affairs are in a desperate situation. Sometimes he gets
terribly misanthropic : all grown people seem conspiring
against him ; he is called away from his serious business so
often, and his attention distracted with such trifling matters, that he is indignant. He is rushing through the passage in hot haste, hands full of nails, strings, and twine,
and Mary seizes him and wants to brush his hair ; he is interrupted in a burst of enthusiasm, and told to wash his
hands for dinner ; or perhaps — a greater horror than all
— company is expected, and he must put on a clean new
suit, just as he has made all the arrangements for a ship-
launching down by the swamp. This dressing and washing he regards with unutterable contempt and disgust ;

secretly, too, he is skeptical about the advantages of going
to school and learning to read ; he believes, to be sure,
when papa and mamma tell him of unknown future advantages to come when he is a " great man ; " but then, the
present he is sure of ; his ships and sloops, his bits of string
and fish-hooks, and old corks and broken railroad cars, and
above all, his new skates; these are realities. And he
knows also what Tom White and Bill Smith say ; and so
he walks by sight more than by faith.

Ah, the child is father of the man ! When he gets older
he will have the great toys of which these are emblems;
he will believe in what he sees and touches — in house,
land, railroad stock — he will believe in these earnestly
and really, and in his eternal manhood nominally and par-
tially. And when his Father's messengers meet him, and
face him about, and take him off his darling pursuits, and
sweep his big ships into the fire, and crush his full-grown
cars, then the grown man will complain and murmur, and
wonder as the little man does now. The Father wants the
future, the Child the present, all through life, till death
makes the child a man.

So, though our Charley has his infirmities, he is a little
bit of a Christian after all. Like you, brother, he has his
good hours, when he sits still and calm, and is told of
Jesus ; and his cheeks glow, and tears come to his eyes ; his
bosom heaves ; and now he is sure he is going to be always
good ; he is never going to be naughty. He will stand still
to have his hair combed ; he will come the first time mother
speaks ; he will never speak a cross word to Katy ; he
repents of having tyrannized over grandmamma, and made
poor mamma's head ache ; and is quite sure that he has now
got the victory over sin. Like the Israelites by the Red
Sea, he beholds his spiritual enemies dead on the sea-shore.
But to-morrow, in one hour even, what becomes of his good
resolutions ? What becomes of yours on Monday ?

With all our Charley's backslidings, he may teach us one thing which we have forgotten. When Jesus would teach his disciples what *faith* was, he took a child and set him in the midst of them. We do not suppose that this child was one of those exceptional ones who have memoirs written. but a common average child, with its smiles and tears, its little naughtinesses and goodnesses ; and its aptness as an example was not in virtue of an exceptional but a universal quality. If you want to study, go to school to *your* Charley. See his faith in you. Does he not believe that you have boundless wealth, boundless wisdom, infinite strength ? Is he not certain of your love to that degree that he cannot be repelled from you ? Does he hesitate to question you on anything celestial or terrestrial ? Is not your word enough to outweigh that of the wisest of the earth ? You might talk him out of the sight of his eyes, the hearing of his ears, so boundless is his faith in you. Even checks and frowns cannot make him doubt your love ; and though sometimes, when you cross him, the naughty murmuring spirit arises, yet in an hour it dissolves, and his little soul flows back, prattling and happy, into your bosom. Be only to God as he is to you, and the fireside shadow shall not have been by your hearth in vain.

But *what is to be done with our Charley?* Yes, that is the question ! The fact is, there seems to be no place in heaven above, or earth beneath, that is exactly safe and suitable, except the bed. While he is asleep, then our souls have rest ; we know where he is and what he is about, and sleep is a gracious state ; but then he wakes up bright and early, and begins tooting, pounding, hammering, singing, meddling, asking questions, and, in short, overturning the peace of society generally, for about thirteen hours out of the twenty-four.

Everybody wants to know what to do with him — everybody is quite sure that he can't stay where they are. The cook can't have him in the kitchen, where he infests the pantry to get flour to make paste for his kites, or melts lead in the new saucepan. If he goes into the wood-shed, he is sure to pull the wood-pile down upon his head. If he be sent up garret, you think for a while that you have settled the problem, till you find what a boundless field of activity is opened amid all the packages, boxes, bags, barrels, and cast-off rubbish there. Old letters, newspapers, trunks of miscellaneous contents, are all rummaged, and the very reign of Chaos and old Night is instituted. He sees endless capabilities in all things, and is always hammering something, or knocking something apart, or sawing or planing, or dragging boxes or barrels in all directions to build cities, or laying railroad tracks, till everybody's head aches, quite down to the lower floor, and everybody declares that Charley must be kept out of the garret.

Then you send Charley to school, and hope you are fairly rid of him, for a few hours at least. But he comes home noisier and busier than ever, having learned of some twenty other Charleys every separate resource for keeping up a commotion that a superabundant vitality of each can originate. He can dance like Jim Smith; he has learned to smack his lips like Joe Brown; Will Briggs has shown him how to mew like a cat; and he enters the house with a new war-whoop learned from Tom Evans. He feels large and valorous; he has learned that he is a boy, and has a general impression that he is growing immensely strong and knowing, and despises more than ever the conventionalities of parlor-life — in fact he is more than ever an interruption in the way of decent folks, who want to be quiet.

It is true that, if entertaining persons will devote themselves to him exclusively, reading and telling stories, he may be kept in a state of quiescence; but then this is discouraging work, for he swallows a story as a dog does a piece of meat, and looks at you for another, and another without the slightest consideration, so that this resource is of short duration ; and then the old question comes up, What is to be done with him ?

But, after all, Charley is not to be wholly shirked, for he is an institution, a solemn and awful *fact ;* and on the answer of the question, What is to be done with him ? depends a future. Many a hard, morose, and bitter man has come from a Charley turned off and neglected — many a parental heart-ache has come from a Charley left to run the streets, that mamma and sisters might play on the piano and write letters in peace. It is easy to get rid of him — there are fifty ways of doing that — he is a spirit that can be promptly laid for a season, but if not laid aright, will come back by and by, a strong man armed, when you cannot send him off at pleasure.

Mamma and sisters had better pay a little tax to Charley now, than a terrible one by and by. There is something significant in the old English phrase, with which our Scriptures make us familiar — a *man* child ! A MAN child ! — there you have the word that should make you think more than twice before you answer the question, What shall we do with Charley ?

For to-day he is at your feet — to-day you can make him laugh, you can make him cry, you can persuade and coax, and turn him to your pleasure ; you can make his eyes fill and his bosom swell with recitals of good and noble deeds ; in short, you can mould him if you will take the trouble.

But look ahead some years, when that little voice shall ring in deep bass tones ; when that small foot shall have a man's weight and tramp ; when a rough beard shall cover that little round chin, and all the strengh of manhood fill out that little form. Then you would give worlds to have the key to his heart, to be able to turn and guide him to your will ; but if you lose that key now he is little, you may search for it carefully with tears some other day, and not find it. Old housekeepers have a proverb, that one hour lost in the morning is never found all day — it has a significance in this case.

One thing is to be noticed about Charley — that, rude, and busy, and noisy as he inclines to be, and irksome as carpet rules and parlor ways are to him, he is still a social little creature, and wants to be where the rest of the household are. A room ever so well adapted for a play-room cannot charm him at the hour when the family is in reunion ; he hears the voices in the parlor, and his play-room seems cold and desolate — it may be warmed by a fire and lighted with gas, but it is *human* light and warmth he shivers for — he longs to take his things down and play by you ; he yearns to hear the talk of the family, which he so imperfectly comprehends, and is incessantly promising that of the fifty improper things which he is liable to do in the parlor, he will not commit one if you will let him stay there.

This instinct of the little one is Nature's warning plea — God's admonition. Oh, how many a mother who has neglected it, because it was irksome to have the child about, has longed, when her son was a man, to keep him by her side, and he would not ! Shut out as a little Arab — constantly told that he is noisy, that he is awkward and meddlesome, and a plague in general — the boy has at last found his own company in the streets, in the highways and hedges where he runs, till the day comes when the parents want their son, the sisters their brother ; and then they are scared at the face he brings back to them, as he comes all foul and smutty from the companionship to which they have doomed him. Depend upon it, mothers, and elder sisters, if it is too much trouble to keep Charley in your society, there will be places found for him, warmed and lighted with no friendly fires, where he who " finds some mischief still for idle hands to do " will care for him if you do not. You may put out a tree, and it will grow aright while you sleep ; but a *son* you cannot treat so. You must take trouble for him, either a little now, or a good deal by and by.

Let him stay with you at least some portion of every day. Put aside your book or work to tell him a story, or read to him from some book. Devise still parlor plays for him, for he gains nothing if he be allowed to spoil the comfort of the whole circle. A pencil and a sheet of paper, and a few patterns, will often keep him quiet for an hour by your side; or in a corner he may build a block house, annoying nobody; and if occasionally he does disturb you now, balance in your own mind which is the greatest evil, to be disturbed by him now, or when he is a man.

Of all that you can give your Charley, if you are a good man or woman, *your presence* is the best and safest thing. God never meant him to do without you, any more than chickens were meant to grow without being brooded.

Then let him have some place in the house where it shall be no sin to hammer, and pound, and saw, and make all the litter that his various schemes of business require. Even if you can ill afford the room, weigh well which is best, to spare him that safe asylum, or take the chance of one which he may find for himself in the street.

Of all devices for Charley which we have tried, a few shelves, which he may dignify with the name of cabinet, is one of the best. He picks up shells, and pebbles, and stones — all odds and ends; nothing comes amiss; and if you give him a pair of scissors and a little gum, there is no end of the labels he will paste on, and the hours that he may innocently spend in sorting and arranging. A bottle of liquid gum is an invaluable resource for various purposes; nor must you mind though he varnish his nose and fingers, and clothes, so that he do nothing worse. A cheap paint box, and some engravings to color, is another; and if you will give him some real paint and putty, to paint and putty his boats and cars, he is a made man. All these things make trouble, — to be sure they do, and will, — but Charley *is* to make trouble; that is the nature of the institution. You are only to choose between safe and wholesome trouble and the trouble that comes at last like a whirlwind.

God bless the little fellow, and send us all grace to know what to do with him!

The stories following are some of those with which one mother has beguiled the twilight hours of *one* Charley; they are given in hopes that other mothers may find pleasure in reading them to their Charleys.

TAKE CARE OF THE HOOK

CHARLEY's mother would often sit with him by the fire, before the lamp was lighted in the evening, and repeat to him little pieces of poetry. This is one that Charley used to like particularly. It is written by Miss Jane Taylor.

THE STORY OF THE LITTLE FISH

"Dear mother," said a little fish,
"Pray is not that a fly?
I'm very hungry, and I wish
You'd let me go and try."

"Sweet innocent," the mother cried,
And started from her nook,
"That horrid fly is meant to hide
The sharpness of the hook!"

Now, as I've heard, this little trout
Was young and silly too;
And so he thought he'd venture out,
To see what he could do.

And round about the fly he played,
With many a longing look;
And often to himself he said,
"I'm sure that's not a hook.

"I can but give one little pluck
To try, and so I will."
So on he went, and lo, it stuck
Quite through his little gill.

And as he faint and fainter grew,
With hollow voice he cried,
"Dear mother, if I'd minded you,
I should not thus have died."

After this was finished, Charley looked gravely into the fire, and began his remarks upon it. "What a silly fellow that little trout was! He might have known better."

"Take care, Charley," said his mamma; "there are a great many little boys just as silly as this trout. For instance, I knew a little boy, a while ago, whose mamma told him not to touch green apples or currants, because they would make him sick. He did not mean to touch them, for he knew that it is very disagreeable to be sick and take medicine, but yet he did the very same thing that this little trout did.

"Instead of keeping far away, he would walk about under the trees and pick up the green apples to look at, and feel of the green currants, just as the fish would play round the hook. By and by he said, 'I really don't think they will hurt me; I will just take one *little* taste.' And then he ate one, and then another, till finally he got very sick. Do you remember?"

"Oh, mamma, that was I. Yes, I remember."

"Now, Charley, hear what I tell you: nobody does very wrong things because he means to at first. People begin by little and little, just tasting and trying what is wrong, like this little fish.

"There is George Johnson, a very fine boy, a bright boy, and one who means to do right; but then George does not always keep away from the hook. You will see him sometimes standing round places where men are drinking and swearing. George does not mean ever to drink or to swear; he only stands there to hear these men sing their songs and tell their stories, and sometimes he will drink just a little sip of sugar and spirits out of the bottom of a tumbler; but George never means really to be a drunkard. Ah, take care, George; the little fish did not mean to be caught either, but he kept playing round and round and round the hook, and at last he was snapped up; and so you will be if you don't take care.

"Then William Day means to be an honest boy, and you could not make him more angry than to tell him he would ever be a thief; and yet William *plays too much round the hook*. What does he do? Why, he will take little things out of his father's desk or shop, or out of his mother's basket or drawers, when he really does not want his father or mother to see him or find it out. William thinks, 'Oh, it's only a little thing; it isn't much matter; I dare say they had just as lief I had it as not.' Ah, William, do you think so? Why do you not go to your parents and ask for it, then? No; the fact is that William is learning to steal, but he does not believe it is stealing any more than the little fish believed that what looked like a fly was in fact a dreadful hook. By and by, if William does n't take care, when he goes into a shop or store, he will begin to take little things from his master just as he did from his father and mother; and he will take more and more, till finally he will be named and disgraced as a thief, and all because, like the little fish, he *would play around the hook*."

"Mamma," said Charley, " who are George Johnson and William Day? Did I ever see them?"

"My dear, I must use names in a story; I am just making this up to show Charley what I meant by *playing round the hook*. And now let me teach you a text out of the Bible that means the same thing: 'He that despiseth small things shall fall by little and little.'"

ONE bright morning, when the yellow dandelions were shining out like so many gold dollars in the green grass, and the brooks were chattering and purling to each other, and small eyebrights were looking up from the turf like flocks of little white sheep, a little boy, whom we shall call Jamie, found, all of a sudden, that his school had stopped, and he had come to the first day of his vacation.

So says Jamie to himself, "What shall I do all day long?" After a while he thought he would take a basket, and go over into a neighboring field. and gather some eyebrights and violets to dress flower vases for his mamma.

Well, over the fence he went, and wandered far off into the field; and there he met two strange boys, larger than he, whose names were Will Drake and Charley Jones.

"Hulloa!" said one of the boys to him; "come along with us — we are going to have fun. We have got our pockets full of stones, and we are going to kill birds with them; it's the best fun in the world."

Now Jamie was a thoughtless little fellow, and when another boy asked him to do a thing, at it he went at once, without so much as thinking whether it was right or not; so he filled his pockets with stones, and began running and shouting with the other boys. "Hulloa! there's a chipping bird," said one; "I'll hit him." "Look at the robin!" bawled another; "send a stone at him. Oh, there's a bluebird! now for him!" I am happy to say that these boys missed their hits, generally, for they intended much worse than they were able to do.

While they were thus running about a nice white cat came stepping along the top of a fence, putting down her paws as daintily as any lady. "Hulloa! there's a cat; now for fun!" shouted Will Drake, as he let fly a stone, and then dashed after the cat. Puss was frightened, and scampered with all her might; and all three of the boys joined chase after her, and came tumbling, one after another, over the back-yard fence of the place where Jamie lived.

But Jamie's mother had been sitting at her window watching the whole affair; and now she stood up, and called, in a very quiet way, "Jamie, come up here; I have something to show you."

The other two boys slunk away a little. Jamie came up into his mother's room, all panting and hot, and began, "Mamma, what do you want to show me?"

Now Jamie's mamma was a very kind and tender-hearted woman, and nothing seemed more dreadful to her than cruelty to any animal. Some mothers, who felt as she did, would have seized Jamie by the arm, and said, "Here, you naughty boy; I saw you stoning birds over in the lot; if you ever do such a thing again, I shall punish you." But Jamie's mother had reflected about these things, and made up her mind that when little boys did cruel things, it was more because they were *thoughtless*, than because they at heart were cruel; and, therefore, instead of blaming him harshly, she set out to make him *think*.

So, when Jamie came in, she washed his heated face and hands, and then took from a drawer a small black box, which she wound up with a key like a watch-key. As soon as the box was set down, it began to play a most beautiful tune, and Jamie was astonished and delighted.

"What a curious box!" said he; "who did make it?"

"I do not know," said his mother; "but why do you think it is curious?"

"Why, it is curious to see a musical instrument shut up in such a little box. Why, I could carry this about in my pocket. I wish 't was mine, and I'd set it a going, and put it in my pocket some day, and then I could make the boys stare."

"But," said his mother, "if you think it strange to see a musical instrument put in a little box, what would you think if I could tell you of one which was so small as to be put in a bird's throat?"

"In a bird's throat!" said Jamie; "who ever heard of such a thing?"

"Well," answered his mother, "there is a boy in this room who has been listening this morning to a little instrument which is inside of a bird's throat, and which can make sweeter music than this box; and yet he did not seem to wonder at it at all."

Jamie looked wondering at his mother. "When you went into the fields, did you not hear robins and bluebirds playing on little instruments in their throats, and making all sorts of sweet sounds? Look now at your little canary bird hanging in the window, and see, when he sings, how his throat trembles."

"Oh, I know what you mean now," said Jamie: "you mean my little canary bird is like a music-box. Well, but what sort of an instrument has he got in his throat? I'm sure I don't know."

"Why, he has a little, fine, soft flute, that can play as many notes as a flute with silver keys."

"A flute in his throat," said Jamie, laughing; "what a funny idea!"

"It is even so," said his mother. "The little pipe through which the canary bird plays his tunes is more curiously made than any flutes which any instrument-maker ever formed; it is so small, yet so perfect; it fits into his throat so easily as never to interrupt his eating or breathing; and it turns whichever way he bends his head. Did you ever hear of any musical instrument that was as curious as this?"

"It is very strange," said Jamie; "I might have heard a bird sing a month, and never have thought of all this; but now I do think of it, it seems very curious. But, mother, what is this little flute made of?"

"It is made of little elastic rings."

"Elastic! what is that?" said Jamie.

"Why, like India rubber, springy and easily bent; and its being made of so many little elastic rings is the reason why he can turn and bend his throat without any inconvenience, which he could not do if it were a straight, stiff pipe like a flute.

"But," continued his mother, "these little bright eyes that your bird has are more wonderful than anything I have yet told you of; but the contrivance is so very complicated that I do not think I can make you understand it."

"What is *complicated?*" said Jamie.

"The machinery in the inside of my watch is *complicated;* that is, it is made up of a great many parts which answer many different purposes. And there is a machinery inside of one of those little birds' eyes that is more complicated still."

"What, that little dot of an eye, not bigger than a pin head?"

"Well, let me tell you; inside of that little eye is a contrivance by which, when the bird is looking at you, an exact picture of you is painted on the back of his eye."

"It must be a very *small* picture," said Jamie.

"Of course it is," said his mother, "but still it is a picture exactly like you; every line and every color in your face is painted exactly on the back of that little eye."

"Pray, how is it done?" said Jamie.

"That, my dear boy, is the machinery which I told you

was so complicated that I cannot hope to make you understand it. There is a contrivance just like it in your own eye, and in the eye of every animal; but it is more curious in a bird's eye because it is so very small."

"What, do we all have pictures painted on the back of our eyes? Is that the way we see?"

"Yes, that is the way; and when you are older you will be able to understand the wonderful and beautiful contrivance by which this is done. It has cost learned men much study to find it out, and they have discovered that the way in which the eye of a bird is made is in some respects more curious than our own."

"Well, mamma," said Jamie, "there's one thing; and that is, that there is a great deal more to be learned about a little bird than I ever supposed."

"But, Jamie, I have not yet told you half. Every bone in this little bird's body is as carefully made and finished as if that *bone* were the only thing the Creator had to make; and the joints of them are curiously contrived, so that the little fellow can hop, and spring, and turn all day, and yet nothing grates or gets out of order. They all move so springily and easily, that I doubt whether he ever thought whether he had a joint in his body or not. Then he has contrivances in his little stomach for dissolving his food, and turning it into blood, and he has blood vessels to carry it all over his body, and he has nerves to feel with, and he has muscles to move with."

"Now, mother, I don't know what nerves and muscles are," said Jamie.

"Nerves are what you feel with. You eat, and the nerves of your mouth give you your *taste*. The nerves of your nose give you *smell*. The nerves of your eyes *see*, and the nerves of your ears enable you to *hear*, and the nerves that cover your whole body enable you to feel. These nerves all come from a very large nerve that runs down through the middle of your back-bone, and is called the spinal marrow ; and they go through the whole body, dividing and branching out, till they form a network covering over the whole of it, so that you cannot put the point of a pin anywhere without touching a nerve."

" Mother, has a bird just such nerves ? "

" Very much the same."

" And what are muscles ? "

" Did you ever pull a piece of lean meat into little strings ? " said his mother.

" Yes," said Jamie.

" Well, a muscle is a bundle of such little strings, and these strings generally end in a strong, tough cord, called a tendon. This muscle has the power of shrinking up short, like India rubber ; and when it shrinks it pulls the tendon and the tendon pulls whatever it is fastened to. I can show you some tendon in a moment. Pull the back of your hand ; don't you find that there is a tough, hard cord runs down from every finger ? these are tendons. Now take hold tight round your arm, and shut up your hand."

Jamie did so, and exclaimed, " Oh, mother, when I shut up my hand, I feel something move up here by my elbow."

" That is the muscle," said his mother ; " you feel it drawing up short, and it pulls the tendons, and these tendons pull down your fingers."

Jamie amused himself some time with opening and shutting his hand, and then he said, —

" Well, are all the movements that we make done in the same way, by muscles and tendons ? "

" Yes," said his mother, " and all the motions of the animals. There are dozens and dozens of muscles, shrinking, and stretching, and pulling about in little Cherry every few moments, and yet none of them wear out, or break, or get out of order or give him the least trouble."

" I guess Cherry don't think much about them," said

Jamie, as he watched the little fellow hopping about in his cage.

"Poor little Cherry," said his mother, "he cannot understand how much God has done for him, with what watchful care he has made his little body, how carefully he has guarded it from all kinds of suffering, and how many beautiful contrivances there are in it to make him happy."

"No, indeed," said Jamie; "if he did he would love God."

"Well, Jamie," said his mother, "how should you feel, if you had contrived some curious and beautiful little plaything, and just as you had it all nicely finished off, some boy should come along with a great stick, and knock it all to pieces ? "

"Feel ? " said Jamie; " why, I should be mad enough ! "

"And suppose that some gentleman should invite you and two or three other boys to his house, and should show you into a large hall full of most beautiful pictures and looking-glasses, and flowers, and every kind of beautiful things, and you should amuse yourselves with breaking his looking-glasses, and beating down his flowers, and pulling to pieces all his curious and beautiful things ; how do you think he would feel ? "

"Why, I should think he would feel very angry, to be sure."

"Well, Jamie, when little boys go out into the woods and fields which God has filled with beautiful trees and flowers, and with hundreds of little happy birds, all so curiously and beautifully made, and amuse themselves only with throwing stones at them, and killing them, must not God be displeased ? "

"Certainly, I should think he must," said Jamie. After a few minutes, he added, " And it is a great deal worse to kill little birds than it is to break looking-glasses and such things, because little birds can *feel*, you know."

"Yes," said his mother, "and the care with which God has made them shows how much he has thought about them, and how careful he has been to do all he can to make them happy. The Bible says, his *tender* mercies are over all his works ; he is not merely good to everything, but he is tender and careful in all he does, as a mother is tender in taking care of a little helpless infant. Now," said his mamma, "I am going to read you a little story."

IT was a bright and beautiful morning in April. The snows had melted into the little brooks, and the little brooks ran rattling and gurgling about among the green, mossy stones. The violet had opened its fair blue eyes to look forth from its tufts of leaves; the broad blades of the water-flag and the blue lily were shooting up fresh and green; the yellow dandelions spotted the grass, and tufts of golden cowslips grew close by the water. The little leaves had just begun to show themselves, and looked like a thin green veil spread over the trees. The little birds had come back a long way through the air from the various countries where they had been spending the winter, and were filling the whole air with music.

On a mossy rail, a part of the orchard fence, sat two beautiful bluebirds, enjoying the bright sunshine, and twittering and chattering to each other with all their might. This very pair of birds, the last year, had made their nest in this very orchard, and brought up a whole family of little birds. All winter they had been chirping about and enjoying themselves among the warm, sunny valleys of the Bahama Isles; and now they had come back again to go to house-keeping in the old orchard.

Right in the middle of this peaceful orchard was a spreading apple-tree, whose bending branches almost touched the ground all around. The tall grass and clover grew up so high under this tree as to mix with the leaves and fruit on the end of these boughs, and underneath there was a delicious cool little room roofed by the branches, where all

summer long no creature had admission but the birds, and
the little flies, and the honey-bees — for this tree stood in
the very middle of the orchard, and Farmer Brown kept good
watch that no boys should get into it to trample down the
long grass before mowing time. Well, in the trunk of this
old tree, just where the branches parted, was a snug little
hole. It was exactly big enough for a bird to build its nest
in, and it was so situated that any one standing under the
tree and looking up could not have thought of there being
any hole there. A safer little house for a bird could never
have been found ; and here these little birds had concluded
to build their nest.

So they set to work and picked out all the rubbish and
dry sticks that had fallen into the hole, and after they had
nicely cleaned it out, they laid the foundation of their little
house with small twigs, which they plastered firmly together
with mud ; then they picked up straw and hay for the next
layer, and wove them into a little round nest; and after
that they flew all over the neighborhood to pick up any
stray feathers and soft bits of wool or moss that they could
find, to line the inside and make it soft and warm.

It took these bluebirds two or three days before their
nest was finished. But on the evening of the third day,
just as the long, bright beams of the setting sun were darting between the apple-trees of the old orchard, the two
little birds might have been seen chirping and chatting
together over their finished nest, in the happiest manner in
the world.

"What a lucky thing it was, my dear." said the little
wife, "that you found such a snug hole ! I am sure nobody
will ever find us out here. We can fly all about under this
great tree, and nobody will ever see us or suspect what we
are doing."

"And, my dear," said the little husband, "I am delighted with your weaving here. in the inside of the house.

How nicely you have worked in that little bit of red silk on one side! I had no idea, when the good woman swept that piece out of doors. that you could make so much of it. Then, how soft and warm the wool is! Ah, very few bluebirds can make a handsomer nest than this."

" Yes," said the wife, " and there is almost a yard of lace woven into it. I picked it off from a bush, where an old lady had hung it on purpose for me."

When the old apple-tree began to put forth its pink buds, after a few days five little blue eggs made their appearance in the nest, and then the mother bird began to set; while her mate spent all his time either in flying about to look up food for her, or perching about in different parts of the tree, and entertaining her with his music. At length the buds on the old tree opened, and it grew white with fragrant blossoms, and five little downy birds were to be seen in the nest. Nobody can say how delighted both parents were. They carefully picked out all the broken bits of the eggs from their nest, and then, while one would sit with wings outspread to keep the little creatures warm, the other would range about and get flies and worms to feed them. Little birds are amazingly hungry; and when either parent returned with food, you might have seen five little red mouths gaping wide open, all ready to receive their portion. And when their hunger was fully satisfied, the mother would nestle over them with her warm feathers, and the father bird would sit beside her, and they would admire the beautiful sheet of white blossoms over their heads, and have long talks about their little family, and how soon they would be learning to fly, and then what journeys they would take with them, and what good times they would have.

One beautiful morning, while the dew-drops were yet twinkling among the blossoms, the father bird prepared to go on one of his journeys after food. He bade good morning to his pretty family in a sweet song which he sung on the highest branch of the apple-tree, and then soared off into the blue sky, as happy a bird as ever was seen.

Just at the same time a man with a large bag slung over his shoulder, and a long gun in his hand, made his appearance in the fields. Pretty soon he saw our bright father bluebird, as he was sitting on the top of a tree with a worm in his mouth, which he was just going to carry home to his family.

So he drew up his gun and fired, and down fell the poor little bluebird. The man walked to the spot and picked him up — the shot had gone through his head and he was quite dead.

"What could he want to shoot the little birds for?" said Jamie.

"My dear boy, some people have an absurd way of thinking that birds will injure the fruit; and as there were one or two ripe cherry-trees in this orchard, the man thought they would get his cherries. It is a very foolish idea; for the birds, in fact, do more good by devouring the grubs and insects that injure trees and plants, than all the harm they can do by helping themselves now and then to a little fruit."

Well, it came noon, and the mother bird remained in the old apple-tree, still brooding and tending her little ones, and wondering that their poor father did not return as he had promised. Very soon the long shadows stretched to the east, and showed that the afternoon was far spent; and still he did not return, and the mother bird wondered, and the little birds began to call for their food. So the mother left the little birds, and went to the top of the tree, and began to call on her husband; but she could not make him hear. She fluttered around among the trees of the orchard, looking for him, and calling him; but in vain. Then she picked up some food for her little ones, and returned home weary and sad. The dark night came, but no kind father returned. And in the morning there was no merry song in the old tree, for the father was gone and the mother was silent. But she took up the burden of supporting her family, and went flying about in the orchard picking up food for her little ones as well as she was able.

While she was thus flying about one day, the same man, with the gun on his shoulder, came spying about the old orchard, for he had said that it was an excellent place to shoot birds. Pretty soon he saw the poor mother picking worms from a mossy rail, and pointed his gun at her. The shot struck her wing and went into her side; but still she was not killed; and all bleeding as she was, she thought she would try to get home to her birdies once more. When she came to the old apple-tree, her little strength was quite spent — her feathers were dripping with blood; and when she had put the food she had gathered into their mouths, she fell down at the foot of the tree. She fluttered a few moments, and then her soft little eyes closed, and the poor mother bird was dead.

A great while after, when the old apple-tree was loaded with bright yellow apples, the farmer's men mowed the grass under the tree, and one of the boys thought he would go up and shake off some apples. While he was climbing, he put his hand into the hole and found our birds' nest.

He drew it out, and there were five little dead birds in it! So much for shooting the pretty bluebirds!

THE HAPPY CHILD

"Papa," said Edward Thompson to his father, "you don't know what beautiful things James Robertson has, of all kinds."

"Oh, yes," said little Robert, "when we were there yesterday, he took us up into a little room that was all full of playthings, just like a toy-shop."

"He had little guns, and two drums, and a trumpet, and a fife," said Edward; "and one of the drums was a real one, papa, such as men play on."

"And, papa, he had railroad cars, with a little railroad for them to go on, and steam-engine, and all," said Robert.

"And a whole company of wooden soldiers," said Edward.

"And all sorts of blocks to build houses," said Robert.

"And besides, papa," said Edward, "he has a real live pony to ride on; such a funny little fellow you never saw; and he has such a pretty little riding-stick, and a splendid saddle and bridle."

"Really," said their father, "you make out quite a list of possessions."

"Oh, but, papa, we have not told you half; he has a beautiful flower-garden, and a gardener to cultivate it for him, so that he don't have to take any trouble with it, and he can do anything with the flowers he chooses."

"Oh, and, papa, he has rabbits and a beautiful gray squirrel, with a cage fixed so nicely; and the squirrel plays so many droll tricks; and he has a parrot that can talk, and laugh, and call his name, and say a great many funny things."

"Well," said their father, "I suppose you think that James is a very happy boy."

"Oh, yes, indeed, papa; how can he help being happy?" said both boys. "Besides, his mamma, he says, lets him do very much as he likes about everything."

"Indeed!" said their father; "and was he so very happy all day when you were there?"

"Why, no, not all day," said Edward; "but then there was a reason for it; for in the morning we had planned to go out to the lake to fish, and it rained, and it made James feel rather cross, I suppose."

"But," said his father, "I should have thought, by your account, that there were things enough in the house to have amused you all."

"But James said he was so used to all those things that he did not want to play with them," said Robert; "he called some of the prettiest things that he had 'ugly old things,' and said he hated the sight of them."

"Well," said their father, "I suspect, if the truth was known, James is not so much to be envied after all. I have been a week at a time at his father's house, and I have thought that a more uncomfortable, unhappy-tempered little fellow I never saw."

"Well, that is strange," said Edward; "I am sure I would be happy if I was in his place."

"I am afraid you would not," said his father; "for I believe it is having so many things that makes him unhappy."

"Having so many things, papa!" said both boys.

"Yes, my sons; but I will explain this more to you some other time. However, this afternoon, as you are going to have a ride with me, I think I will take you over to see a little boy who is a very happy boy, as I think," said their father.

.   .   .   .

"I wonder if this can be the house?" said Edward to Robert, as the carriage stopped before a very small brown house.

Their father got out, and asked them to walk in with him. It was a very little house, with only two rooms in it; and in the one they entered they saw a very pale, thin little boy, lying on a small, low bed in front of the door. His face was all worn away by disease, and his little hands, which were folded on the outside of the bed, were so thin one could almost see through them. He had a few playthings lying by him on the bed, and on a little stand near him was a cracked brown mug, in which were some sweet peas, and larkspurs, and lavender, and bright yellow marigolds; beside which lay a well-worn Bible and hymn-book. His mother was ironing in the next room; but when she saw the boys and their father, she came forward to receive them.

" Well, my little fellow," said Mr. Thompson, " how do you do to-day ? "

" Oh, pretty comfortable," he said, cheerfully.

" I have brought my boys to see you," said Mr. Thompson.

The sick boy smiled, and reached out one of his thin little hands to welcome them. Edward and Robert took his hand, and then turned and looked anxiously at their father.

" Papa, how long has he been so sick ? " asked Robert.

" More than a year, young gentlemen," said his mother; " it 's a year since he has been able to sit up : and it 's four months since he has been able to be turned at all in bed ; he has to lie all the time, just as you see, on his back."

" Oh, what a long, long time ! " said Edward ; " why can't you turn him. and let him lie on his side ? "

" Because it hurts him to lie on either side."

" What is the matter with him ? " asked Robert.

" Why, the doctor says it 's a complaint of the bone ; it began more than two years ago, down in his foot, and they had to cut the foot off, in hopes that that would stop it ; but it did n't ; and then they cut off the leg above the knee, and that did n't stop it; and it 's creeping up, up, up, and finally it will be the death of him. He suffers dreadfully at nights; sometimes no sleep at all for two or three nights."

"Oh, father, how dreadful!" said Edward, pressing close to his father.

"Papa," said Robert, looking up and whispering, "I thought we were going to see a little boy that was very happy."

"Wait a while," said Mr. Thompson, "and you will see;" and then he turned to the sick boy.

"My little fellow," said he, "you find it very tiresome lying here so long."

"A little so," said the boy, smiling very pleasantly; "but then I have so many things to make me comfortable."

"What things?"

"Oh, I have a knife, and I can whittle a little at a time, and I have this little china dog that a lady gave me. I play with that sometimes; and then, don't you see my flowers?"

The little boy pointed to a small bed of flowers just before the door, where there were some pinks, and some larkspurs, and marigolds, and sweet peas; it was weeded very clean, and the flowers made it bright enough.

"Mother planted all those flowers for me in the spring," he said, "and she has watered and weeded them every night after she has done her work; they grow beautifully, and I lie here every day and look at them. Sometimes, when the rain is falling, or in the morning when the dew is on them, they look so bright and fresh! Mother puts some in the mug to stand by me every day."

"But don't you suffer a great deal of pain?"

"Sometimes I do; but then, sir, I know that God would not send it if it was not best for me, so I am willing to bear it; besides, I know that the Lord Jesus Christ suffered more pain for me than I suffer. There are some beautiful hymns about it in this book," he added, taking up his little hymn-book; " and then I have my Bible. Oh, I don't know how I could get along if it were not for that."

" But are you never unhappy when you see other boys jumping and playing about ? "

" No, I am not ; I know God knows what is best for me; besides, my Saviour comforts me. I love to lie here, when it is all still, and I think about him."

" Don't you hope that sometime you will get well, and be able to go about again ? "

" No, I know that I can't ; I shall not live a great while ; they all say so."

" And don't you feel afraid to die ? "

" Oh, no ; I feel as if I would be glad to. I long to see my Saviour. All I feel sad about is, that mother will be lonesome when I am gone."

" Well, my little boy, if there is anything that I can send you to make you more comfortable, I shall be glad to."

" Oh, thank you, sir ; but I don't know as I want anything."

" I wish I could relieve your pains, my little fellow," said Mr. Thompson.

" God would do it in a minute, if it was only best for me," said the boy ; " and if it is not best, I had rather he would not do it. Besides, I think I am happier now than I used to be when I was well."

" Ah ! how can that be ? "

" I did not love God so much then, and I used to forget to read my Bible. I had not so much pleasure in thinking about heaven," said the little boy.

" You remember," said Mr. Thompson, " it says in the Bible, ' Before I was afflicted I went astray ; but now have I kept thy word.' "

" That is just it, sir." said the boy ; " just the way I feel. Oh, I 've been very happy since I have been sick here."

Edward and Robert looked at their father, at these words. Mr. Thompson now rose to go.

"If you please, sir, perhaps the boys would like some of my flowers; there is a beautiful root of pinks there, and some roses," said the sick boy.

"Oh, no," said Edward, "we won't take them away from you."

"Oh, I like to give them away," said the boy, earnestly; "do take some."

"Take some, my dear children; it will please him," said Mr. Thompson, in a low voice, as he picked a few and gave to each of the boys; and then added aloud, "We will keep them to remember you by, my dear little fellow."

As they parted with the little boy, he smiled sweetly, and put out his hand, and added, —

"If you'll come when my latest rose-bush is in blossom, I'll give you some roses."

.   .   .   .

"Papa," said Edward, "that poor little boy really does seem to be happy, and yet he is poor and sick and in pain; and he has very few things, too. It is strange; he is certainly a great deal happier than James Robertson."

"Well, I can tell you the reason," said his father. "It is because James Robertson is a *selfish boy* that he is unhappy; from morning till night he thinks of nothing but how to please himself. His father and mother have spent all their lives in contriving ways to please him, and have never required him to give up his own will in anything; and now he is so selfish that he is always unhappy. He does not love God, and he does not love his parents, nor anything else, so well as he loves himself; and such a boy will always be unhappy. And the reason that this poor little sick boy is happy, is because he has learned to love God, his Saviour, better than anything else, and to find all his pleasure in trying to do *His* will instead of his own.

This is what makes him *peaceful*. If he did not love God, and love to give up his will to Him, and to bear and suffer whatever He thought best, how miserable he would be now !"

"He would be very fretful, I suppose," said Edward ; " I 'm afraid I should be."

"Yes," said his father ; " but now, when he has learned to give up entirely to the will of his heavenly Father, see how he seems to enjoy his flowers, and his hymn-book, and his few little playthings. He enjoys them more than James Robertson enjoys all his elegant things. Now, my dear boys, remember this : The way to be happy is to have a *right heart*, and not to have everything given to us that we want."

LITTLE CAPTAIN TROTT

It has become fashionable to write sketches of the lives of really existing worthies, who are at present acting their parts with more or less success on the stage of this mortal life. Among them all there is none who, as we think, exerts a more perceptible influence, makes more commotion, more confusion, more comfort, more perplexity, more laughing, and more crying than our sprightly, ingenious, omnipresent, ever-active little friend, Captain Trott.

His title indicates that he is in a position of responsibility and command. Nobody would infer this, from his short body, his dumpy little hands, and his square, padding little feet, his curly head, his ivory-fine complexion, and his rather singular modes of treating the English language; yet, should the question be put at this moment by the electric telegraph, to the million families of our land, " Who governs and rules you ? " the reply would come back, as with the voice of many waters, " Little Trott." Little Trott has more influence at this hour in these United States than General Grant himself !

In giving a sketch of his personal appearance, we are embarrassed by the remembrance of the overweening admiration he always contrives to excite in the breasts of the feminine part of creation. A million women, we do believe, at this very hour, if we should draw his picture, would be ready to tear our eyes out for the injustice done him. That the picture of our little Trott, forsooth ? What is the woman thinking of ? She does not know, she never can know, she had no senses to perceive, half how beautiful he is ! So say all the mothers ; and the grandmothers double-say it, and are ready to shoot you if you doubt it ; and the aunties and sisters reiterate it ; and even the papas — who, as heads of the women and lords of creation, are supposed to take more sensible and impartial views of matters and things — go hook and line, bob and sinker into the general current. The papas are, if anything, even sillier and more beside themselves with admiration than the mammas. Trott is, in their eyes, a miracle of nature. They gaze at him with round eyes of wonder ; they are really ashamed of themselves for their inebriate state of admiration, and endeavor to draw over it a veil of reticent gravity ; but it leaks out of every cranny, and oozes out of every pore, that the man is, as our negro friends say, "done gone over" in admiration of little Trott. His administration, therefore, is a highly popular one, and we run some risk in instituting anything like a criticism upon it. There is, of course, as in all popular governments, an opposition party, composed principally of older brothers and sisters, crabbed old bachelors, and serious-minded maiden ladies, who feel it their duty, with varying success, to keep up a protest against Trott's proceedings, and to call on his besotted admirers to be on their guard against his wiles, and even go so far as to prophesy that, if not well looked after, he may one day ruin the country. Under these circumstances, it is a delicate matter to deliver our opinion of Trott, but we shall endeavor to do it with impartial justice. We shall speak our honest opinion of his accomplishments, his virtues. and his vices, be the consequences what they may.

And first we think that nobody can refuse to Captain Trott the award of industry and energy.

He is energy itself. He believes in early rising, and, like all others who practice this severe virtue, is of opinion that it is a sin for anybody to sleep after he is awake. Therefore he commences to whistle and crow, and pick open

the eyes of papa and mamma with his fat fingers, long before " Aurora crimsons the east." as the poet says. For
those hapless sinners who love the dear iniquity of morning
naps Trott has no more mercy than a modern reformer;
and, like a modern reformer, he makes no exceptions for
circumstances. If he is wide-awake and refreshed, it makes
no difference to him that mamma was up half a dozen
times the night before to warm his milk and perform other
handmaid offices for his lordship; or that papa was late at
his office, and did not get asleep till twelve o'clock. Up
they must get; laziness is not to be indulged; morning
naps are an abomination to his soul; and he wants his
breakfast at the quickest conceivable moment, that he may
enter on the duty of the day.

This duty may be briefly defined as the process of culti-
vating the heavenly virtue of patience in the mind of his
mother and of the family and the community generally.
He commences the serious avocations of the day after a
shower of kisses, adorned by fleeting dimples and sparkling
glances. While mamma is hastily dressing, he slyly upsets
the wash-pitcher on the carpet, and sits a pleased spectator
of the instant running and fussing which is the result. If
there is a box of charcoal tooth-powder within reach,
he now contrives to force that open and scatter its contents
over his nightgown and the carpet, thus still further increas-
ing the confusion. If he is scolded, he immediately falls
on his mother's neck, and smothers her with sooty kisses.
While taking his bath, he insists on sucking the sponge,
and splashing the water all over his mother's neat morning-
wrapper. If this process is stopped, he shows the strength
of his lungs in violent protests, which so alarm the poor
woman for the character of the family, that she is forced to
compromise with him by letting him have a bright pincush-
ion, or her darling gold watch, or some other generally forbidden object to console him. This, of course, he splashes

into the water forthwith, and fights her if she attempts to take it away ; for Trott is a genuine red republican in the doctrine of his own right to have his own way. Then he follows her up through the day, knowing exactly when and where to put himself in her way, in fulfilment of his important mission of perfecting her in patience. If she be going up-stairs with baby in her arms, Trott catches her about the knees, or hangs on to her gown behind, with most persistent affection.

In the kitchen, if she be superintending verdant Erin in the preparation of some mysterious dish, Trott must be there, and Trott must help. With infinite fussing and tip-toe efforts, he pulls over on his head a pan of syrup, — and the consequences of this movement all our female friends see without words.

Is there company to dinner, and no dessert, and stupid Biddy utterly unable to compass the difficulties of a boiled custard, then mamma is to the fore, and Trott also. Just at the critical moment, — the moment of projection, — a loud scream from Trott announces that he has fallen head first into the rain-water butt ! The custard is spoiled, but the precious darling Trott is saved, and wiped up, and comes out, fresh and glowing, to proclaim to his delighted admirers that he still lives.

Thus much on Trott's energy and industry, but who shall describe the boundless versatility of his genius ? Versatility is Trott's forte. In one single day he will bring to pass a greater variety of operations than are even thought of in Congress, — much as they may do there, — and he is so persevering and industrious about it !

He has been known, while mamma is busy over some bit of fine work at her sewing-machine, to pad into the pantry and contrive machinery for escalading the flour-barrel, which has enabled him at last to plump himself fairly into the soft, downy interior, which he can now throw up over his head in chuckling transport, powdering his curls till he looks like a cherub upon a Louis Quatorze china teacup. Taken out, while his mother is looking for fresh clothes in the drawer, he hastens to plunge his head into the washbowl to clean it. He besets pussy, who runs at the very sight of him. He has often tried to perform surgical operations on her eyes with mamma's scissors; but pussy, having no soul to save, has no interest in being made perfect through suffering, and therefore gives him a wide berth. Nevertheless, Trott sometimes catches her asleep, and once put her head downward into a large stone water-jar, before she had really got enough awake to comprehend the situation. Her tail, convulsively waving as a signal of distress, alone called attention to the case, and deprived her of the honor of an obituary notice. But, mind you, had pussy died, what mamma and grandma and auntie would not have taken Trott's part against all the pussies in the world? "Poor little fellow! he must do something;" and "After all, the cat was n't much of a mouser; served her right; and was n't it cunning of him?" And, my dear friend, if Trott some day, when you are snoozing after dinner, should take a fancy to serve you as Jael did Sisera, your fate would scarcely excite any other comment. The "poor dear little fellow" would still be the hero of the house, and you the sinner, who had no business to put yourself in his way. This last sentence was interpolated here by my crabbed bachelor uncle, Mr. Herod Killchild, who cannot, of course, be considered as dispassionate authority. In fact, an open feud rages between Uncle Herod and Trott; and he only holds his position in the family circle because the women-folks are quick-witted enough to perceive that, after all, he is in his heart as silly about Trott as any of them. He has more than once been detected watching the little captain's antics over the top of his newspaper, and slyly snickering to himself as he followed his operations while at the same moment his mouth was ostensibly full of cursing and bitterness. Once, when Trott was very, very sick indeed, Uncle Herod lost his rest nights, — he declared it was only indigestion ; his eyes watered, — he declared that it was only a severe cold. But all these symptoms marvelously disappeared when Trott, as his manner is, suddenly got well and came out good as new, and tenfold more busy and noisy than ever. Then Uncle Herod remarked dryly that " he had hoped to be rid of that torment," and mamma laughed. Who minds Uncle Herod ?

We have spoken of Trott's industry, energy, and versatility ; we must speak also of his perseverance. This is undeniably a great virtue, as all my readers who have ever written in old-fashioned copy-books will remember. Trott's persistence and determination to carry his points and have his own way are traits that must excite the respect of the beholder.

When he has a point to carry, it must be a wise mamma, and a still wiser papa, that can withstand him, for his ways and wiles are past finding out. He tries all means and measures, — kissing, cajoling, coaxing ; and, these proving ineffectual, storming, crying, threatening, fighting fate with both of his chubby fists, and squaring off at the powers that be with a valor worthy of a soldier.

There are the best hopes of the little captain, if he keeps up equal courage and vigor, some future day, when he shall lead the armies of the republic.

If, however, Trott is routed, as sometimes occurs, it is to be said to his credit that he displays great magnanimity. He will come up and kiss and be friends, after a severe skirmish with papa, and own himself beaten in the handsomest manner.

But, like a true, cunning politician, when beaten, he does not give up. There is many a reserved wile under his mat of curls yet, and he still meditates some future victory ;

and, sooth to say, after a running fire of some weeks, Trott often carries his point, and establishes his right to take certain household liberties, in spite of the protest of the whole family republic.

"Well, what can you do with him? we can't be fighting him always," are the usual terms which announce the surrender.

And did not our Congress do about the same thing with President Johnson? The fact is, when you've got a chief magistrate, you can't fight him all the time, and Trott is the chief magistrate of the family state.

The opposition party in the government, consisting always of people who never had or are like to have Trotts of their own to take care of, are always largely blaming those who submit to him. They insist upon it that minute rules should be made, and Trott made to understand what is meant by the reign of law.

Law? We would like to see the code that could compass and forbid Trott's unheard-of inventions. He always surprises you by doing just the thing you never could have conceived of, and through it all his intentions are so excellent! He sees mamma rubbing her head with hair-oil, and forthwith dips his hand in a varnish-pot and rubs his own mat of curls. He sees Biddy squeeze bluing into the rinsing-water, and, watching his opportunity, throws the bluing-bag into the soup-kettle. You have oil paints put away in a deep recess in the closet. Of course he goes straight to them, squeezes all the tubes together, and makes a pigment with which he anoints his face and hands and the carpet, giving an entirely new view of a work of art. "Who would have thought, now, that he could have?" etc., is the usual refrain after these occurrences.

The maxim that "silence is golden" does not apply to Trott. Much as his noise may make mamma's head ache, it is nothing to the fearful apprehensions excited by his silence. If Trott is still ten minutes, or even five, look out for a catastrophe. He may be tasting bug-poison, or clawing the canary-bird out of the cage, or practicing writing on papa's last Art Union, or eating a whole box of pills, or picking mamma's calla bud, or, taken with a sudden fit of household usefulness, be washing the front of the bureau drawer with a ten-dollar bill which he has picked out of it !

Sleep is usually considered a gracious state for Trott, but he has too intense a sense of his responsibility to lose much time in this way, especially if mamma is to have company to dinner, or has any very perplexing and trying bit of household work to do. Under these circumstances Trott never can sleep. He is intensely interested ; he cannot let her go a moment.

There have been as many books written as there are stars in the skies concerning the vexed question of Trott's government, and concerning the constitutional limits of his rights and those of the older and bigger world.

And still that subject seems to be involved in mystery. Some few points only are clear, — Trott must *not* be allowed to make a bonfire of the paternal mansion, or stick the scissors in his mother's eyes, or cut his own throat with his father's razor. Short of this " the constitutional limits," as we say, are very undefined. And if you undertake to restrict him much, you will have all the fathers and mothers in the land on your back, who with one voice insist that, though Trott may have his faults, like all things human, yet he is a jolly little fellow, and they prefer, on the whole, to let him do just about as he does do, and don't want any advice on that subject.

Of course, his administration bears hard on the minority, and it is sometimes a question whether anybody else in the house has any rights which Trott is bound to respect. So much the worse for the minority. We should like to know what they are going to do about it ?

There is one comfort in this view of the subject. All the wonderful men of the world have been Trotts in their day ; have badgered and tormented their mammas till they trained them up into a meetness for Heaven, and then have come, in their turn, to be governed by other Trotts, — for in this kingdom the king never dies, or, rather, to put it in a modern form, in this republic there is always a president.

Well, after all, our hearts are very soft towards the little deluding Captain. The very thought that the house might some day be without his mischief and merriment and the patter of his little stubbed feet, causes us a hard lump in our throats at once. No noise of misrule and merriment, however deafening, where Trott reigns triumphant, can be so dreadful as the silence in the house where he once has been, but is to be no more.

> " The mother in the sunshine sits
> Beside the cottage wall,
> And, slowly, slowly as she knits,
> Her quiet tears down fall.
> *Her little hindering thing is gone,*
> And undisturbed she may knit on."

When we think of those short little mounds in Greenwood and Mount Auburn, we go in for patient submission to Trott with all his faults, rather than the dismalness of being without him. His hold is on our heart-strings, and reign over us he must.

We are reminded, too, how, years and years ago, the Dearest, Wisest, and Greatest that ever lived on earth took little Trott on his knee, and said, "Whosoever shall receive one of such children, in my name, receiveth me " ; " for of such is the kingdom of heaven."

Trott was doubtless as full of motion and mischief in those days as in these ; but the Divine eyes saw through it all, into that great mystery making little Trott the father of whatever is great and good in the future.

CHRISTMAS; OR, THE GOOD FAIRY

"Oh, DEAR! Christmas is coming in a fortnight, and I have got to think up presents for everybody!" said young Ellen Stuart, as she leaned languidly back in her chair. "Dear me, it's so tedious! Everybody has got everything that can be thought of."

"Oh, no," said her confidential adviser, Miss Lester, in a soothing tone. "You have means of buying everything you can fancy; and when every shop and store is glittering with all manner of splendors, you cannot surely be at a loss."

"Well, now, just listen. To begin with, there's mamma. What can I get for her? I have thought of ever so many things. She has three card cases, four gold thimbles, two or three gold chains, two writing desks of different patterns; and then as to rings, brooches, boxes, and all other things, I should think she might be sick of the sight of them. I am sure I am," said she, languidly gazing on her white and jeweled fingers.

This view of the case seemed rather puzzling to the adviser, and there was silence for a few minutes, when Ellen, yawning, resumed : —

"And then there's cousins Jane and Mary: I suppose they will be coming down on me with a whole load of presents; and Mrs. B. will send me something — she did last year; and then there's cousins William and Tom — I must get them something; and I would like to do it well enough, if I only knew what to get."

"Well," said Eleanor's aunt, who had been sitting quietly rattling her knitting needles during this speech, "it's a pity that you had not such a subject to practice on as I was when I was a girl. Presents did not fly about in those days as they do now. I remember, when I was ten years old, my father gave me a most marvelously ugly sugar dog for a Christmas gift. and I was perfectly delighted with it, the very idea of a present was so new to us."

"Dear aunt, how delighted I should be if I had any such fresh, unsophisticated body to get presents for! But to get and get for people that have more than they know what to do with now; to add pictures, books, and gilding when the centre tables are loaded with them now, and rings and jewels when they are a perfect drug! I wish myself that I were not sick, and sated, and tired with having everything in the world given me."

"Well, Eleanor," said her aunt, "if you really do want unsophisticated subjects to practice on, I can put you in the way of it. I can show you more than one family to whom you might seem to be a very good fairy, and where such gifts as you could give with all ease would seem like a magic dream."

"Why, that would really be worth while, aunt."

"Look over in that back alley," said her aunt. "You see those buildings?"

"That miserable row of shanties? Yes."

"Well, I have several acquaintances there who have never been tired of Christmas gifts or gifts of any other kind. I assure you, you could make quite a sensation over there."

"Well, who is there? Let us know."

"Do you remember Owen, that used to make your shoes?"

"Yes. I remember something about him."

"Well, he has fallen into a consumption, and cannot work any more; and he, and his wife, and three little children live in one of the rooms."

" How do they get along ? "

" His wife takes in sewing sometimes, and sometimes goes out washing. Poor Owen! 1 was over there yesterday; he looks thin and wasted, and his wife was saying that he was parched with constant fever, and had very little appetite. She had, with great self-denial, and by restricting herself almost of necessary food, got him two or three oranges; and the poor fellow seemed so eager after them."

" Poor fellow ! " said Eleanor, involuntarily.

" Now," said her aunt. " suppose Owen's wife should get up on Christmas morning and find at the door a couple of dozen of oranges, and some of those nice white grapes, such as you had at your party last week; don't you think it would make a sensation ? "

" Why, yes, I think very likely it might; but who else, aunt ? You spoke of a great many."

" Well, on the lower floor there is a neat little room, that is always kept perfectly trim and tidy ; it belongs to a young couple who have nothing beyond the husband's day wages to live on. They are, nevertheless, as cheerful and chipper as a couple of wrens ; and she is up and down half a dozen times a day, to help poor Mrs. Owen. She has a baby of her own about five months old, and of course does all the cooking, washing, and ironing for herself and husband ; and yet, when Mrs. Owen goes out to wash, she takes her baby, and keeps it whole days for her."

" I'm sure she deserves that the good fairies should smile on her," said Eleanor ; " one baby exhausts my stock of virtues very rapidly."

" But you ought to see her baby," said Aunt E. ; " so plump, so rosy, and good-natured, and always clean as a lily. This baby is a sort of household shrine ; nothing is too sacred or too good for it ; and I believe the little thrifty woman feels only one temptation to be extravagant, and that is to get some ornaments to adorn this little divinity."

" Why, did she ever tell you so ? "

" No: but one day, when I was coming down stairs, the door of their room was partly open, and I saw a peddler there with open box. John, the husband, was standing with a little purple cap on his hand, which he was regarding with mystified, admiring air, as if he did n't quite comprehend it, and trim little Mary gazing at it with longing eyes.

" ' I think we might get it,' said John.

" ' Oh, no,' said she, regretfully ; ' yet I wish we could, it 's so pretty ! ' "

" Say no more, aunt. I see the good fairy must pop a cap into the window on Christmas morning. Indeed, it shall be done. How they will wonder where it came from, and talk about it for months to come ! "

" Well, then," continued her aunt, " in the next street to ours there is a miserable building, that looks as if it were just going to topple over ; and away up in the third story, in a little room just under the eaves, live two poor, lonely old women. They are both nearly on to ninety. I was in there day before yesterday. One of them is constantly confined to her bed with rheumatism ; the other, weak and feeble, with failing sight and trembling hands, totters about, her only helper ; and they are entirely dependent on charity."

" Can't they do anything ? Can't they knit ? " said Eleanor.

" You are young and strong, Eleanor, and have quick eyes and nimble fingers ; how long would it take you to knit a pair of stockings ? "

" I ? " said Eleanor. " What an idea ! I never tried, but I think I could get a pair done in a week, perhaps."

" And if somebody gave you twenty-five cents for them, and out of this you had to get food, and pay room rent, and buy coal for your fire, and oil for your lamp —"

" Stop, aunt, for pity's sake ! "

" Well, I will stop ; but they can't : they must pay so much every month for that miserable shell they live in, or be turned into the street. The meal and flour that some kind person sends goes off for them just as it does for others, and they must get more or starve ; and coal is now scarce and high priced."

" O aunt, I 'm quite convinced, I 'm sure ; don't run me down and annihilate me with all these terrible realities. What shall I do to play good fairy to these old women ? "

" If you will give me full power, Eleanor, I will put up a basket to be sent to them that will give them something to remember all winter."

" Oh, certainly I will.   Let me see if I can't think of something myself."

" Well, Eleanor, suppose, then, some fifty or sixty years hence, if you were old, and your father, and mother, and aunts, and uncles, now so thick around you, lay cold and silent in so many graves — you have somehow got away off to a strange city, where you were never known — you live in a miserable garret, where snow blows at night through the cracks, and the fire is very apt to go out in the old cracked stove — you sit crouching over the dying embers the evening before Christmas — nobody to speak to you, nobody to care for you, except another poor old soul who lies moaning in the bed.   Now, what would you like to have sent you ? "

" O aunt, what a dismal picture ! "

" And yet, Ella, all poor, forsaken old women are made of young girls, who expected it in their youth as little as you do, perhaps."

" Say no more, aunt.   I 'll buy — let me see — a comfortable warm shawl for each of these poor women ; and I 'll send them — let me see — oh, some tea — nothing goes down with old women like tea : and I 'll make John wheel some coal over to them; and, aunt, it would not be a very bad thought to send them a new stove. I remember, the other day, when mamma was pricing stoves, I saw some such nice ones for two or three dollars."

"For a new hand, Ella, you work up the idea very well," said her aunt.

"But how much ought I to give, for any one case, to these women, say?"

"How much did you give last year for any single Christmas present?"

"Why, six or seven dollars for some; those elegant souvenirs were seven dollars; that ring I gave Mrs. B. was twenty."

"And do you suppose Mrs. B. was any happier for it?"

"No, really, I don't think she cared much about it; but I had to give her something, because she had sent me something the year before, and I did not want to send a paltry present to one in her circumstances."

"Then, Ella, give the same to any poor, distressed, suffering creature who really needs it, and see in how many forms of good such a sum will appear. That one hard, cold, glittering ring, that now cheers nobody, and means nothing, that you give because you must, and she takes because she must, might, if broken up into smaller sums, send real warm and heartfelt gladness through many a cold and cheerless dwelling, through many an aching heart."

"You are getting to be an orator, aunt; but don't you approve of Christmas presents, among friends and equals?"

"Yes, indeed," said her aunt, fondly stroking her head. "I have had some Christmas presents that did me a world of good — a little book mark, for instance, that a certain niece of mine worked for me, with wonderful secrecy, three years ago, when she was not a young lady with a purse full of money — that book mark was a true Christmas present; and my young couple across the way are plotting a profound

surprise to each other on Christmas morning. John has
contrived, by an hour of extra work every night, to lay by
enough to get Mary a new calico dress ; and she, poor soul,
has bargained away the only thing in the jewelry line she
ever possessed, to be laid out on a new hat for him.

"I know, too, a washerwoman who has a poor lame boy
— a patient, gentle little fellow — who has lain quietly for
weeks and months in his little crib, and his mother is going
to give him a splendid Christmas present."

"What is it, pray ? "

"A whole orange ! Don't laugh. She will pay ten
whole cents for it ; for it shall be none of your common
oranges, but a picked one of the very best going ! She has
put by the money, a cent at a time, for a whole month ;
and nobody knows which will be happiest in it, Willie or
his mother. These are such Christmas presents as I like
to think of — gifts coming from love, and tending to produce love ; these are the appropriate gifts of the day."

"But don't you think that it's right for those who *have*
money to give expensive presents, supposing always, as you
say, they are given from real affection ? "

"Sometimes, undoubtedly. The Saviour did not condemn
her who broke an alabaster box of ointment — very precious
— simply as a proof of love, even although the suggestion
was made, 'This might have been sold for three hundred
pence, and given to the poor.' I have thought he would
regard with sympathy the fond efforts which human love
sometimes makes to express itself by gifts, the rarest and
most costly. How I rejoiced with all my heart, when
Charles Elton gave his poor mother that splendid Chinese
shawl and gold watch ! because I knew they came from the
very fulness of his heart to a mother that he could not do
too much for — a mother that has done and suffered everything for him. In some such cases, when resources are
ample, a costly gift seems to have a graceful appropriateness ;

but I cannot approve of it if it exhausts all the means of doing for the poor ; it is better, then, to give a simple offering, and to do something for those who really need it."

Eleanor looked thoughtful ; her aunt laid down her knitting, and said, in a tone of gentle seriousness, " Whose birth does Christmas commemorate, Ella ? "

" Our Saviour's, certainly, aunt."

" Yes," said her aunt. " And when and how was he born ? In a stable ! laid in a manger ; thus born, that in all ages he might be known as the brother and friend of the poor. And surely, it seems but appropriate to commemorate his birthday by an especial remembrance of the lowly, the poor, the outcast, and distressed ; and if Christ should come back to our city on a Christmas day, where should we think it most appropriate to his character to find him ? Would he be carrying splendid gifts to splendid dwellings, or would he be gliding about in the cheerless haunts of the desolate, the poor, the forsaken, and the sorrowful ? "

And here the conversation ended.

.   .   .   .

" What sort of Christmas presents is Ella buying ? " said Cousin Tom, as the waiter handed in a portentous-looking package, which had been just rung in at the door.

" Let 's open it," said saucy Will. " Upon my word, two great gray blanket shawls ! These must be for you and me, Tom ! And what 's this ? A great bolt of cotton flannel and gray yarn stockings ! "

The door bell rang again, and the waiter brought in another bulky parcel, and deposited it on the marble-topped centre table.

" What 's here ? " said Will, cutting the cord. " Whew ! a perfect nest of packages ! oolong tea ! oranges ! grapes ! white sugar ! Bless me, Ella must be going to house-keeping ! "

" Or going crazy ! " said Tom ; " and on my word," said

he, looking out of the window, " there's a drayman ringing at our door, with a stove, with a teakettle set in the top of it ! "

" Ella's cook stove, of course," said Will ; and just at this moment the young lady entered, with her purse hanging gracefully over her hand.

" Now, boys, you are too bad ! " she exclaimed, as each of the mischievous youngsters was gravely marching up and down, attired in a gray shawl.

" Did n't you get them for us ? We thought you did," said both.

" Ella, I want some of that cotton flannel, to make me a pair of pantaloons," said Tom.

" I say, Ella," said Will, " when are you going to housekeeping ? Your cooking stove is standing down in the street ; 'pon my word, John is loading some coal on the dray with it."

" Ella, is n't that going to be sent to my office ? " said Tom ; " do you know I do so languish for a new stove with a teakettle in the top, to heat a fellow's shaving-water ! "

Just then, another ring at the door, and the grinning waiter handed in a small brown paper parcel for Miss Ella. Tom made a dive at it, and staving off the brown paper, developed a jaunty little purple velvet cap, with silver tassels.

" My smoking cap, as I live ! " said he ; " only I shall have to wear it on my thumb, instead of my head — too small entirely," said he, shaking his head gravely.

" Come, you saucy boys," said Aunt E., entering briskly. " what are you teasing Ella for ? "

" Why, do see this lot of things, aunt ! What in the world is Ella going to do with them ? "

" Oh, I know ! "

" You know ! Then I can guess, aunt, it is some of your charitable works. You are going to make a juvenile Lady Bountiful of El. eh ? "

Ella, who had colored to the roots of her hair at the *exposé* of her very unfashionable Christmas preparations, now took heart, and bestowed a very gentle and salutary little cuff on the saucy head that still wore the purple cap, and then hastened to gather up her various purchases.

"Laugh away," said she, gayly; "and a good many others will laugh, too, over these things. I got them to make people laugh — people that are not in the habit of laughing!"

"Well, well, I see into it," said Will; "and I tell you I think right well of the idea, too. There are worlds of money wasted, at this time of the year, in getting things that nobody wants, and nobody cares for after they are got; and I am glad, for my part, that you are going to get up a variety in this line; in fact, I should like to give you one of these stray leaves to help on," said he, dropping a ten dollar note into her paper. "I like to encourage girls to think of something besides breastpins and sugar candy."

But our story spins on too long. If anybody wants to see the results of Ella's first attempts at *good fairyism*, they can call at the doors of two or three old buildings on Christmas morning, and they shall hear all about it.

LITTLE FRED, THE CANAL BOY

PART I

In the outskirts of the little town of Toledo, in Ohio, might be seen a small, one-story cottage, whose external architecture in no way distinguished it from dozens of other residences of the poor, by which it was surrounded. But over this dwelling, a presiding air of sanctity and neatness, of quiet and repose, marked it out as different from every other.

The little patch before the door, instead of being a loafing ground for swine, and a receptacle of litter and filth, was trimly set with flowers, weeded, watered, and fenced with dainty care. The scarlet bignonia clambered over the mouldering logs of the sides, shrouding their roughness in its gorgeous mantle of green and crimson, and the good old-fashioned morning glory, laced across the window, unfolded every day tints whose beauty, though cheap and common, the finest French milliner might in vain seek to rival.

When, in traveling the western country, you meet such a dwelling, do you not instinctively know what you shall see inside of it? Do you not seem to see the trimly-sanded floor, the well-kept furniture, the snowy muslin curtain? Are you not sure that on a neat stand you shall see, as on an altar, the dear old family Bible, brought, like the ancient ark of the covenant, into the far wilderness, and ever overshadowed, as a bright cloud, with remembered prayers and counsels of father and mother, in a far-off New England home?

And in this cottage there was such a Bible, brought from the wild hills of New Hampshire, and its middle page recorded the marriage of James Sandford to Mary Irving; and alas! after it another record, traced in a trembling hand — the death of James Sandford, at Toledo. And this fair, thin woman, in the black dress, with soft brown hair parted over a pale forehead, with calm, patient blue eyes, and fading cheek, is the once energetic, buoyant, light-hearted New Hampshire girl, who has brought with her the strongest religious faith, the active practical knowledge, the skillful, well-trained hand and head, with which cold New England portions her daughters. She had left all, and come to the western wilds with no other capital than her husband's manly heart and active brain — he young, strong, full of hope, prompt, energetic, and skilled to acquire — she careful, prudent, steady, no less skilled to save; and between the two no better firm for acquisition and prospective success could be desired. Everybody prophesied that James Sandford would succeed, and Mary heard these praises with a quiet exultation. But alas! that whole capital of hers — that one strong, young heart, that ready, helpful hand — two weeks of the country's fever sufficed to lay them cold and low forever.

And Mary yet lived, with her babe in her arms, and one bright little boy by her side; and this boy is our little brown-eyed Fred — the hero of our story. But few years had rolled over his curly head, when he first looked, weeping and wondering, on the face of death. Ah, one look on that awful face adds years at once to the age of the heart; and little Fred felt manly thoughts aroused in him by the cold stillness of his father, and the deep, calm anguish of his mother.

"O mamma, don't cry so, don't," said the little fellow. "I am alive, and I can take care of you. Dear mamma, I pray for you every day." And Mary was comforted even in her tears and thought, as she looked into those clear, loving brown eyes, that her little intercessor would not plead in vain: for saith Jesus, "Their angels do always behold the face of my Father which is in heaven."

In a few days she learned to look her sorrows calmly in the face, like a brave, true woman, as she was. She was a widow, and out of the sudden wreck of her husband's plans but a pittance remained to her, and she cast about, with busy hand and head, for some means to eke it out. She took in sewing — she took in washing and ironing; and happy did the young exquisite deem himself whose shirts came with such faultless plaits, such snowy freshness, from the slender hands of Mary. With that matchless gift which old Yankee housewives call faculty, Mary kept together all the ends of her raveled skein of life, and began to make them wind smoothly. Her baby was the neatest of all babies, as it was assuredly the prettiest, and her little Fred the handiest and most universal genius of all boys. It was Fred that could wring out all the stockings, and hang out all the small clothes, that tended the baby by night and by day, that made her a wagon out of an old soap box, in which he drew her in triumph; and at their meals he stood reverently in his father's place, and with folded hands repeated, "Bless the Lord, O my soul, and forget not all his mercies;" and his mother's heart responded amen to the simple prayer. Then he learned, with manifold puffing and much haggling, to saw wood quite decently, and to swing an axe almost as big as himself in wood splitting; and he ran of errands, and did business with an air of bustling importance that was edifying to see; he knew the prices of lard, butter, and dried apples, as well as any man about, and, as the storekeeper approvingly told him, was a smart chap at a bargain. Fred grew three inches higher the moment he heard it.

In the evenings, after the baby was asleep, Fred sat by

his mother with slate and book, deep in the mysteries of
reading, writing, and ciphering; and then the mother and
son talked over their little plans, and hallowed their nightly
rest by prayer; and when, before retiring, his mother knelt
with him by his little bed and prayed, the child often
sobbed with a strange emotion, for which he could give no
reason.   Something there is in the voice of real prayer that
thrills a child's heart, even before he understands it; the
holy tones are a kind of heavenly music, and far off, in distant years, the callous and worldly man often thrills to his
heart's core when some turn of life recalls to him his
mother's prayer.

So passed the first years of the life of Fred. Meanwhile his little sister had come to toddle about the cottage
floor full of insatiable and immeasurable schemes of mischief.   It was she that upset the clothes basket, and pulled
over the molasses pitcher on to her own astonished head,
and with incredible labor upset every pail of water that by
momentary thoughtlessness was put within reach.   It was
she that was found stuffing poor, solemn old pussy head
first into the water jar, that wiped up the floor with her
mother's freshly-ironed clothes, and jabbered, meanwhile, in
most unexampled Babylonish dialect, her own vindications
and explanations of these misdemeanors.   Every day her
mother declared that she must begin to get that child into
some kind of order; but still the merry little curly pate
contemned law and order, and laughed at all ideas of retri-
butive justice, and Fred and his mother laughed and de-
plored. in the same invariable succession, the various direful results of her activity and enterprise.

But still, as Mary toiled on, heavy cares weighed down
her heart.   Her boy grew larger and larger, and her own
health grew feebler in proportion as it needed to be stronger.
Sometimes a whole week at a time found her scarce able to
crawl from her bed, shaking with ague, or burning with

fever; and when there is little or nothing with which to replace them, how fast food seems to be consumed, and clothing to be worn out! And so at length it came to pass that, notwithstanding the labors of the most tireless of needles, and the cutting, clipping, and contriving of the most ingenious of hands, the poor mother was forced to own to herself that her darlings looked really shabby, and kind neighbors one by one hinted and said that she must do something with her boy — that he was old enough to earn his own living; and the same idea occurred to the spirited little fellow himself.

He had often been along by the side of the canal, and admired the horses; for between the horse and Fred there was a perfect magnetic sympathy, and no lot in life looked to him so bright and desirable as to be able to sit on a horse and drive all day long; and when Captain W., pleased with the boy's bright face and prompt motions, sought to enlist him as one of his drivers, he found a delighted listener. "If he could only persuade mother, there was nothing like it." For many nights after the matter was proposed, Mary only cried; and all Fred's eloquence, and his brave promises of never doing anything wrong, and being the best of all supposable boys, were insufficient to console her.

Every time she looked at the neat, pure little bed, beside her own, that bed hallowed by so many prayers, and saw her boy, with his glowing cheeks and long dark lashes, sleeping so innocently and trustfully, her heart died within her, as she thought of a dirty berth on the canal boat, and rough boatmen, swearing, chewing tobacco, and drinking; and should she take her darling from her bosom and throw him out among these? Ah, happy mother! look at your little son of ten years, and ask yourself, if you were obliged to do this, should you not tremble! Give God thanks, therefore, you can hold your child to your heart till he is old enough to breast the dark wave of life. The poor must throw them in, to sink or swim, as happens. Not for ease — not for freedom from care — not for commodious house and fine furniture, and all that competence gives, should you thank God so much as for this, that you are able to shelter, guide, restrain, and educate the helpless years of your children.

Mary yielded at last to that master who can subdue all wills — necessity. Sorrowfully, yet with hope in God, she made up the little package for her boy, and communicated to him with renewed minuteness her parting counsels and instructions. Fred was bright and full of hope. He was sure of the great point about which his mother's anxiety clustered — he should be a good boy, he knew he should; he never should swear; he never should touch a drop of spirits, no matter who asked him — that he was sure of. Then he liked horses so much : he should ride all day and never get tired, and he would come back and bring her some money; and so the boy and his mother parted.

Physical want or hardship is not the great thing which a mother need dread for her child in our country. There is scarce any situation in America where a child would not receive, as a matter of course, good food and shelter; nor is he often overworked. In these respects a general spirit of good nature is perceptible among employers, so that our Fred meets none of the harrowing adventures of an Oliver Twist in his new situation.

To be sure he soon found it was not as good fun to ride a horse hour after hour, and day after day, as it was to prance and caper about for the first few minutes. At first his back ached, and his little hands grew stiff, and he wished his turn were out, hours before the time ; but time mended all this. He grew healthy and strong, and though occasionally kicked and tumbled about rather unceremoniously by the rough men among whom he had been cast, yet, as they said, " he was a chap that always came down on his feet, throw him which way you would;" and for this reason he was rather a favorite among them. The fat, black cook, who piqued himself particularly on making corn cake and singing Methodist hymns in a style of unsurpassed excellence, took Fred into particular favor, and being equally at home in kitchen and camp-meeting lore, not only put by for him various dainty scraps and fragments, but also undertook to further his moral education by occasional luminous exhortations and expositions of Scripture, which somewhat puzzled poor Fred, and greatly amused the deck hands.

Often, after driving all day, Fred sat on deck beside his fat friend, while the boat glided on through miles and miles of solemn, unbroken old woods, and heard him sing about "de New Jerusalem," about "good old Moses, and Paul, and Silas," with a kind of dreamy, wild pleasure. To be sure it was not like his mother's singing; but then it had a sort of good sound, although he never could very precisely make out the meaning.

As to being a good boy, Fred, to do him justice, certainly tried to very considerable purpose. He did not swear as yet, although he heard so much of it daily that it seemed the most natural thing in the world; and although one and another of the hands often offered him tempting portions of their potations, as they said, "to make a man of him," yet Fred faithfully kept his little temperance pledge to his mother. Many a weary hour, as he rode, and rode, and rode through hundreds of miles of unvarying forest, he strengthened his good resolutions by thoughts of home and its scenes.

There sat his mother; there stood his own little bed; there his baby sister, toddling about in her night gown; and he repeated the prayers and sung the hymns his mother taught him, and thus the good seed still grew within him. In fact, with no very distinguished adventures, Fred achieved the journey to Cincinnati and back, and proud of his laurels, and with his wages in his pocket, found himself again at the familiar door.

Poor Fred! a sad surprise awaited him. The elfin shadow that was once ever flitting about the dwelling was gone; the little pattering footsteps, the tireless, busy fingers, all gone; and his mother, paler, sicker, sadder than before, clasped him to her bosom, and called him her only comfort. Fred had brought a pocketful of sugar plums, and the brightest of yellow oranges to his little pet; alas! how mournfully he regarded them now!

How little do we realize, when we hear that such and such a poor woman has lost her baby, how much is implied to her in the loss! She is poor; she must work hard; the child was a great addition to her cares; and even pitying neighbors say, " It was better for her, poor thing! and for the child too." But perhaps this very child was the only flower of a life else wholly barren and desolate. There is often, even in the humblest and most uncultured nature, an undefined longing and pining for the beautiful. It expresses itself sometimes in the love of birds and of flowers, and one sees the rosebush or the canary bird in a dwelling from which is banished every trace of luxury. But the little child, with its sweet, spiritual eyes, its thousand bird-like tones, its prattling, endearing ways, its guileless, loving heart, is a full and perfect answer to the most ardent craving of the soul. It is a whole little Eden of itself; and the poor woman whose whole life else is one dreary waste of toil, clasps her babe to her bosom, and feels proud, and rich, and happy. Truly said the Son of God, " Of such is the kingdom of heaven."

Poor Mary! how glad she was to see her boy again — most of all, that they could talk together of their lost one! How they discoursed for hours about her! How they cried together over the little faded bonnet, that once could scarce be kept for a moment on the busy, curly head! How they treasured, as relics, the small finger marks on the doors, and consecrated with sacred care even the traces of her merry mischief about the cottage, and never tired of telling over to each other, with smiles and tears, the record of the past gleesome pranks!

But the fact was, that Mary herself was fast wearing away. She had borne up bravely against life; but she had but a gentle nature, and gradually she sank from day to day. Fred was her patient, unwearied nurse, and neighbors — never wanting in such kindness as they can understand — supplied her few wants. The child never wanted for food, and the mantel shelf was filled with infallible specifics, each one of which was able, according to the showing, to insure perfect recovery in every case whatever; and yet, strange to tell, she still declined. At last, one still autumn morning, Fred awoke, and started at the icy coldness of the hand clasped in his own. He looked in his mother's face; it was sweet and calm as that of a sleeping infant, but he knew in his heart that she was dead.

PART II

MONTHS afterwards, a cold December day found Fred turned loose in the streets of Cincinnati. Since his mother's death he had driven on the canal boat; but now the boat was to lie by for winter, and the hands, of course, turned loose to find employment till spring. Fred was told that he must look up a place; everybody was busy about their own affairs, and he must shift for himself; and so, with half his wages in his pocket, and promises for the rest, he started to seek his fortune.

It was a cold, cheerless, gray-eyed day, with an air that pinched fingers and toes, and seemed to penetrate one's clothes like snow water — such a day as it needs the brightest fire and the happiest heart to get along at all with; and, unluckily, Fred had neither. Christmas was approaching, and all the shops had put on their holiday dresses; the confectioners' windows were glittering with sparkling pyramids of candy, with frosted cake, and unfading fruits and flowers of the very best of sugar. There, too, was Santa Claus, large as life, with queer, wrinkled visage, and back bowed with the weight of all desirable knickknacks, going down chimney, in sight of all the children of Cincinnati, who gathered around the shop with constantly-renewed acclamations. On all sides might be seen the little people, thronging, gazing, chattering, while anxious papas and mammas in the shops were gravely discussing tin trumpets, dolls, spades, wheelbarrows, and toy wagons.

Fred never had heard of the man who said, "How sad a thing it is to look into happiness through another man's eyes!" but he felt something very like it as he moved through the gay and bustling streets, where everybody seemed to be finding what they wanted but himself.

He had determined to keep up a stout heart; but, in spite of himself, all this bustling show and merriment made him feel sadder and sadder, and lonelier and lonelier. He knocked and rang at door after door, but nobody wanted a boy; nobody ever does want a boy when a boy is wanting a place. He got tired of ringing door bells, and tried some of the shops. No, they did n't want him. One said if he was bigger he might do, another wanted to know if he could keep accounts; one thought that the man around the corner wanted a boy, and when Fred got there he had just engaged one. Weary, disappointed, and discouraged, he sat down by the iron railing that fenced a showy house, and thought what he should do. It was almost five in the afternoon: cold, dismal, leaden-gray was the sky — the darkness already coming on. Fred sat listlessly watching the great snow feathers, as they slowly sailed down from the sky. Now he heard gay laughs, as groups of merry children passed; and then he started, as he saw some woman in a black bonnet, and thought she looked like his mother. But all passed, and nobody looked at him, nobody wanted him. nobody noticed him.

Just then a patter of little feet was heard behind him on the flagstones, and a soft baby voice said, " How do 'oo do ? " Fred turned in amazement; and there stood a plump, rosy little creature of about two years, with dimpled cheek, ruby lips, and long, fair hair curling about her sweet face. She was dressed in a blue pelisse, trimmed with swan's down, and her complexion was so exquisitely fair. her eyes so clear and sweet, that Fred felt almost as if it were an angel. The little thing toddled up to him, and holding up before him a new wax doll, all splendid in silk and lace, seemed quite disposed to make his acquaintance.

Fred thought of his lost sister, and his eyes filled up with tears. The little one put up one dimpled hand to wipe them away, while with the other holding up before him the wax doll, she said, coaxingly, " No no ky."

Just then the house door opened, and a lady, richly dressed, darted out, exclaiming, " Why, Mary, you little rogue, how came you out here ? " Then stopping short, and looking narrowly on Fred, she said, somewhat sharply, " Whose boy are you ? and how came you here ? "

" I 'm nobody's boy," said Fred, getting up, with a bitter choking in his throat ; " my mother 's dead ; I only sat down here to rest me for a while."

" Well, run away from here," said the lady ; but the little girl pressed before her mother, and jabbering very earnestly in unimaginable English, seemed determined to give Fred her wax doll, in which, she evidently thought, resided every possible consolation.

The lady felt in her pocket and found a quarter, which she threw towards Fred. " There, my boy, that will get you lodging and supper, and to-morrow you can find some place to work, I dare say ; " and she hurried in with the little girl, and shut the door.

It was not money that Fred wanted just then, and he picked up the quarter with a heavy heart. The sky looked darker, and the street drearier, and the cold wind froze the tear on his cheeks as he walked listlessly down the street in the dismal twilight. " I can go back to the canal boat, and find the cook," he thought to himself. " He told me I might sleep with him to-night if I could n't find a place ; " and he quickened his steps with this determination. Just as he was passing a brightly lighted coffee house, familiar voices hailed him, and Fred stopped ; he would be glad even to see a dog he had ever met before, and of course he was glad when two boys, old canal boat acquaintances, hailed him, and invited him into the coffee house. The blazing fire was a brave light on that dismal night, and the faces of the two boys were full of glee, and they began rallying Fred on his doleful appearance, and insisting on it that he should take something warm with them.

Fred hesitated a moment ; but he was tired and desperate, and the steaming, well-sweetened beverage was too tempting.

" Who cares for me ? " thought he, " and why should I care ? " and down went the first spirituous liquor the boy had ever tasted ; and in a few moments he felt a wonderful change.   He was no longer a timid, cold, disheartened, heart-sick boy, but felt somehow so brave, so full of hope and courage, that he began to swagger, to laugh very loud, and to boast in such high terms of the money in his pocket, and of his future intentions and prospects, that the two boys winked significantly at each other.   They proposed, after sitting a while, to walk out and see the shop windows. All three of the boys had taken enough to put them to extra merriment ; but Fred, who was entirely unused to the stimulant, was quite beside himself.   If they sung, he shouted ; if they laughed, he screamed ; and he thought within himself he never had heard and thought so many witty things as on that very evening.   At last they fell in with quite a press of boys, who were crowding round a confectionery window, and, as usual in such cases, there began an elbowing and scuffling contest for places, in which Fred was quite conspicuous.   At last a big boy presumed on his superior size to edge in front of our hero, and cut off his prospect ; and Fred, without more ado, sent him smashing through the shop window.   There was a general scrabble, every one ran for himself, and Fred, never having been used to the business, was not very skillful in escaping, and of course was caught and committed to an officer, who, with small ceremony, carried him off and locked him up in the watch house, from which he was the next morning taken before the mayor, and after examination sent to jail.

This sobered Fred. He came to himself as out of a dream, and he was overwhelmed with an agony of shame and self-reproach. He had broken his promise to his dead mother — he had been drinking! and his heart failed him when he thought of the horrors that his mother had always associated with that word. And then he was in jail — that place that his mother had always represented as an almost impossible horror, the climax of shame and disgrace. The next night the poor boy stretched himself on his hard, lonely bed, and laid under his head his little bundle, containing his few clothes and his mother's Bible, and then sobbed himself to sleep.

Cold and gray dawned the following morning on little Fred, as he slowly and heavily awoke, and with a bitter chill of despair recalled the events of the last two nights, and looked up at the iron-grated window, and round on the cheerless walls; and, as if in bitter contrast, arose before him an image of his lost home — the neat, quiet room, the white curtains and snowy floor, his mother's bed, with his own little cot beside it, and his mother's mild blue eyes, as they looked upon him only six months ago. Mechanically he untied the check handkerchief which contained his few clothes, and worldly possessions, and relics of home.

There was the small, clean-printed Bible his mother had given him with so many tears on their first parting; there was a lock of her soft brown hair; there, too, were a pair of little worn shoes and stockings, a baby's rattle, and a curl of golden hair, which he had laid up in memory of his lost little pet. Fred laid his head down over all these, his forlorn treasures, and sobbed as if his heart would break.

After a while the jailer came in, and really seemed affected by the distress of the child, and said what he could to console him; and in the course of the day, as the boy "seemed to be so lonesome like," he introduced another boy into the room as company for him. This was a cruel mercy; for while the child was alone with himself and the memories of the past, he was, if sad, at least safe, and in a few hours after his new introduction he was neither. His new companion was a tall boy of fourteen, with small. cunning, gray eyes, to which a slight cast gave an additional expression of shrewdness and drollery. He was a young gentleman of great natural talent, — in a certain line, — with very precocious attainments in all that kind of information which a boy gains by running at large for several years in the city's streets without anything particular to do, or anybody in particular to obey — any conscience, any principle, any fear either of God or man. We should not say that he had never seen the inside of a church, for he had been, for various purposes, into every one of the city, and to every camp-meeting for miles around; and so much had he profited by these exercises, that he could mimic to perfection every minister who had any perceptible peculiarity, could caricature every species of psalm-singing, and give ludicrous imitations of every form of worship. Then he was *au fait* in all coffee house lore, and knew the names and qualities of every kind of beverage therein compounded; and as to smoking and chewing, the first elements of which he mastered when he was about six years old, he was now a *connoisseur* in the higher branches. He had been in jail dozens of times — rather liked the fun; had served one term on the chain-gang — not so bad either — should n't mind another — learned a good many prime things there.

At first Fred seemed inclined to shrink from his new associate. An instinctive feeling, like the warning of an invisible angel, seemed to whisper, "Beware!" But he was alone, with a heart full of bitter thoughts, and the sight of a fellow-face was some comfort. Then his companion was so dashing, so funny, so free and easy, and seemed to make such a comfortable matter of being in jail, that Fred's heart, naturally buoyant, began to come up again in his breast. Dick

Jones soon drew out of him his simple history as to how he came there, and finding that he was a raw hand, seemed to feel bound to patronize and take him under his wing. He laughed quite heartily at Fred's story, and soon succeeded in getting him to laugh at it too.

How strange! — the very scenes that in the morning he looked at only with bitter anguish and remorse, this noon he was laughing at as good jokes — so much for the influence of good society! An instinctive feeling, soon after Dick Jones came in, led Fred to push his little bundle into the farthest corner, under the bed, far out of sight or inquiry; and the same reason led him to suppress all mention of his mother, and all the sacred part of his former life. He did this more studiously, because, having once accidentally remarked how his mother used to forbid him certain things, the well-educated Dick broke out, —

"Well, for my part, I could whip my mother when I wa'n't higher than that!" with a significant gesture.

"Whip your mother!" exclaimed Fred, with a face full of horror.

"To be sure, greenie! Why not? Precious fun it was in those times. I used to slip in and steal the old woman's whiskey and sugar when she was just too far over to walk a crack — she'd throw the tongs at me, and I'd throw the shovel at her, and so it went square and square."

Goethe says somewhere, "Miserable is that man whose *mother* has not made all other mothers venerable." Our new acquaintance bade fair to come under this category.

Fred's education, under this talented instructor, made progress. He sat hours and hours laughing at his stories — sometimes obscene. sometimes profane, but always so full of life, drollery, and mimicry that a more steady head than Fred's was needed to withstand the contagion. Dick had been to the theatre — knew it all like a book, and would take Fred there as soon as they got out; then he had a

first-rate pack of cards, and he could teach Fred to play;
and the gay tempters were soon spread out on their bed,
and Fred and his instructor sat hour after hour asborbed
in what to him was a new world of interest. He soon
learned, could play for small stakes, and felt in himself the
first glimmering of that fire which, when fully kindled,
many waters cannot quench, nor floods drown !

Dick was, as we said, precocious. He had the cool eye
and steady hand of an experienced gamester, and in a few
days he won, of course, all Fred's little earnings. But
then he was quite liberal and free with his money. He
added to their prison fare such various improvements as his
abundance of money enabled him to buy. He had brought
with him the foundation of good cheer in a capacious bottle
which emerged the first night from his pocket, for he said
he never went to jail without his provision ; then hot
water, and sugar, and lemons, and peppermint drops were
all forthcoming for money, and Fred learned once and again,
and again, the fatal secret of hushing conscience, and
memory, and bitter despair in delirious happiness, and, as
Dick said, was " getting to be a right jolly 'un that would
make something yet."

And was it all gone, all washed away by this sudden
wave of evil ? — every trace of prayer, and hope, and sacred
memory in this poor child's heart ? No, not all ; for
many a night, when his tempter slept by his side, the child
lived over the past , again he kneeled in prayer, and felt
his mother's guardian hand on his head, and he wept tears
of bitter remorse, and wondered at the dread change that
had come over him. Then he dreamed, and he saw his
mother and sister walking in white, fair as angels. and would
go to them ; but between him and them was a great gulf
fixed, which widened and widened, and grew darker and
darker, till he could see them no more, and he awoke in
utter misery and despair.

Again and again he resolved, in the darkness of the night, that to-morrow he would not drink, and he would not speak a wicked word, and he would not play cards, nor laugh at Dick's bad stories.   Ah, how many such midnight resolves have evil angels sneered at and good ones sighed over! for with daylight back comes the old temptation, and with it the old mind; and with daylight came back the inexorable prison walls which held Fred and his successful tempter together.

At last he gave himself up.   No, he could not be good with Dick — there was no use in trying! — and he made no more midnight resolves, and drank more freely of the dreadful remedy for unquiet thoughts.

And now is Fred growing in truth a wicked boy.   In a little while more and he shall be such a one as you will on no account take under your roof, lest he corrupt your own children; and yet, father, mother, look at your son of twelve years, your bright, darling boy, and think of him shut up for a month with such a companion, in such a cell, and ask yourselves if he would be any better.

And was there no eye, heavenly or earthly, to look after this lost one?   Was there no eye which could see, through all the traces of sin, the yet lingering drops of that baptism and early prayer and watchfulness which consecrated it? Yes; He whose mercy extends to the third and fourth generations of those who love him, sent a friend to our poor boy in his last distress.

It is one of the most refined and characteristic modifications of Christianity, that those who are themselves sheltered, guarded, fenced by good education, knowledge, and competence, appoint and sustain a pastor and guardian in our large cities to be the shepherd of the wandering and lost, and of them who, in the Scripture phrase, "have none to help."   Justly is he called the "City Missionary," for what is more truly missionary ground?   In the hospital, among the old, the sick, the friendless, the forlorn — in the prison, among the hardened, the blaspheming — among the discouraged and despairing, still holding with unsteady hand on to some forlorn fragment of virtue and self-respect, goes this missionary to stir the dying embers of good, to warn, entreat, implore, to adjure by sacred recollections of father, mother, and home, the fallen wanderers to return. He finds friends, and places, and employment for some, and by timely aid and encouragement saves many a one from destruction.

In this friendly shape appeared a man of prayer to visit the cell in which Fred was confined. Dick listened to his instructions with cool complacency, rolling his tobacco from side to side in his mouth, and meditating on him as a subject for some future histrionic exercise of his talent.

But his voice was as welcome to poor Fred as daylight in a dungeon. All the smothered remorse and despair of his heart burst forth in bitter confessions, as, with many tears, he poured forth his story to the friendly man. It needs not to prolong our story, for now the day has dawned and the hour of release is come.

It is not needful to carry our readers through all the steps by which Fred was transferred, first to the fireside of the friendly missionary, and afterwards to the guardian care of a good old couple who resided on a thriving farm not far from Cincinnati. Set free from evil influences, the first carefully planted and watered seeds of good began to grow again, and he became as a son to the kind family who had adopted him.